CALLED TO ACCOUNT

CALLED TO ACCOUNT

How Corporate Bad Behaviour
and Government Waste Combine
to Cost Us Millions

MARGARET HODGE

Little, Brown

LITTLE, BROWN

First published in Great Britain in 2016 by Little, Brown

13 5 7 9 10 8 6 4 2

A CIP catalogue record for this book
is available from the British Library.

ISBN 978-1-4087-0807-1

Typeset in Bembo by M Rules
Printed and bound in Great Britain by
Clays Ltd, St Ives plc

Papers used by Little, Brown are from well-managed forests
and other responsible sources.

MIX
Paper from
responsible sources
FSC
www.fsc.org FSC® C104740

Little, Brown
An imprint of
Little, Brown Book Group
Carmelite House
50 Victoria Embankment
London EC4Y 0DZ

An Hachette UK Company
www.hachette.co.uk

www.littlebrown.co.uk

'Our lives begin to end the day we become silent about things that matter.'

Martin Luther King, Jr

Contents

Contents

Acknowledgements

This book would never have been written without the substantial and generous support of many people. The book belongs to them as much as it does to me and I am immensely grateful to everyone concerned.

Professor Anthony King and Steve Bundred spent many hours reading the early draft chapters. Their detailed and meticulous comments, suggestions and ideas were invaluable and their advice over lunch, supper and a glass of wine was hugely important.

Lisa Tremble has been the most wonderful friend and brilliant adviser over many years and her reading of the drafts, which she did together with her colleague Hayley Geffin, helped to ensure that the book is accessible and readable.

Niamh O'Kane was brilliant at checking the accuracy of everything I wrote and did a wonderfully thorough job for me. I am also grateful to Dr Ben Wilkinson for the support he gave Niamh and me through King's College, London.

The excellent Liz Bradshaw, who worked as my researcher during the five years that I chaired the Public Accounts Committee, contributed in an important way to my early thinking. She also helped to research the history of both the committee and the National Audit Office.

I could not have completed the book without the constant, even-tempered and common-sense hard work of Jess Mullins, who worked with Liz during my time as chair and then became my head of office in 2015. She helped me to stay the course and contributed enormously by sourcing facts and relevant material, commenting and helping to manage the process of writing a book.

Tom Bergin, Richard Brooks, Richard Murphy and Sol Picciotto were very helpful in making sure that what I wrote made sense and was accurate.

The House of Commons library and its staff have provided immense support by identifying and sourcing relevant material.

Harriet Harman and Ann Coffey have been absolutely brilliant friends throughout, staying with me through both the good times and the difficult moments and always ready to give advice and support. It has been good fun – and productive – to sit with Harriet at our kitchen tables, as I wrote this book and she wrote her memoir, comparing our word counts and reading extracts as we wrote them.

My wonderful family have provided constant encouragement and support and put up with all my questions, moans, panics and obsessions. I am particularly grateful to two sons-in-law, James Lyons and Joe Caluori, for their ideas and their help.

A final thank you to those who made this book possible by giving me the opportunity to serve as chair of the Public Accounts Committee; the people of Barking and Dagenham from whom I have learned so much and whose priorities were always at the back of my mind when I asked questions; and my fellow Members of Parliament who elected me to the position of chair and gave me the privilege to enjoy one of the most interesting and rewarding times in my career.

1

The Unlikely Leader of the PAC

I grew up in a family that knew more than most about what it was like to live in fear of extremism and intolerance. My parents were Jews who had emigrated from Europe to Egypt in the 1930s only to find that after the Second World War and the founding of Israel they were unwelcome there.

My family were grateful to find sanctuary in Britain but arriving here in 1949 from Alexandria we were confronted with the rigid British class system which left me bewildered and thinking of myself as an outsider. That sense remains with me to this day, despite all that has happened; from becoming a government minister, to being appointed as a member of the Privy Council and, eventually, a Dame Commander of the Order of the British Empire.

My childhood experience also instilled in me a fierce anger at injustice and a determination to strive for fairness and equality. Democracy cannot just be a game where the winner takes it all.

At the same time, as a woman who came of age in the sixties, I have always felt optimistic. I believed that with determination and co-operation we could make the world a better place. Striving to challenge privilege and eradicate inequality guided my work and my choices.

When we came to the UK, I was four, the middle child of five – all of us born in Egypt except for my youngest sister. The photograph of the family in Egypt shows me at the centre, lots of curly hair, but pretty determined, cheeky and confident.

Someone had hurled a stone through the window of the steel stockyard my father ran and with memories of the Holocaust still very fresh in his mind, he decided it was time for us to leave. He struggled to find a country that would accept a large Jewish family and we found ourselves rejected by the United States and Canada. My dad was forever grateful to Britain for allowing us to come and live here.

That immigrant identity and experience dominates the memories of my early years. I remember the bed and breakfast we lived in when we first arrived, with the horrid porridge and the tasteless, overcooked greens we had to eat – very different from the spicy food and succulent fresh fruits I had been used to in Egypt. I remember the man who screamed at my father, who had a strong foreign accent, calling him 'a useless bloody foreigner' after my dad was involved in a minor car accident.

I remember the bizarre process we had to go through to secure our British passports. By that time I was nine years old, my younger sister was six and my other siblings were away at university and boarding school. My father was at work and my mother was terminally ill in hospital when we went through a test devised by the British immigration authorities. An inspector came to tea at our house, to ascertain how 'British' these two young girls had become before we were granted citizenship.

Tea at home was never served in the sitting room. It usually consisted of a soft-boiled egg with fingers of toast eaten in the kitchen, but on this occasion my father organised cucumber sandwiches and fruitcake, served from a trolley in the sitting room. I loathed fruitcake, but my father told us we had to pretend that the cake and the cucumber sandwiches had become our traditional fare just to show how British we now were!

So we sat through this awkward occasion, nibbling at the fruitcake, while we were questioned about the books we read, the friends we had and the games we played. We passed the test and got our British passports, but I am not sure the process was any more welcoming then in 1954 than are the immigration controls used today to keep out as many immigrants as we can. We were definitely made to feel like outsiders.

After my mother died when I was ten, I became an impossible teenager and was bundled off to a boarding school in Oxford. That was where the British class system really impinged on my consciousness. The school was a direct grant school and had a mixed intake, with girls whose parents worked at the car plant in Cowley learning alongside the children of middle-class academics from the university. The Cowley girls mixed with the Cowley girls; the middle-class girls mixed with the middle-class girls. The Cowley girls didn't mix with the middle-class girls and I didn't mix with either lot. I hated the way girls were pigeon-holed on the basis of their background. Again I was definitely the misfit and outsider, struggling to find my identity and not feeling I belonged.

But moving from that background to becoming a Member of Parliament and then chair of arguably the most important committee in the House of Commons would appear to make me a typical member of the British establishment. Yet I have never felt myself to be an establishment insider. I still feel like an outsider and, perhaps like others, an outsider visiting the inside.

As an outsider it has been second nature for me to challenge the establishment whether in politics, business or the Civil

Service, and as I have challenged it, I have come to understand how strong the establishment is in protecting its own.
Whatever wrong someone may have committed, however
foolish they may have been, the unwritten establishment rules
assume that you don't criticise people publicly if you went to
school or university with them, if you worked with them, if
they gave you a job or a public appointment, or if they live
nearby and you mingle in the same social circles. You may
censure them under the radar or behind their backs, but it is
a betrayal to challenge their behaviour or judgement publicly.
That's the establishment rule but I never bought into it. I never
felt part of it.

I drifted into politics by chance. When I had my first child in
1971, I gave up work, partly because that was still the accepted
norm, but also because my work involved foreign travel that I
felt I couldn't manage with bringing up babies.

Much as I love children (and I am now the very proud
mother of four children and grandmother of eleven), I became
frustrated as a stay-at-home mum. It was a friend who suggested I should stand for Islington council in 1973. In her
words, 'it would keep me sane while I was changing nappies!'

Forty years later I am not sure about my sanity, but it has
helped me to enjoy a purposeful and fulfilling working life.
Even in those early days I focused on the practical delivery of
council services. For me, the most fertile ground for developing new policy ideas came from the hands-on experience of
delivering for local residents.

In the mid-1970s I became chair of Islington's housing committee. I inherited the challenge of what to do with over ten
thousand beautiful Islington properties, mainly Georgian or
early Victorian houses that the council had bought from the
private sector. Most of them had no inside toilet and bathroom;

some still used gas as the only form of energy for lighting in the home.

At the time that I took on the responsibility for this rehabilitation and renewal programme, we were only completing a meagre dozen newly renovated homes annually from that stock of houses. Within twelve months we had accelerated the programme so that we were delivering 1600 newly modernised homes each year. This effort complemented a new building programme, delivering around 2000 new homes. Thus we were creating between 3000 and 4000 decent homes per annum at a rent people could afford, extraordinary by today's standards.

That early experience taught me about the essential ingredients for the successful implementation of a complex project: proper planning, clear milestones, strong and consistent leadership, appropriate commercial and technical skills; and ensuring that those responsible for delivering a programme were also accountable for it.

I was leader of Islington council for a decade from 1982–92, a difficult time, when Margaret Thatcher was bearing down on public spending and was determined to smash the power of both the trades unions and Labour councils. We found ourselves caught up in the battles around rate capping and were hounded by the press for what they deemed 'Loony Left' antics.

Much of what was then described as 'Loony Left' has become accepted orthodoxy today. For instance, we introduced childcare facilities for our employees, which was condemned as extreme profligacy then but is widely accepted as good practice today. We monitored the allocation of council homes to ensure that there was no discrimination, which was ridiculed as 'political correctness gone mad' and is commonplace today.

We brought together early years education and childcare so that services were delivered around the needs of children and families, rather than around the requirements of professionals – work that I later developed into the children centres model as Children's Minister.

Of course, as was much publicised at the time, we also did do some mad things, like declaring Islington a Nuclear Free Zone and banning foxhunting on the A1, which came through the borough – and this was long before Islington residents were troubled by the current proliferation of urban foxes.

Equally, many of the mad things we were alleged to have said or done were pure fiction, invented by journalists who lived and drank in Islington pubs and made the stories up over a pint of beer. So we never banned the singing of 'Baa Baa Black Sheep' in council-run nurseries on the grounds that it was racist. But the power of the media meant that some of our nursery workers read it in the papers and assumed it must be true and so denied young children in their care the joy of singing one of their favourite nursery rhymes. With so many media folk living in Islington and with 'Loony Left' stories making such good copy, we were rarely out of the spotlight and received endless criticism.

I learned important lessons from this period. Most obviously, you couldn't make the world a better place by passing resolutions in the council chamber. Labour nationally lost not just the 1979 General Election but those of 1983, 1987 and 1992. For many people, their only experience of Labour in power was the Labour-controlled authorities. Our performance locally could influence Labour's prospects nationally. We would not be trusted as a party if we did not demonstrate that we could deliver value-for-money services for the taxpayer. So we in local government had to stop thinking we could change the world by proclamations from the council platform and we had to start showing our competence in answering phones, replying to letters and making sure dustbins were collected efficiently and on time.

We were lambasted daily by the local and national press, and by 1992, when Labour had lost its fourth General Election in a row, I had had enough and was preparing to leave politics.

At that very moment, as I was coming to the end of a ten-year stint as the leader of the council, the *Evening Standard* published an exposé with allegations of paedophile activity in Islington's children's homes.

I took the allegations seriously and carried out lengthy and, as I thought, appropriate investigations. Although it seems incredible today, my colleagues and I did what was normal at the time. We questioned the professionals, the social workers and the police, but we failed to talk directly to the children who were the victims of the abuse.

I accepted the strong assurances given to me by my officials that there was no paedophile activity in our children's homes. Whether those officials knew and were covering up, or whether they themselves believed that the allegations made by the children were unfounded, I will never know. But our naivety then seems incredible today. It was only after an inquiry some three years later that I learned the allegations were true.

After that experience I was determined never to make the same kind of mistake again. It transformed my whole approach to politics and government in two important ways. First, I now understood how important it was to talk to the users of services, in this case the children, when trying to get at the truth. Similarly, talking directly to the elderly about what is happening in care homes, or to benefit claimants about the service they experience in jobcentres, is vital to an understanding of the effectiveness of those public services.

Second, I became deeply sceptical of the way in which officials can account for themselves and therefore determined to
be more rigorous and persistent in my questioning of them,
particularly when I suspected that they were covering up mistakes or being 'economical with the truth'.

That scepticism influenced me and was reinforced by my
time as both a minister and chair of the Public Accounts
Committee.

I was a minister through most of the Blair/Brown years,
serving in a range of roles in a variety of government departments. I was the first Minister for Children. I held two other
portfolios in education. I also held the welfare-to-work brief
in the Department for Work and Pensions. My last job was
as Minister for Culture and the Creative Industries in the
Department for Culture, Media and Sport. I saw at first
hand the dedication and brilliance of many civil servants and
learned that success depends on a strong and positive working
partnership with your civil servants. However, my experience
also persuaded me that the *Yes Minister* sitcom has too much of
the truth in it for comfort!

The reality is that the Civil Service is permanent and ministers are transient. If they don't like what you are doing, they
can either conveniently forget to implement your directions
in the hope that you will also forget, or they can delay and
delay in the hope that you will become bored, be reshuffled
or sacked before your decisions can be implemented. They
can also recommend a radical rethink after you depart. The
rhetoric of Civil Service professionalism all too often hides the
reality of where much of the power and authority lies. You
have to be pretty determined and persistent if the civil servants
disapprove of what you want to do.

I had one memorable experience of how civil servants

regarded ministers when I was Minister for Children. I was determined to improve the quality of the service provided by the Children and Family Court Advisory and Support Service (CAFCASS). Its job was to support the child's interests in all court proceedings but as a result of a sloppy amalgamation it was causing considerable delays by failing to provide courts with the appropriate social work reports on the children in a timely manner.

I decided we needed radical action and wanted to change the entire board and start again. I had to talk to Lord Falconer about doing this, because he was then Lord Chancellor and we shared responsibility for CAFCASS. The responsible official working to me could not be present when the two of us spoke on the phone. So she sent what she thought was a helpful note to my private office. In it she said: 'I have drafted up a one page of "what to say" and "what not to say". That sounds very Sir Humphrey . . . but if there are any awkward questions it's entirely open to Margaret just to say – That's a matter for you, Lord Falconer. In fact, she would be wise to do so. Sympathetic nods, "mm interesting" and "I see" are good too.'

I was left in no doubt that my role was seen as that of the puppet on the string controlled by the Civil Service.

Another memorable experience came in my final job, as Minister for Culture. One of the minister's tasks is to oversee public appointments to our national museums and art galleries. On assuming the responsibility, I discovered that only 26 per cent of the new appointments went to women. There seemed no reason whatsoever for our not being able to ensure equal representation on the boards of these national cultural bodies and I was determined to change this. Working with officials, we compiled a list of strong women candidates. We then talked to the chairs and the members of the individual bodies who had direct responsibility for short-listing and interviewing. I told them that I wanted to change the profile of the boards and made clear that I was prepared to use my authority to turn down their recommendations if they did not show that they had achieved a better balance on the boards.

Achieving the change involved many struggles. Initially officials told me that what I was trying to do was impossible and illegal. I sought advice from the Solicitor General and that proved very helpful in overcoming opposition from the Civil Service. Then some of the chairs of the boards put up resistance. They thought it was simply political correctness. It was extraordinary how many of the men really thought that introducing more women would mean a lower-calibre board. However, with determination and persistence I won through, and within a year we had achieved my goal. Just under 50 per cent of the new appointments went to women.

It was then in 2008 that my husband Henry was diagnosed with leukaemia. I wanted to spend my time with him in his fight against cancer. It was my close friend Harriet Harman who suggested asking the Prime Minister, Gordon Brown, for compassionate leave and an assurance that I could return to the job. To his great credit, Gordon agreed. No minister had ever been granted compassionate leave before, so it was an important first, which simply would not have happened without Harriet's strong support.

About a year later, after Henry died, I did return as Minister for Culture, with less than a year to go to the 2010 General Election. Picking up the issues in my portfolio again, I was taken aback to discover that, within a year, the department had reverted to its old habits. Only a quarter of the public appointments made during the year that I was on compassionate leave had been given to women. That really taught me how fleeting the influence of ministers sometimes is – and how entrenched the Civil Service culture can be.

Which isn't to say that I did not enjoy really constructive relationships with many civil servants, but the stories are illustrative of the deep-seated problems that I shall explore in this book.

Of course, my time as a minister would influence the way I chaired the Public Accounts Committee. I was accustomed to obfuscation, the failure to answer questions directly and attempts just to get through meetings saying as little as possible. At PAC hearings, I wanted to extract as many full and honest answers as I could.

While I was a government minister things became very tough in my constituency. I was elected the MP for Barking in 1994. At the time, the local Labour Party basically told me not to worry about what happened in Barking and Dagenham, but to put my energies into Westminster. The seat was a safe Labour seat and the party had become used to weighing rather than counting the votes in at elections.

The then Labour leader of the local council had been a member of the Labour Party since the 1930s, when he had joined the Labour League of Youth, but he had never knocked on a single door to canvass support at election time.

The party in Barking and Dagenham was inward-looking. It had close links to the trades unions both at Ford in Dagenham and among the council workers, but it was unrepresentative of the community as a whole. It was chock-a-block with white middle-aged men who spent their time talking and bickering among themselves instead of engaging with the people they were elected to represent.

At the same time the borough was undergoing a rapid transformation. To illustrate the point, data from the census carried out by the Office for National Statistics (ONS) charted the change. The ONS only started collecting data on ethnicity in

1991 but the figures from then onwards are stark. In 1991, 93.2 per cent of the borough's population was white. Twenty years later the percentage had dropped to 58.3 per cent. In 1991, 2.2 per cent of the people living in Barking and Dagenham were black; twenty years later that had risen to 19.9 per cent. In 1991, 4.1 per cent of the citizens were classified as Asians; by 2011 that had risen to 15.9 per cent.

All of us find change difficult. It is unsettling and challenging when your neighbours suddenly change, when the food sold in the local shops changes, when there are many more minority ethnic community faces in the playgrounds.

This change coincided with the decline of Ford in Dagenham. Unemployment soared and at the same time finding alternative work was made more difficult by an entrenched culture of low aspirations for educational attainment.

All of this was further exacerbated by a huge decline in the council's housing stock as tenants exercised their right to buy. And nobody was building decent homes for the sons and daughters of those for whom Barking and Dagenham council had provided down the generations at a price local people could afford.

Finally, the physical condition of many of the council estates was poor and neglected. The lifts smelled of urine; condoms and needles from drug injections littered the common areas. The 1997 Labour government had been busy building new schools and hospitals, but had neglected the important investment people wanted in their local environment.

With this toxic mix of rapid demographic change, high unemployment, the loss of traditional industrial jobs and a lack of housing – all coupled with a Tammany Hall-style council and a moribund Labour Party – it is no wonder the people of Barking and Dagenham revolted against the Labour Party. Out of anger, not apathy, and in part as a protest at Labour's failure to listen and respond to their concerns and their aspirations, they turned to the British National Party.

In 2006, the BNP won twelve seats on the council. It was utterly obvious to me that I had to radically change the way I did politics in the constituency if we were to halt the slide away from Labour and stop in its tracks the growing support for the BNP. Failure to change could have led to my losing the parliamentary seat.

So I stopped spending my time in small rooms talking to Labour activists; I stopped going to meetings in the town hall or cutting ribbons at openings. Instead I operated on the principle that every activity I undertook had to pass my simple reconnection test. Just one simple question – would it help to re-establish trust with those whose support I needed to retain and to see off the BNP?

I knew that my constituents were fed up with politicians who refused to talk about immigration and its impact on their community. Understanding their concerns and engaging with the issues that mattered to them did not mean conceding anything to the BNP's racist agenda. Indeed, I believed that the only way to beat the BNP was by democratic means and open debate.

I started holding regular coffee afternoons, during which I didn't come and lecture constituents on what they should be thinking about. I didn't preach to them about the latest hot issue that the Labour leadership in the Westminster bubble had instructed MPs to focus on. People simply talked and I simply listened. Their concerns often arose from what was happening in their immediate area. I was able to respond to many local issues, such as broken pavements or the siting of a bus stop. By listening, responding and taking action where I could and then telling people what I had done, I started to rebuild trust and draw people away from the BNP and back to Labour.

None of this was rocket science but it was hard work and it took time. Indeed, it took me four years to really rebuild trust and the techniques I used then, whether coffee afternoons, street meetings, campaigns on local issues, or door-to-door canvassing, are things I still do today.

In the autumn of 2009, Nick Griffin, the then BNP leader, decided he would challenge me at the election in the following year. He had clearly calculated that Barking was the place where he was most likely to secure a seat in Parliament. Battling for Barking became the most important event in my long political life. I continued to focus on reconnecting with people and I talked about immigration.

Unlike the leaders of the mainstream political parties, I never promised we could reduce immigration numbers. With increasing globalisation, there will inevitably be more migration. Just as capital becomes global and crosses national borders, so people will cross borders more often and in greater numbers. Migration is a feature of globalisation.

The Chinese are poised to fund and build a new nuclear power station, the Germans are building our trains and the French run some of our energy companies. Similarly, our hospitals are staffed with people from all over the world, our hotels and restaurants are kept going on migrant labour, and our infrastructure is designed and constructed by an international workforce.

Pledging that you can cut immigration numbers in a global environment is a pledge all governments make but find they can't keep. Yet when politics is held in such disrepute and politicians enjoy so little trust, our leaders keep promising what they cannot deliver and so lose the very trust they need to inspire.

I learned from fighting the BNP that offering a false prospectus simply doesn't work. You have to be straight with people. So I did not pledge to turn the clock back on the numbers of migrants coming to Barking and Dagenham. But I could and did talk about rationing access to public goods, whether it was social housing or welfare benefits, so that the time someone had spent in a place like Barking and Dagenham was as important as 'need' in determining whether or not they were eligible for housing from the local council or benefits from the government.

By suggesting that there should be a link between the time spent in a place and entitlement to public services, I was able to lance the boil that the BNP had exploited – the perceived unfairness felt by long-standing residents that newly arrived migrants were jumping the queue. This was highly controversial in 2008 but has been widely accepted today. It was a way of promoting tolerance rather than inviting division.

We crushed the BNP in the election, and I increased both my numerical vote to nearly 25,000 and my share of the total vote in what was a very difficult election for the Labour Party. Nick Griffin was pushed into third place with only 6620 votes. The BNP also lost all the seats it had won on the council.

Our triumph was the most important achievement of my political lifetime. Smashing the BNP in Barking helped lead to the rapid decline of the BNP as a force in British politics – for the time being.

My experience in Barking transformed my approach to politics. I learned how important it was to be direct and straight and not to use the pompous and somewhat obscure language often associated with politicians and parliamentary debates. I learned how vital it was to raise the issues and ask the questions that my constituents and people like them wanted answered, instead of the ones that the Westminster elite believed were important. I learned that, if we wanted to restore some credibility to politics and politicians, we had to do our politics in a different way, one that connected with voters candidly and honestly. I tried to take those lessons with me into the work of the PAC.

I made sure that I took the opportunity, whenever possible, to ensure that issues raised with me by local people set the agenda for the Public Accounts Committee. For instance, two constituents came to me to complain about the cost of using 0845 numbers when contacting their GP. Ringing a premium 0845 telephone number from a mobile phone can cost 11p a minute; one of my constituents had accumulated a £30 bill trying to get appointments for her disabled son. We challenged the Cabinet Office at a PAC hearing on the use of 0845 numbers by public bodies.

It is mainly poor people who contact public services because it is the poor who are more likely to use and rely on such services. Charging them premium rates is wrong and regressive. Exposing that injustice publicly through the Public Accounts Committee led the civil servants to agree to instruct all those who provide public services to offer 01, 02 or 03 telephone numbers. Not only did my constituents benefit from the change forced on GPs, but anybody contacting any government department no longer has to pay extra for that phone call.

While campaigning against the BNP I was also nursing my husband Henry through his battle with leukaemia, a struggle he tragically lost when he died at the early age of sixty-five in June 2009. The emotions I experienced during his illness and the utter misery I felt at his death gave me a very different slant on politics and Westminster. Playing the traditional political games seemed utterly irrelevant and wasteful.

Immediately after Henry died, I was thrown into the struggle against Nick Griffin and the BNP, so my time was filled with political campaigning. Fighting the extreme right did feel worthwhile and important. But after the 2010 General Election, I felt empty and wondered what on earth I could do with my life. The vacuum left by Henry's death was gigantic and finding a purpose that would help me through the trauma seemed impossible. Yet my early experience as an immigrant and self-defined outsider had always led me to seek out a purpose rather than to accept the hand circumstances dealt me.

Although the 2010 election had been a triumph for me personally, it had been a disaster for the Labour Party nationally. I am not a natural Opposition politician and the thought of becoming a member of the Opposition frontbench team filled me with gloom. I had spent eighteen long years in the 1980s and 1990s surviving in Opposition and working on new policies for the Labour Party, and frankly didn't have the appetite to do it again.

By chance I was having a cup of tea with an old friend of mine. He suggested I put my hat in the ring for election as chair of the Public Accounts Committee. It had never occurred to me that I might enjoy what at first sight appeared to be very dry audit work, monitoring government spending. But at that particular moment I simply knew I had to be busy if I were to have any chance of managing life without Henry. Spurred on by the encouragement, I went directly to my office and wrote out my CV for the job. I had no idea whether or not I could win.

2

Following the Taxpayer's Pound

Having just emerged from the gruelling fight against the BNP, I suddenly found myself thrown into a new electoral battle. Traditionally the chair and members of all the select committees, including the Public Accounts Committee, had been patronage appointments agreed by the party whips and party leaders. This changed in 2010, with Parliament deciding to introduce elections for these positions.

The rivals for the chairmanship of the Public Accounts Committee were thus the first candidates to confront the need to be elected by all of our parliamentary colleagues. There were six of us, all Labour MPs, because the post had to be filled by a member of the Opposition. However, all six of us had to compete to win the support of a majority of our 649 colleagues across all the political parties in Parliament. The strongest contenders appeared to be Brian Donohoe, a popular Scottish colleague who could count on the Scottish Labour vote, and Hugh Bayley, who had apparently had his eye on the job for many years. I was the only woman and had decided to enter the race at the last minute. I felt daunted by the challenge. I had only a couple of weeks to convince my colleagues I was the right person.

Not on the face of it a great time to go on holiday! But I was exhausted from the General Election campaign, I was still trying to come to terms with my husband's death and probably a little part of me wanted a plausible excuse when inevitably someone else got the job. I decided the week's holiday was a must. Having written out a CV, I sent it to every Member of Parliament and went away on holiday.

It came as no surprise, when I returned, to find that the others in the race were well ahead of me. I started canvassing as many MPs as I could. Two things worked in my favour – first, trouncing Nick Griffin helped me to win votes across every political divide, and second, I was a woman. To every female MP I simply said: 'I'm a woman. There's never been a woman chairing the Public Accounts Committee. Vote for me please!'

It was during this frenetic campaign that I encountered Richard Bacon, the Tory MP who had been a member of the Public Accounts Committee since 2001 and who was by then its senior Conservative member and, in effect, its vice-chair. Not having come across him before, I had not understood his role. 'What do you think of Amyas Morse?' he asked. I hadn't a clue what he was talking about. Only a little later did I discover that Amyas Morse had recently been appointed the Comptroller and Auditor General at the National Audit Office, a person with whom I would need to work closely. I should have done my homework. I pleaded ignorance and immediately lost Richard's vote. Fortunately that didn't prove fatal and we became good colleagues and friends. He is an extremely able, voluble and knowledgable man who should be a minister but has probably always been too independent-minded for any Prime Minister.

I am very much a Marmite politician and there were plenty of people on the Labour side who would always vote against a metropolitan, middle-class woman, so my expectations were not high. The outcome was incredibly difficult to call, but to my surprise I beat Hugh Bayley in the fifth round by just five votes to become the first woman chair in the Public Accounts Committee's 150-year history.

The first thing that I learned was that I would have to move into the office reserved for the chair of the committee. I had just secured an office in the modern Portcullis House near all my close political friends. The last thing I wanted was to change offices and become isolated from my soulmates. But I forced myself to go and have a look at what was on offer.

The office turned out to be a splendid Pugin-style room on the upper committee corridor of the original Palace of Westminster. 'Chairman of the Public Accounts Committee' was engraved in gilded lettering over the door. There was a stunning view over the River Thames and Pugin wallpaper adorns the walls. It was love at first sight so, a little guiltily, I deserted my friends for the office that would become my working home for the next five years.

One wall of the room was covered with photographs of my predecessors. Among them was Harold Wilson, who chaired the committee from 1959 until 1963, becoming Prime Minister the following year. I couldn't understand why he had done the job at that point in his political career. Then somebody explained the reason to me. During Harold Wilson's time, Opposition Members of Parliament did not have offices. Everybody was allocated an old-style school desk with a chair physically attached to it. These desks lined the committee corridors and were where MPs were expected to work. The only person to be allocated a room of their own was the chair of the Public Accounts Committee. Harold Wilson took the job to get the room. Legend has it that he used to hold regular drinking sessions there with loud renditions of 'The Red Flag' echoing down the committee corridor.

The Public Accounts Committee is the oldest select committee of the House of Commons, founded by William Gladstone when he was Chancellor of the Exchequer in 1861. The Standing Order establishing the committee originally said 'That there shall be a Standing Committee to be designated the Committee of Public Accounts, for the examination of the Accounts showing the appropriation of sums granted by Parliament to meet the Public Expenditure.'

Reading those words, I was not surprised to learn that Gladstone thought the committee's duties would be of 'a dry and repulsive kind'.

I got a similar reaction when I told my brilliant and loyal researcher, Liz Bradshaw, that I was going to chair the committee for the entire five years of the new Parliament. She pulled a face and told me that she thought the work would be excruciatingly boring.

I thought it might be too. Little did we both know how wrong we were.

As we quickly found, there were good reasons for Peter Hennessy, the historian, bestowing on the committee the title of 'Queen of the Select Committees'.

The role of the Public Accounts Committee is to hold the government to account for the way in which it spends public money. My regular mantra thus became – we follow the taxpayer's pound, wherever it goes. The committee does not take evidence from ministers but requires accounting officers – for the most part, the permanent secretaries who head up government departments – to give evidence on whether taxpayers' money is spent efficiently and effectively. That convention of not taking evidence from politicians, but calling bureaucrats to account, makes for more effective accountability. On the whole, heads of departments give a more honest version of events; they are less susceptible to immediate political and media pressure, and their tenure in post is more secure. Of course that is not true of all the senior civil servants, all of the time, as some of the stories in this book will reveal. But during my five years, we took evidence from ministers only once and that session did not yield much, maybe because politicians were more skilled at not answering questions.

In 1861, the Public Accounts Committee was responsible for overseeing some £69 million of public spending – less than £8 billion in today's money. Today we oversee more than £700 billion of public spending. In fact, the budget for 2016–17 has been set at £772 billion.

In the early years most public money was spent directly by or through the big government departments. It was relatively straightforward to hold these departments to account. Today over half of the expenditure on goods and services (as opposed to expenditure on pensions or benefits) is channelled through private sector companies. Furthermore, many public sector organisations are much more fragmented than they were even a generation ago. We now have a plethora of independent institutions such as foundation trust hospitals, free schools, academy schools, private university colleges and so on, all spending the taxpayer's pound. Following that pound has become much more difficult and complex.

When the Public Accounts Committee was first founded in the nineteenth century, it met only between December and May and reported once a year in the summer, covering all government expenditure during the previous financial year. In the five years between 2010 and 2015, we met throughout the parliamentary year, held 276 evidence sessions and published 246 unanimous reports.

Our work was immensely varied, the tapestry vast. In our two hearings each week, we might hear evidence on major defence projects on a Monday and examine how the NHS was responding to diabetes on a Wednesday; at the same time we considered draft reports on anything from tax avoidance to rural broadband. We only failed to agree on one report, covering the highly contentious sale of Royal Mail. Achieving unanimity was hugely important and although it was sometimes challenging, we worked hard to find agreement – and succeeded.

There is much in the committee's history that we would recognise today. On one memorable occasion in 1887, the committee raised concerns about the taxpayer being ripped off by a private contractor. They could have been talking about the revelations of 2013 when G4S and Serco overcharged the Ministry of Justice tens of millions of pounds on their electronic-tagging contract; the MOJ paid out taxpayers' money for tagging prisoners, but included in the bills were people who had been discharged from prison and even ex-prisoners who had died.

The scandal in 1887 involved the War Office and a contract with a company called Davis and Co. that supplied ribbon to the army, for which it was charged twenty shillings, when the previous contract with Thorp and Son had cost only fourteen shillings – an increase of over 40 per cent. Then, as so often happens now, the committee met with considerable resistance from the department as it tried to get to the bottom of the situation and establish whether the taxpayer had been cheated. The War Office refused to reply to questions, claiming that the Comptroller and Auditor General had no powers 'to enter upon matters of administration'. The Public Accounts Committee responded: 'If, in the course of his audit, The Comptroller and Auditor General becomes aware of facts that appear to him to indicate an improper expenditure or waste of public money, it is his duty to call the attention of Parliament to them.' We could have penned identical words today.

In 1881, the Public Accounts Committee ordered a Colonel Synge, who was a British adviser to the Ottoman gendarmerie, to personally refund money paid as a ransom to rescue him in Turkey. The sum was £24,000, the equivalent of nearly half a million pounds today.

In 1920, the committee found that an officer at the Ministry of Information had approved a number of payments totalling £101 6s 3d, described as 'personal remuneration and allowances', without obtaining the proper authorisation from the Treasury. Colonel Buchan had been asked to close down the Ministry of Information after Armistice Day. He overruled the accounting officer at the Ministry of Information and paid out money to a number of individuals. In one case, he paid £7 11s 6d to one officer to travel into London from his country home. In another, he paid two men £35 in lieu of notice although they had been working abroad during their notice period and had already been paid for that. Another payment was for accounting work not sanctioned by the Treasury. A year later the committee ordered that the money be repaid, and reported: 'We are glad to know that the disallowance recommended in Paragraph 61 of our third report 1920 has been duly effected. The Accounting Officer of the Ministry of Information having repaid the exchequer from his own pocket the sum of £101 6s 3d.' In those days those responsible were also made to account for their actions – a link that is much weaker today.

In 1960, Harold Wilson – as chair of the committee – took the Ministry of Defence to task for spiralling costs and delays in the Blue Streak missile programme, commenting: 'I think that the House must agree that the system of control and the estimating in this case have been utterly deplorable.' More than fifty years later I could have made an identical speech in the House of Commons about the failures of successive governments on the Queen Elizabeth aircraft carrier project. That enduring and depressing failure to learn the lessons of the past was one of the most frustrating aspects of my experience as chair of this historic and important committee, to which I shall return later.

Looking back through the long history of the committee, I found that many colourful characters served as its chair. Curiously there have been more assassinations of chairs of the Public Accounts Committee than there have been of Prime Ministers. Lord Frederick Cavendish (who chaired the PAC between 1877 and 1880) was stabbed to death in one of the so-called Phoenix Park Murders. It later transpired that it was a case of mistaken identity and his assassins, a group known as the Irish National Invincibles, had actually wanted to kill Cavendish's companion, Thomas Henry Burke, the most senior British civil servant in Ireland.

In 1944, another parliamentarian, Walter Guinness, Lord Moyne, who had chaired the committee twenty years earlier, fell victim to terrorism. He was shot and killed in Cairo by members of the Zionist militant group Lehi, more commonly known as the Stern Gang.

Three chairs, all Labour MPs, served time in prison. Morgan Jones (1931–8) became the first conscientious objector to be elected to Parliament after the First World War, having been imprisoned for his pacifist views during the conflict. Frederick William Pethick-Lawrence (1938–41) served a six-month prison sentence in 1912 for his involvement in the campaign for women's suffrage, and George Benson (1952–9) was imprisoned as a conscientious objector during the Second World War.

The first Labour chair was a man called Frederick William Jowett (1923). He was a Christian Socialist and one of the founders of the Labour Party, who during his time as a councillor in Bradford pioneered the first ever free school meals programme. Unlike most of his predecessors, who had been educated at the country's top public schools, Jowett left school at the age of just eight and first worked in a textile mill.

Another well-known chair was Sir Edward du Cann (1974–9), a prominent Conservative politician in the Thatcher era, who led the Public Accounts Committee for five years. He later managed to leave a trail of financial disasters behind him in his associations with Keyser Ullman Bank and an endowment policy company called Home Assured, and he was finally declared bankrupt. Not all PAC chairs have been saints.

Harold Wilson was the most famous politician to hold the post. Even somebody as tough as he was, regarded the committee's style of questioning as occasionally brutal: 'My colleagues ... are normally kind-hearted men, kind to animals and men, who in their private lives, would not hurt a fly'; 'When they enter Committee Room 16 upstairs they take on what Shakespeare's Henry V called a terrible aspect and enter on their duties in the Committee hunting season ... in a way which less understanding observers might regard as sublimated blood lust.' We still meet in Committee Room 16.

During my political life there have been a range of eminent individuals who have chaired the committee, from Joel Barnett – of Barnett formula fame – to Edmund Dell and Robert Sheldon, who was probably the longest-serving chair (1983–97). Most recently I was preceded by David Davis (1997-2001) and Sir Edward Leigh (2001-10), both of whom continue to be powerful voices in the House of Commons and are strong advocates for parliamentary accountability.

I knew when I took the job that I had a hard act to follow. During my time as chair I often met people who were well aware of our high-profile inquiries, but who had never previously heard of the Public Accounts Committee and were curious to understand how we worked. The committee is a cross-party committee. While it is chaired by an Opposition MP, its membership reflects the composition of the House of Commons, with the result that it always has an in-built majority for the government of the day. During my tenure, there were seven Conservative MPs, five Labour members (including me) and one Liberal Democrat.

There was some turnover of members as individuals were promoted or could no longer cope with the workload.

Matthew Hancock, the extremely ambitious and young-looking Conservative MP who had worked as chief of staff for George Osborne before entering Parliament in 2010, was the only member who invariably prioritised the Conservative Party interest over the public interest. He quickly secured promotion.

Boris Johnson's younger brother, the Conservative MP Jo Johnson, was promoted at the same time, but his contribution to the committee's work was far greater. He was a clear, lateral thinker with an urbane and civil manner who was prepared to express independent views based on the facts.

Some of the Conservatives remained on the committee for a number of years and contributed much to our success. Among them was our effective vice-chair Richard Bacon, who always sat next to me and played a key role in keeping us together as a group. While he strongly believes in a small state and is vigorously anti-European and I am both pro-Europe and pro-public expenditure, we nearly always agreed about everything to do with value for money and tax avoidance. If the Conservatives on the committee felt that the criticism of a government programme in a particular report was too strident, he would single-mindedly focus on the evidence and seek a compromise in the wording that everybody could support.

We were a very cohesive group and spent a lot of time together – I grew to like them all. Conservatives who worked hard on the committee included Stewart Jackson, the colourful MP for Peterborough, who certainly didn't fit the Cameron mould with his strident views on immigration, Europe and gay marriage, and who often asked direct and incisive questions that might have embarrassed the government; Chris Heaton-Harris, who had spent ten years as a Member of the European Parliament before entering Westminster to campaign against Europe, and who in a very nice way tried to curb my over-zealous instincts but who did see his role as minimising the damage our reports might inflict on the Conservative-led government; and Jackie Doyle-Price, who was the only Conservative woman on the committee. She often contributed towards the end of any hearing, perhaps because she wrongly lacked the confidence to intervene earlier; she and I shared a great deal in that we represented neighbouring constituencies with similar challenges. The sole Liberal Democrat, Ian Swales, gave me consistent support; I thought he felt more comfortable with his Labour colleagues than with his coalition partners and his extensive experience outside Parliament meant he always asked penetrating questions.

On the Labour side, Dame Anne McGuire provided brilliant support to me personally and she had a very gentle but firm manner that made her a fearsome interrogator; she constantly gave good and honest advice; Fiona Mactaggart was also a wonderful friend and supporter. She saw her role as being a bridge builder across the political divide, seeking out common ground and persuading people, especially the Conservatives, to accept critical findings and recommendations. Her propensity to deafness often helped us get over difficult moments. Austin Mitchell, who reached his eightieth birthday in 2014, always attended the committee, was completely dependable and was very funny. He never missed the opportunity to take a swipe at the government but he also recognised the importance of reaching a consensus. Meg Hillier joined the committee in October 2011 and used the time to enhance her skills and knowledge so that she could take over chairing the committee after I retired in 2015.

Having been elected as chair for the whole five years of the Parliament, I enjoyed better security of tenure than I had ever enjoyed as a minister. Knowing I had five years made a huge difference to my approach to the job. It allowed me to pace the work and time the inquiries in a much more structured and effective manner. We were still able to respond quickly to topical issues of public concern.

I worked hard to build and maintain consensus. We all had widely differing views and came from different wings of our parties. We might never agree on Europe or gay rights. But unanimity in every report was important to us all, as unanimous reports from a cross-party committee carry much more weight in Parliament, with the government and with the public. We wanted our recommendations to be implemented and we had a greater chance of success if we produced unanimous reports.

There were many reasons that helped make consensus possible. First, our task was to hold government to account for all its expenditure, so we mostly looked at the past record, rather than trying to develop new policy ideas. Our job was not to question government policy but to examine how it was implemented and to assess whether the government was getting value for money. Clearly the line between formulating and delivering policy is blurred and we often found ourselves trespassing into the policy domain. But we tried to focus on whether government, in putting a policy choice into practice, was acting efficiently and effectively. It was this focus on implementation that helped keep crude tribal politics at bay and establish consensus.

Second, we were all elected by our peers and not appointed by party leaders and that gave us a new-found authority and confidence to act independently of the party machines, leaving our political loyalties outside the door of the committee room. Coalition government also helped to change the culture and break down traditional party loyalties. It gave MPs greater freedom to come to their own views.

Third, following the dreadful impact of the 2009 expenses scandal on the reputation of all Members of Parliament, many MPs felt a determination to restore our credibility among voters. We believed that demonstrating independence of thought on a committee of Parliament and calling the executive to proper account would help to rebuild trust and confidence, showing people we were really working on their behalf.

Finally, I believe that my personal approach to the work also helped build unanimity. In the very early days of my tenure we looked back at the record of the Labour government, of which I had been a part. Indeed, one of our earliest inquiries was into the welfare-to-work programme for people with disabilities, for which I had briefly held ministerial responsibility. The report by the National Audit Office was critical of the design of the programme and of the outcomes achieved. The evidence was clear, and I accepted the unfavourable judgements, which were then reflected in our published report. Similarly, when we took our first look at the aircraft carrier programme initiated by the Labour government, it was absolutely clear that the Labour government's actions had led to a terrible waste of taxpayers' money, and I was as tough as anyone in my criticism.

That willingness to be critical of the actions of the Labour government – indeed, to be critical of my personal involvement – almost certainly reassured the Conservatives on the committee that I was genuinely focused on the quest for better value for money and was not trying to use the committee for party political advantage. This determination to make judgements based on objective evidence helped secure cross-party support for our reports.

That brings me to the role of the National Audit Office. Our hearings were mostly based on reports prepared by this independent body, headed by the Comptroller and Auditor General. The Audit Office staff of eight hundred people were mostly auditors – auditing government accounts – with some economists, statisticians and social scientists employed to focus on the value-for-money work. Their reports provided us with the uniquely reliable and independent evidence that was necessary to enable us to do our job. Few ever quarrelled with the facts set out in those reports, which were mostly agreed with the government departments before they were published.

The Audit Office evidence informed our judgements. On that basis I was prepared to criticise the aircraft carrier programme of the Labour government and the Conservatives were willing to criticise the Conservative flagship Work Programme, aimed at moving people off welfare and into employment. The National Audit Office began life in 1866 as a rather different creature from the one we know today. It was then the Exchequer and Audit Department, another of Gladstone's innovations. The Act that brought it into being also established the job of the person with the somewhat pompous-sounding title of Comptroller and Auditor General.

The earliest reference to a public official responsible for auditing public expenditure dates back as far as 1314 and variations of this role have existed ever since. What was important about the 1866 Act was that, for the first time, government departments were required to produce annual accounts, to be audited by the Auditor General, who would then report to Parliament. This

was a major step towards strengthening parliamentary accountability and improving the capacity of the legislature to hold the
executive to account.

One can find examples of how it all worked at that time.
During the Boer War the Comptroller and Auditor General
undertook a high-profile inquiry into expenditure on horses. He
discovered that the agent sourcing horses for the British Army in
Spain (we had run out of horses) was being paid a commission
both by the British Army and by the dealer selling the horses.

It was the Conservative patrician Norman St John-Stevas
who in 1983, working from the backbenches after being sacked
from the Cabinet by Margaret Thatcher, put the Comptroller
and Auditor General on a modern footing. He steered the
National Audit Act through the Houses of Parliament and
established today's National Audit Office. The Act made clear
that the Auditor General is an officer of Parliament, accountable
to MPs, and that his staff are independent of the Civil Service.
It is this mandate that has enabled the Audit Office under the
direction of the Comptroller to publish value-for-money studies on issues right across the public sector. These studies have
formed the basis of much – but not all – of the Public Accounts
Committee's programme of work.

When I became chair, the National Audit Office was recov-
ering from a low point in its history, following the resignation
of Sir John Bourn, who had held the job for twenty years. His
resignation followed huge controversy over his expenses, with
a series of exposés in *Private Eye* detailing lavish foreign trips,
full of five-star hotels and first-class flights, and a personal
chauffeur, all funded by the British taxpayer. This unsavoury
episode dealt a blow to the National Audit Office's reputation.
However, both the interim leader, Tim Burr, and the current
Auditor General, Sir Amyas Morse – appointed in 2009 – have
worked successfully to restore the organisation's reputation.

During the early days in the job I had a somewhat fractious relationship with Amyas Morse. Amyas is a highly intelligent man, always well dressed and well groomed, who had spent most of his life at PricewaterhouseCoopers. The early tensions between us arose more from our similarities than our differences; we were both strong and determined people. We both liked to get our own way. We shared similar views on the importance of value for money, the failings in government and the reforms necessary to secure better value for the taxpayer's pound.

But I inherited ways of working that I felt inhibited my committee. The Audit Office would produce a report, the Public Accounts Committee would hold a hearing based on that report, and the Audit Office would then – believe it or not – write the Public Accounts Committee report, which would then be duly published. Every now and then, with really scandalous issues, that way of proceeding could give us three opportunities to capture the public's attention. But it felt that, as a committee, we were the end of a sausage machine, created and controlled by the Auditor General and the Audit Office, and that we were not adding much value to the work.

I was determined not to become a mere mouthpiece for the National Audit Office. I wanted us to be genuinely independent, to look at issues we thought mattered, to seek evidence from sources other than the Audit Office and to come to our own conclusions on the issues we considered. I wanted us to champion taxpayers' and citizens' interests. I wanted us to make a difference.

That change of approach did lead to some difficult moments. For instance, I wanted the committee to appoint a couple of advisers to work directly with us, independently of the National Audit Office. Our committee staff had no time to provide independent advice and support; they were hard pressed to ensure we all received the right papers at the right time and that the right witnesses turned up when asked. With such an active committee, their time was filled by the bureaucratic logistics that were essential to ensure its smooth running.

I talked to members of the committee individually to persuade them that advice and support independent of the National Audit Office would strengthen our effectiveness. I thought I had convinced all of them of the case.

However, the proposal was just too threatening to the Auditor General and the National Audit Office. They saw it as weakening their influence. So the Auditor General – completely inappropriately in my view – talked to the Conservative members of the committee privately, without my knowledge, seeking to dissuade them from making the new appointments I thought necessary.

I arrived at the next full committee meeting, when we were to thrash out the details of how and whom we would appoint, only to find that I had lost the support of the Conservative members – a majority of the committee.

I was furious, but the episode made me even more determined to act independently of the National Audit Office. So, unbeknown to most of the committee members, I recruited three experts I knew personally to provide me with advice and to act as regular sounding boards. We met every week on a Thursday morning in my office and spent a couple of hours reflecting on what had happened during the previous week, planning for the following week's hearings and discussing issues that were important or causing me concern.

The three became known in my office as the 'Three Wise Men'. I had known Steve Bundred since the 1970s, when we had been councillors together on Islington council. Highly intelligent and very private, he went on to spend time as the chief finance officer at Birkbeck College, London, moving to become chief executive of Camden council and then chief executive at the Audit Commission. I had known Tony Travers, who is a professor at the London School of Economics, for years; with a brilliant brain and a great ability to cut to the core, he is universally respected as a leading expert on public finance and the public sector. David Walker is also an old and valued friend, who is always highly critical of all governments, and has spent most of his professional life writing books and articles about the public sector.

I could not have asked for better support. They gave of their time freely and generously, with only the odd croissant for breakfast or a celebratory meal in my local bistro pub as a reward. It was not just their policy insights that helped; they often helped frame the questions I went on to ask in our evidence sessions – killer questions that would bring the sessions alive.

My effectiveness in committee was largely dependent on the superb work of my young researcher Liz Bradshaw, my brilliant parliamentary assistant Jess Mullins, and on the advice and support I received from my Three Wise Men. Sometimes when I thought about the mountain of preparation and backing that some of our witnesses enjoyed (from the bosses of Serco, Google and HSBC to experienced Cabinet secretaries and permanent secretaries), I was more than a little intimidated; the scales seemed grotesquely unbalanced. I was able to hold my own because of the brilliant work of Liz, Jess, Steve, Tony and David. Ironically, the NAO's determination to be the committee's only source of advice ended up with one member of the committee finding a much better way of dealing with the problem.

The second occasion when conflicts with the National Audit Office and its leadership threatened relationships arose from my concerns about the adequacy of public audit.

As part of the 'bonfire of the quangos', the government

abolished the Audit Commission, which had been responsible for assessing value for money in local government and the health service. Until that time the National Audit Office had focused on central government expenditure. The government argued that voters were best placed to judge efficiency and effectiveness and instructed local authorities to publish all items of expenditure of £500 and over. While I am a strong supporter of transparency, the idea that a whole army of armchair auditors would spend their evenings wading through reams of invoices to check value for money was laughable. The government conceded the force of this argument, changing legislation so that the National Audit Office would take on some of the value-for-money functions of the Audit Commission, carrying out each year what I deemed to be a limited number of pretty superficial value-for-money studies.

So the National Audit Office became the only body responsible for auditing public expenditure and assessing all value for money across all of the public sector. This was a massive job, made even more difficult by the fragmentation of public services that had resulted from government policies. Discussions with my Three Wise Men convinced me that we should hold a review of the adequacy of public audit in Britain. We devised an innovative way of proceeding, whereby the work would be undertaken by both government and Parliament, working in partnership, to evaluate public audit in the UK.

I discussed this possibility with the two relevant Cabinet ministers, Francis Maude at the Cabinet Office and Danny Alexander in the Treasury. I also talked to committee members, all of whom seemed supportive initially. Of course, I shared my ideas with Amyas Morse. Unsurprisingly, he thought the review threatened his empire. Again he set about scuppering the proposal by persuading Conservative members of the Public Accounts Committee that it was unnecessary.

The Conservative members clearly talked to the ministers, who concluded that there was no consensus, and the review never happened.

Describing these tussles suggests that the relationship with Amyas Morse was and remained fragile. Fortunately that was not true. In time we got to know and like each other; we developed a great mutual respect as we both came to understand that neither of us could succeed without the other succeeding and that co-operation, rather than conflict, would be to our benefit.

The same cannot be said of my relationship with Gus O'Donnell and some senior civil servants. Threatened by the new level of scrutiny of senior civil servants, which tradition-ally had been reserved only for politicians, the Civil Service used the full force of its pressure. Following a particularly bruising PAC hearing with Anthony Inglese, the senior legal adviser in Revenue and Customs, Cabinet Secretary Gus O'Donnell wrote me a letter that was highly critical of the way in which we conducted our inquiries. (I discuss this letter in the chapter on Goldman Sachs.) I assumed the letter was private, but quickly found out that it had been agreed by all the permanent secretaries and had been sent to the Clerk of the House of Commons.

I replied saying: 'It is the duty of the committee to pursue fearlessly the public and taxpayers' interest whenever and wherever we deem it necessary.'

Unfortunately that was not the end of the matter. Unbe-known to me, the Civil Service had commissioned the recently established Institute for Government to conduct interviews with committee members and senior officials seeking their views of the Public Accounts Committee.

Their researcher, with whom I had worked when I was a min-ister, insisted on coming to see me. She was only officialdom's messenger, but her message from senior civil servants was blunt. She showed me her findings, which left me aghast, not because of what they said about me, but because of what that revealed about civil servants and their approach to accountability and to their own power.

Her findings included a litany of criticism. Anonymous senior civil servants said: 'NAO/PAC are modelled on the red guards – not a convincing grown up model of government, for example swearing on the King James Bible.'

'Chair is an abysmal failure – Committee is very divided. She is the worst Chair I have ever seen.'

'MH is informed by friends in the media e.g. Polly Toynbee.'

'PAC becomes a political theatre . . . MH is heavy handed . . . seen as ridiculous . . .'

'PAC has mistaken their role and should focus on the regulatory aspects of expenditure. It is under appreciated how important dull committees are.'

The final paragraph read: 'Should the PAC be broken up?' The explicit threat the researcher relayed to me was that if we did not change how we held civil servants to account, we would be closed down. Shut up or we will shut you down. That was what left me aghast: the civil servants' apparent belief that they could dictate and control how politicians behaved and that they would legislate us out of existence if we did not abide by their interpretation of the world. The views of the most senior civil servants were both arrogant about their own position and lacking in respect for Members of Parliament.

I shared the report with all the members of the committee and with Sir Edward Leigh, who had preceded me as chair. They were unanimous in saying that the views expressed were completely inappropriate, reflecting a completely mistaken view of the power of the Civil Service and the role of Parliament. The approach taken by Gus O'Donnell had backfired and the committee became even more determined to hold civil servants to account in the way we saw fit, whether they liked it or not.

Our powers were actually very limited. We asked witnesses to come and give evidence to us. If witnesses turned down our invitation, we could command them to attend the hearing. That involved me signing a bit of paper ordering their presence. I did that three or four times.

I always felt nervous about the authority behind the order. I asked my clerk what would happen if the prospective witness chose to ignore the order requiring their presence. I was told that in those circumstances I could take the matter through the House of Commons and, with the consent of the House, the offending witness could be incarcerated in the Clock Tower under Big Ben for a period of time to reflect on their failures ... happily, we never tested that historical sanction. Apparently the House has not imprisoned a non-Member since 1880, although the power was widely used in the sixteenth, seventeenth and eighteenth centuries. Indeed, there were even eighty cases of committal between 1810 and 1880.

But I was conscious of the limits of our powers. An Institute for Public Policy study in 2006 said that while officials might dread their appearances before the committee, they were confident that it would never really 'change the price of fish'.

I was determined to change the price of fish. I was determined we would do things differently. My experience in Barking taught me just how out of touch with the public we in Westminster were. I wanted to reconnect Parliament with people as voters, taxpayers and citizens by giving a voice to the issues that mattered to them. This meant that as well as taking evidence on reports produced by the National Audit Office, we would ask the NAO to carry out swift studies on matters of public interest – whether a scandal over the potential misuse of funds by an academy school, the failure of G4S to provide the security guards needed for the Olympics, or, of course, allegations of tax avoidance by multinational companies. Members of the committee suggested inquiries arising out of their constituency or other parliamentary work, which led us to look at a range of issues from the Ebola outbreak to the finances of Peterborough Hospital.

I wanted our work on public services to be rooted in people's experience of those services, so as well as hearing from those responsible for delivery we introduced pre-panels of subject experts to give us their insight – for example, Mencap, when we looked at services for adults with severe learning difficulties; Citizens Advice, on the impact of changes to welfare benefits; and local authorities, involved in implementing the Troubled Families programme.

The Coalition government dramatically expanded the role of the private sector in public service delivery. I was determined that these private providers should be held to account just as rigorously as were the public sector – no matter how many feathers that ruffled in private companies unused to being accountable to anybody but their shareholders and, in many cases, unused to being held to account on quality rather than simply on profit margin. We took evidence from companies such as Atos, on its catastrophic implementation of the new Personal Independence Payment scheme for people with disabilities; Capita, on its failure to deliver court interpretation services; G4S, on the quality of accommodation provided to vulnerable asylum seekers; and Serco, on its misreporting of performance data in its contract to deliver out-of-hours GP services in Cornwall.

Even when it came to hearing evidence from civil servants, I discovered ludicrous conventions that inhibited our ability to hold individuals to account.

For instance, the convention was that the person answerable to Parliament for a particular programme had to be the accounting officer who held the job at the time of the parliamentary hearing, regardless of whether they had been in charge when the programme was implemented. This bizarre practice emerged when we wanted to consider a report on the failures of the Rural Payments Agency. Helen Gosch, the permanent secretary who had been in charge of the Department for Environment, Food and Rural Affairs (DEFRA) for five years, was an experienced civil servant, who had just been promoted to the Home Office and so felt that she no longer had to account to Parliament for her actions at DEFRA. She refused two invitations to appear before the committee on the issue. In an email to the committee staff, Mike Lutz from her office wrote: 'Given the passage of time since Helen was Permanent Secretary at DEFRA, and considering that the current permanent secretary of the department is responsible for reporting to the committee, we do not feel that it is appropriate for Helen to appear ... Additionally we are aware of a letter from Edward Leigh to Gus O'Donnell dated 27 March 2006 where the then PAC chair promised to obtain a committee resolution each time a former Accounting Officer is recalled. We are not aware of such a PAC resolution having been passed.' It was only after I ordered her to come and give evidence to us that she reluctantly agreed. This episode led to a change in the convention, which was accepted by both government and senior civil servants. We now do call civil servants to give evidence on programmes for which they were responsible, even if they have moved on.

We challenged other conventions. Rather than just having accounting officers appear before us, usually the permanent secretaries, we called as witnesses those civil servants who were directly responsible for the programme we were reviewing; often their evidence was much more convincing than that of their superiors, because, of course, they knew what they were talking about.

We broke other conventions to strengthen accountability, such as regularly returning to issues where we had particular concerns. We held several sessions on the Rural Broadband programme, a £2 billion taxpayer-funded subsidy to BT aimed at extending broadband access to rural areas; we held three hearings on the progress – or rather the lack of progress – in dealing with nuclear waste at Sellafield; and we frequently returned to evaluate the Work Programme, where I took the view that government was wasting hundreds of millions of pounds on an ineffective intervention.

We set aside time to call back departments and their senior managers if we felt they hadn't implemented the changes we had recommended or if they expressed unreasonable disagreement with our recommendations. The threat of being recalled acted as a strong incentive to both respond and act positively. It helped ensure that our reports did not simply fill the shelves in my office, but led to improvements in public service delivery.

We instituted other changes. The National Audit Office produced landscape reviews for us, which allowed us to understand the full context of a department's work over time, and also helped track the efficiency and effectiveness of complex, long-term projects. This represented a departure from the tradition of just looking back at what had been done in the past. We were able to report regularly as major reform projects progressed and so could exert influence at an earlier stage.

Finally, anybody reading about us in the press or watching our antics on the screen would be forgiven for thinking that we only ever uncovered disasters. We did review successful, well-run projects and programmes that delivered what was intended in an efficient and effective way. Our aim was to improve public service delivery and I wanted us to celebrate success. We created a Public Accounts Committee award for the department or body which showed outstanding service delivery and value for money. This became a regular feature of the Civil Service Awards ceremony.

But getting coverage for good news stories is impossible. I shall never forget the occasion when we produced a report on sixteen- to nineteen-year-olds in education. The report was pretty positive and also contained recommendations for further improvements. I got a phone call from a researcher on BBC Radio 4's *Today* programme asking whether I would agree to appear on the following morning's show to discuss the report's findings. I replied that I would be delighted to do so. She asked me what I would say. I said that I would be pretty complimentary and that I would highlight the areas where things were going well, in addition to talking about the areas we thought required improvement.

'But I thought you were going to be critical,' the researcher exclaimed.

'No,' I replied. 'This is a pretty encouraging assessment.'

'Oh,' she said. 'I'd better go away and read it.'

She came back twenty minutes later to tell me that they had dropped the item from the programme.

In 1960, as the committee approached its centenary, Harold Wilson said that it had 'stood the test of time'. Through the way we approached our work, I and other members of the committee sought to ensure that it continued to do so. I believe that we did a pretty good job and I am confident our successors will take up the mantle and endeavour to do the same.

3

The Start of the Investigation into Tax

Shortly after I was elected to chair the Public Accounts Committee, David Davis, the Conservative MP who had successfully led the committee between 1997 and 2001, approached me offering help and support as I settled into my new job. Since failing in his attempt to become leader of the Conservative Party, David championed many causes from the backbenches, particularly on civil liberties. He often worked closely with MPs from across the political parties. Those outside Westminster may not know about the frequent collaboration that occurs between backbench MPs from different parties. This collegiate approach is rarely talked about, but it is very important, especially for backbenchers; it helps us all do more and do it better. I am grateful to David for the advice he regularly gave me throughout the five years I did the job.

During our initial discussion just after my appointment, I recall him pointing his finger at me and saying, 'Vodafone. You must look at Vodafone and tax.' I couldn't for the life of me understand what he was talking about. How could the tax affairs of a private company impinge on the concerns of a committee charged with following the taxpayer's pound?

Five years on, I am much wiser. Indeed, it was the committee's work on tax and tax avoidance that catapulted us on to the front pages and had a significant impact not just on the public, but on politicians, global corporations and very rich individuals.

The tax affairs of a private company are relevant because how tax liabilities are assessed and how efficiently the money owed is collected impacts on the effectiveness of HM Revenue and Customs (HMRC) – the government department responsible for collecting tax. Not only is tax collection clearly within the remit of the Public Accounts Committee, it is also hugely important. How good the department is at collecting the tax revenues is critical to the public finances and HMRC's failure to collect every pound that is owed impacts negatively on other taxpayers and every public service. It also impacts on everybody's sense of whether they live in a fair society. It is worth quoting some figures to demonstrate the point.

HMRC calculates what it calls the 'tax gap'. The tax gap is its estimate of the difference between what it thinks the Exchequer should receive in revenues and what in practice it does receive. HMRC has been focused on reducing that gap for at least ten years. Under the pre-2010 Labour government, the 2010–15 Coalition government and now the Conservative government, resources and staffing levels have theoretically been concentrated on the effort to reduce the gap. Yet the gap remains stubbornly high. In 2011–12, HMRC admitted to an increase of £1 billion over the year before, with the figure rising to a staggering £35 billion, and by 2013–14, it was still £34 billion. Getting just half of that money in would pay for nearly half of the annual defence budget or enable us to employ over three quarters of a million more nurses for a year.

Every year HMRC writes off around £5 billion in its accounts as uncollectable and gives up on a further £10 billion that it judges it will be unlikely to collect. We are talking big numbers.

The figure of £34 billion is itself contested. Richard Murphy, who is a longstanding tax campaigner and member of the Tax Justice Network, has argued that the figure is probably closer to £120 billion. For example, in his analysis of 2009–10 data, he claimed that a third of the companies registered at Companies House were not asked by HMRC to submit any return for corporation tax purposes. Of those who were asked to submit a return, a further third ignored the request. So of the nearly 2.8 million companies registered at Companies House, fewer than 1.2 million submitted a tax return. Some of these companies would have been dormant, some would have been new, but HMRC appeared – according to Richard Murphy – to turn a blind eye to these companies. They apparently did not know whether any of them should have been paying tax and did not include any assessment of potential tax in their calculation of the tax gap. Goodness knows how much tax those companies owed.

Arriving at an accurate figure for the tax gap is impossible, partly because our tax system is so complex, but also because there is no access to the information. The law requires that all information pertaining to any taxpayer remains secret and confidential, so we are left trying to construct an accurate picture from the little that is in the public domain.

HMRC does provide overall figures, which show that the amount being paid by large companies in corporation tax is going down, though profits are going up. In 2010–11, HMRC collected £43 billion through corporation tax; two years later that had dropped to £40.5 billion. This drop can partly be explained by the government's decision to cut the headline rate from 28 per cent in 2010 to 20 per cent in 2016 with a promise that it will further reduce to 17 per cent by 2020.

Although the government argued that a lower rate would increase tax revenues that did not happen and corporation tax now contributes a smaller slice of the total tax take than it did six years ago. And this despite the fact that the economy is now well past the 2008 bank-fuelled recession.

HMRC also provides data on their current disputes with the biggest companies. At the end of 2010–11, there were over 2700 separate issues with large companies subject to dispute, involving a potential tax value of £25.5 billion. Again, we are talking very big figures.

Furthermore, HMRC fail to include in their assessment of the tax gap the tax that most of us believe companies like Amazon, Google and Starbucks should pay on the profits they make from economic activity they undertake in the British jurisdiction. These multinationals, as I shall describe in future chapters, create an artificial structure of companies across the world with the sole purpose of shifting profits out of the UK to avoid paying tax. HMRC tells us that under the current law, they are not required to pay more tax in the UK and therefore HMRC does not include the potential tax from these companies in their tax gap calculation. As the reader will see in the discussion on Google, the issue of whether or not these companies are liable, even under current rules, remains an open question. And how much the Exchequer could collect if the international rules changed is also important.

With tax being so secret, all we can do is make an intelligent guess at the sums lost to the UK Exchequer. So, for example, an analysis by *Financial Mail* journalists in 2012 looked at the accounts filed in the USA for the 2010 financial year by five Internet giants: Apple, Google, Amazon, eBay and Facebook. Their analysis led the *Financial Mail* to assert that by using a complex net of offshore companies to receive payments from UK customers, the Internet companies hid a total of over

£12 billion in revenues earned from UK customers and nearly £2.5 billion profits made from this business. The journalists calculated that the companies should have paid some £685 million in corporation tax on those profits, but ended up paying just £19 million, an effective rate of 0.8 per cent on the profits they earned from their UK business.

The *Financial Mail* analysis may be rough and ready and the figures tax campaigners use are probably overstated, but equally I do not have much confidence in HMRC's own assessment of the tax gap. So even if we settle somewhere in the middle of £34 billion (the HMRC figure) and £120 billion (the tax campaigners' figure), the sums are enormous. There is a huge amount of tax at stake and hence the importance of the debate.

What is surprising is that these issues have not been more central to our thinking in the past. The Public Accounts Committee hearings on tax were groundbreaking in many ways. For the first time we focused on how taxes are collected as well as how they are spent. And we did not allow complexity to deter us.

The ridiculous complexity of the tax system has acted as a shield, preventing most people from understanding how the system works. That same complexity has allowed the richest and most powerful in our society, supported by a wealthy and well-established tax-avoidance industry comprising advisers, accountants, lawyers and bankers, to find clever ways aimed solely at helping the rich pay less than their proper share of tax.

Our public hearings helped to shine a light on what had been going on for years. We helped to stimulate public debate and encourage greater scrutiny of the workings of the tax system. Tax professionals and large multinationals, whose behaviour had been unchallenged for decades, found they had to justify their actions in public. This was not about being anti-business. Far from it. Some of those most damaged by the aggressive tax avoidance of global multinationals were UK businesses employing British workers – from John Lewis to the high street bookshop to the community-based coffee shop – most of whom paid their taxes. In fact, small businesses today feel hounded by the taxman for every last penny they owe.

Our inquiries were about being pro-fairness. Nobody should be so big that they can negotiate secret, favourable terms with HMRC. Nobody should be so important that they can aggressively avoid tax and get away with it. Every person and every company should be treated equally by the tax authorities.

Our hearings attracted much attention both nationally and internationally and reflected the public mood. In part this was because most people pay their contribution without question and without choice. In Britain 85 per cent of the population pay their individual taxes automatically through the PAYE system, with tax deducted from their earnings at source. To discover that an extremely rich individual or a large global corporation can choose to opt out of paying taxes is simply seen as unfair and offensive. The very people who should be paying the most into the common pot for the common good are getting away with not paying what they owe. The issue has added potency at this time, when many families are under pressure to both maintain their standard of living and pay all their bills. At the same time, the impact of public service cuts is affecting many communities, and again that influences attitudes and strengthens hostility to those who deliberately avoid tax.

A frequent rebuke I encountered when arguing that there was a moral dimension to paying your taxes, was that it was absurd for me to inveigh against the immorality of tax avoidance. After all, as a Member of Parliament I was responsible for writing the law. That was my job. If I wanted individuals or companies to behave differently, I should write the laws differently.

How could I expect people voluntarily to pay more taxes than the law required? Surely directors of companies had a duty to maximise their profits, which meant that they had to minimise their tax bill? Paying tax, my opponents argued, was nothing to do with morality and was entirely a question of legality.

Of course, there is some substance in the argument, but only a little. Some of the laws introduced by Parliament are unworkable and unfair, and Parliament should write simpler, clearer, better and fewer laws.

Nevertheless, in my view paying tax is both a moral and a legal issue – and the moral arguments trump the legal arguments every time. Being a member of a community, a citizen of a country, or a person living in a particular tax jurisdiction involves entering into a compact and agreeing to a system of rules and regulations that makes all of our lives better. So we all have a duty to contribute to the system; in order to gain, we all have a responsibility to give.

Indeed, it is especially important for the richest and most powerful in society to stick to the spirit and not just the letter of the law, because they gain the most from the system, in terms of their individual or corporate wealth. The latest data from the Office for National Statistics suggests that the richest 1 per cent of the population own as much wealth as the poorest 55 per cent put together.

A vital component in the compact we make with each other is that we agree to contribute through taxation into the common pot for the common good. The level of taxation and who pays is determined through democracy, by the government of the day.

Those who pay their taxes through PAYE have little choice over whether to do so but to see others take advantage of legal loopholes to avoid paying is grossly unfair. This is not about companies breaking the law by 'evading' tax. It is about offending the intention and spirit of the law by 'aggressively avoiding' tax. That is where morality comes in.

How can it be right for big corporations and wealthy individuals to ride roughshod over the intentions of Parliament? If Parliament had intended Google to pay a mere £130 million in corporation tax on the revenue of $24 billion – around £16.5 billion – they earned in the UK over the ten years from 2005 to 2015, they would have laid that out in legislation. Parliament didn't intend that and Google, along with others, is deliberately exploiting loopholes in the law to avoid paying the tax that Parliament intended.

Claiming that you are not breaking the law and not evading tax does not make you a good company or an upright citizen. You should work within the spirit and intention of the law as well as its letter. For tax, that means you should contribute a proper share, as decided by Parliament, according to your income, wealth or profits, into the collective funds of the jurisdiction where you have made that money. What would happen if everybody decided to behave like Google? The public coffers would collapse and public services would disintegrate. Ensuring the sustainability of our collective infrastructure depends on collective responsibility.

Of course lawmakers have a responsibility to try to write clear and unambiguous laws, but to suggest that we deliberately pass poorly drafted laws is absurd. The reality is that it is impossible to draw up a set of tax rules that are so tight as to cover every eventuality. Setting out watertight legislation is impracticable. The people who understand that best are the very people who scream from the rooftops that questioning the morality of what they do constitutes cynical bullying or grandstanding.

HMRC, in written evidence to the Public Accounts Committee, admitted: 'Because the application of tax law to a particular set of complex circumstances is not straightforward, there may be more than one possible answer as to how the issue in dispute should be resolved.'

Jane McCormick, head of tax at KPMG, admitted in evidence to us when asked how she drew the line between legitimate tax planning and egregious tax avoidance: 'There is this grey area. We have difficulty in definitions.'

Many of those who complain about the ambiguities in the law are the people who make their living out of identifying and using those ambiguities. Think of the army of accountants, lawyers, advisers and bankers who earn huge salaries for providing advice to corporations and individuals on how to avoid tax. The four big accountancy firms alone told us that together, their tax business in the UK was worth £2 billion a year to them.

The lawyers and accountants who claim that the problem of tax avoidance is down to poorly drafted legislation are the very people who thrive on finding new loopholes and make millions out of the endless inevitable ambiguities. It is hardly in their interest for the law to be clearer or tighter. And anyway, even if we wrote a thousand pages of new law to try to cover every eventuality, they would find a way around it.

What is most perturbing is that often those who exploit the ambiguities and loopholes have had a hand in writing the technical rules and the tax laws. The starkest example of this came from the Public Accounts Committee evidence session that we held with the four big accountancy firms.

It emerged that a corporate tax partner in KPMG, Jonathan Bridges, had been seconded to the Treasury to help write the rules for a new tax relief, christened the Patent Box relief. The government wanted to introduce this new relief to encourage companies to commercialise their patents, and to create jobs and growth by using patents to establish new business activity. When Alistair Darling first launched the tax relief he said in the House of Commons in the 2009 Pre-Budget Report: 'I will introduce a 10 per cent corporation tax rate on income which stems from patents in the UK. This will help maintain jobs in science and technology in this country.'

In a similar vein, the Conservative David Gauke said, as Exchequer Secretary to the Treasury in 2013: 'The Patent Box is a key initiative to make the UK tax regime competitive for high-tech companies. It provides an incentive for them to retain and commercialise existing patents and to develop new, innovative products. Our aim is for this tax relief to encourage companies to create high value jobs in the UK and maintain the UK's competitive position as a world leader in patent technologies.'

The KPMG partner had the technical expertise required to formulate the law and spent eighteen months in the Treasury helping to develop the tax rules. But no sooner had he completed his secondment and returned to KPMG than he helped to produce a brochure entitled: 'Patent Box – what's in it for you.' The brochure was designed to encourage KPMG's clients to exploit the new relief and thereby avoid tax. For example, the brochure claimed: 'Patent Box will enable a more economical use of tax reliefs ... KPMG can advise on the opportunities available in order to maximise the relief.' The brochure went on to stress how KPMG could help 'to maximise Patent Box Revenue' by the 'preparation of defendable expense allocation' and by 'optimising the structuring of licence agreement arrangements'. That was not the purpose intended by Parliament. The KPMG partner had had a hand in creating the legislation with the loopholes it included. A poacher turned gamekeeper and then poacher again.

What to me is so frustrating is that so many talented and experienced experts spend their working lives helping those with the broadest shoulders avoid tax. Both the Organisation for Economic Co-operation and Development (OECD) and the European Commission found that the Patent Box relief was a 'harmful tax practice' that would not encourage new products but would encourage companies simply to shift their profits from other countries to the UK to avoid tax.

Aggressive tax avoidance is thus not the fault of the law-makers alone. Morality also has a role to play. One's moral obligations in this area are independent of one's legal obligations. And surely it is morally wrong to seek to interpret the law not in the way Parliament intended but with the sole purpose of avoiding tax.

There will always be ways of gaming the system and the boundary between legitimate tax planning and aggressive tax avoidance will always be blurred and require judgement. But that does not excuse the current practices of too many businesses and too many rich individuals. It does not make them good citizens.

For companies, being good citizens matters. Reputation impacts on profitability. We saw that clearly with Starbucks. The consumer boycott of their outlets after the exposure of their tax affairs at the Public Accounts Committee shattered their reputation and hit Starbucks hard.

Reputation can impact on the bottom line, so acting morally as well as legally is not only right but can help companies to maximise their profits. Indeed, research by Christian Aid in 2014 found that 85 per cent of British adults believe that tax avoidance is morally wrong even if it is legal. In all, 34 per cent of those questioned in a survey a year earlier said that they were currently boycotting the products or services of a company because it did not pay its fair share of tax in the UK.

The corporate social responsibility agenda that has been embraced by a growing number of companies over the last twenty years reflects a change in approach. Companies acknowledge that being a good corporate citizen enhances their standing and so supports improved profitability. That is why over the years companies have become more sensitive about their employees' terms, conditions, training opportunities and so on; it is why they pay greater attention to their supply chain to ensure they are not exploiting low-paid workers in developing countries; it is why they try to contribute in cash and in kind to their communities. Paying a proper share of tax should become an important element of a company's corporate social responsibility.

The moral arguments do not impinge solely on Britain and other Western countries. Multinationals shift the profits they earn from their economic activities in developing countries to tax havens. This matters even more to developing countries than it does to richer nations, because developing nations need the public investment even more, and corporation taxes form a larger proportion of tax revenues in developing countries than they do in richer jurisdictions. Angela Gurria, Secretary-General of the OECD, stated in November 2008: 'Developing countries are estimated to lose to tax havens almost three times what they get from developed countries in aid.' Poor countries, the OECD claims, could eliminate hunger in just one decade with less than a third of the money they lose to tax avoidance by big corporations.

Greed is part of human nature. Lawmakers cannot design it out. Values and morals have a role to play. What we have to do is argue for and promote a culture where everybody accepts their responsibility to pay their proper share of tax. Avoiding tax should not be seen as rebellious or clever. Paying tax should be seen as decent and honourable – and expected from all, individuals and multinationals alike. Thankfully that is the view that is held by most people in Britain today.

Over the following chapters I describe some of the key injustices that, aided by journalists, whistleblowers and tax campaigners, the Public Accounts Committee exposed. This includes:

- How HMRC agreed, and then attempted to keep secret, special deals with Goldman Sachs.
- The complex smoke-and-mirrors structures used by Starbucks, Google and Amazon, with the sole aim of avoiding paying many millions of pounds of tax in the UK each year.
- The huge sums of money earned by the four big account-ancy firms from advising their clients on how to avoid paying tax.
- The over-cosy relationships and revolving doors between HMRC and tax professionals; the capture of tax policy by multinationals and the tax-avoidance industry, with those involved in drafting the law swiftly turning to become those who are paid to advise others on how to avoid it.
- The shady world of boutique advisers and how they work with QCs and banks to ensure they never lose, even when the schemes they sell are found to be unlawful.
- The role of HSBC in Switzerland in facilitating avoid-ance and even tax evasion by UK citizens using secret bank accounts.
- The absurdly long list of tax reliefs that grows year by year and that enables politicians to fund pet ideas by the back door; reliefs that become another opportunity to

avoid tax, that are ineffectively monitored and evaluated, and that cost the Exchequer £100 billion each year.

In the final chapter on tax I set out some ideas for action that would create a fairer tax system in which we could have confidence that everybody was treated equally under tax law.

Ironically, the one company we never investigated properly was the one that started it all off when David Davis took me aside that morning – Vodafone. To this day I do not know whether they got away with a deal that cost the taxpayer £6 billion or whether they were treated in exactly the same way as the smallest business in my constituency.

4

The Goldman Sachs Deal

Our inquiries started with the Goldman Sachs affair. All the initial intelligence on this tax deal came not from HMRC officials or the National Audit Office, but, believe it or not, from my regular reading of *Private Eye*. It was the stories in *Private Eye* that enabled Members of Parliament to start asking questions.

HMRC consistently claimed that they could not divulge any details and tell us the facts about the case, because that would offend their duty to protect the confidential information given to them by taxpayers – a key issue to which I shall return – but the law requiring confidentiality around any taxpayer's interests meant that all the action HMRC took in relation to collecting tax from individuals or companies was secret and nothing was transparent.

Private Eye was running a story on a tax-avoidance scheme set up in 1997 by over twenty investment banks and other companies, designed to pay their staff offshore and thereby avoid making the necessary National Insurance payments. Goldman Sachs was one of these companies. It had established a company in the British Virgin Islands called Goldman Sachs

Services Ltd. They claimed that their London-based employees were employed by this offshore entity and were only 'seconded' to work in the UK. They used this device both to avoid National Insurance contributions and to hide the size of the bankers' bonuses. At the end of the 1990s, a junior banker at Goldman Sachs could expect to be paid an annual bonus of between £150,000 and £200,000.

To avoid the National Insurance payments, Goldman Sachs (and the other companies) set up an elaborate scheme that involved employee benefit trusts. Their employees were paid through the trusts.

In 2005, HMRC successfully challenged the scheme as a tax-avoidance ruse and all but one of the companies settled and paid up. Goldman Sachs refused to settle, leading HMRC to take legal action against them.

Goldman Sachs were warned that if they did not settle they would incur additional costs arising from the interest charged on the money they owed. Indeed, HMRC's own published litigation strategy, which set out the protocols for dealing with tax avoidance and evasion, made it clear that HMRC was obliged to pursue Goldman Sachs for 100 per cent of the tax and interest owed. After one of the committee hearings where the issue had been raised, Dave Hartnett, Permanent Secretary for Tax, wrote to us and said: 'All disputes must be resolved in accordance with the law; HMRC does not "split the difference" with the taxpayer or enter into "package deals" in which one issue is traded off against another.'

However, the City firm fought HMRC tooth and nail from 2005 onwards. An HMRC document leaked to the committee talked about how Goldman Sachs 'resisted for 5 more years, including as (Case Lawyer) explained making every conceivable point in the Tribunal, and putting up a "stooge" witness when Mr Housden [a senior executive at Goldman Sachs] was the obvious person to answer the question'. Judge Norris, who gave directions at a preliminary hearing in the case, said in his judgement: 'I have tried to avoid being seduced . . . by the blustering intransigence of the other and its determination to litigate everything to the bitter end.' According to other leaked documents, by 2010 the bill owing to HMRC had risen to £40 million.

Then in April 2010, Goldman Sachs lost a tribunal case in the British Virgin Islands when a judge determined that the bankers were not employed by the offshore company and were indeed employees of the UK-based company and therefore liable for National Insurance contributions. Armed with that success, HMRC was advised by a leading QC that this put the government in a strong position to extract all of its money from Goldman Sachs, including all the interest due.

That advice was given in July 2010; yet by November 2010 a deal had been struck between HMRC and Goldman Sachs which appeared to have let the bankers off paying all that was due. It was difficult to establish the facts because, as always, the information was deemed confidential. As far as we could glean, the taxpayer lost between £5 million and £8 million of interest payments in what could only be seen as a 'sweetheart' deal. We were never able to establish the precise figure.

In the context of a tax gap of between £34 billion and £120 billion this is not a great amount, but it was the first time we had any insight into how HMRC dealt with powerful taxpayers and financial institutions. The only public document to which the committee had access was the litigation strategy document produced by HMRC that set out how it would deal in principle with tax disputes. That document clearly stated that settling for anything less than 100 per cent of the tax and interest due was not allowed in cases such as Goldman Sachs.

Armed with the *Private Eye* allegations, which set out the alleged terms of a 'sweetheart' deal, Jesse Norman, the Conservative MP for Hereford and South Herefordshire, was the first MP to raise the issue at a meeting of the Treasury Select Committee. This public hearing took place before the meeting of the Public Accounts Committee. Dave Hartnett, Permanent Secretary for Tax at HMRC, was the witness. Hartnett had joined HMRC in 1976, three years after he left university, rising through the ranks to become the top official on tax. He looked unremarkable, bespectacled, with red cheeks and somewhat dishevelled hair, but despite his ordinary demeanour, he was the most powerful official in government when it came to tax. Under the instructions of Gordon Brown, he had led the effort to secure more tax from the large multinationals and was seen by companies, tax professionals, HMRC staff and ministers as the key official in this area.

Jesse Norman began by asking: 'There has been a deal done with Goldman, I think I am right in saying, in which they were—'

At this point he was interrupted by Dave Hartnett, who said: 'I am really sorry, but I cannot talk about a specific taxpayer. To make sure I could not do that, twice in the last ten days, I have been to see our most senior lawyers to see whether there was anything I could say about the newspaper reports on this, and they have said no.'

Pressed further by Norman on whether he had discussed the issue at a dinner with Goldman Sachs' partners, Dave Hartnett ended up saying: 'I knew nothing of Goldman's tax affairs when I was at that supper. I do not deal with Goldman's tax affairs.'

When Hartnett appeared before the Public Accounts Committee, he stalled in a similar manner and refused to answer any questions we put to him on Goldman Sachs, again hiding behind his legal obligations in relation to taxpayer confidentiality.

We were left frustrated and none the wiser. It seemed that we had hit an insuperable buffer and could not pursue the matter any further.

And then I received a big brown envelope from a whistleblower who worked as a lawyer in HMRC. The envelope contained a huge wad of papers and I was in two minds as to whether I had the time to go through the whole lot. The House of Commons' clerk to the committee must have looked at the papers. He suggested that I should look through the file and that I might find what was in it interesting, so I did.

In the middle of the pile I found a crucial document. It consisted of the minutes of a meeting held in HMRC with the head of law at the Revenue, to discuss the Goldman Sachs deal. The meeting had been held a couple of weeks after the deal was struck. The minutes were astonishing. First, those present at the meeting talked 'about a deal on which DH [Dave Hartnett] had "shaken hands" with GS [Goldman Sachs]'. But Hartnett had claimed categorically to the Treasury Select Committee that he had nothing to do with the tax affairs of Goldman Sachs and did not deal with them.

The minutes also stated that 'the proposed settlement gave GS [Goldman Sachs] no additional penalty for having resisted for 5 more years' and 'AI [Anthony Inglese, the top lawyer at HMRC] said that he would always want to assist DH [Dave Hartnett], but not if this were "unconscionable". He referred to the difficulty all those present at this meeting were having in justifying a settlement without an interest element.'

So we now had evidence from a whistleblower that confirmed the *Private Eye* story and indicated both that the head of tax had misled a parliamentary committee and that the deal the same individual had struck with Goldman Sachs was considered 'unconscionable' by the head of law in HMRC.

Deliberately misleading Parliament is considered a grave offence in our system. Signing up to a sweetheart deal with a powerful financial institution against your own published guidelines is bound to undermine confidence in the tax authorities.

Armed with these minutes we, of course, recalled the head of tax, Dave Hartnett, to what became a highly charged evidence session which began with my saying: 'I am going to start with a rather tough question: it seems to me that you lied when you told the Treasury Select Committee on 12 September that "I do not deal with Goldman's tax affairs."'

Unsurprisingly Hartnett found it difficult to convince us that he had been entirely honest in his previous evidence. He insisted he only met with Goldman Sachs on a single occasion – at the crucial meeting where the strange deal was concluded. He claimed that when he had said he did not deal with Goldman's tax affairs, he meant that he had no 'deep knowledge' of their affairs and that he did not deal with them on a 'regular' basis.

However, he admitted that he had overseen the litigation launched by HMRC against the twenty-two companies referred to earlier to ensure that they did not avoid National Insurance contributions by setting up employee benefit trusts, so he must have known a good deal about Goldman Sachs.

It also became clear that Mr Hartnett had a close working relationship with Goldman Sachs. He admitted accepting corporate hospitality 107 times between 2007 and 2009, mostly from big businesses and their advisers. Indeed, in 2010, Dave Hartnett was named by City University as the most wined and dined civil servant in Britain. He ate with KPMG ten times, accepted hospitality from PricewaterhouseCoopers seven times, and from Ernst and Young four times. He also enjoyed a free lunch, dinner and a reception with Goldman Sachs.

Tax officials do need working relationships with large companies because a great deal of tax is at stake. But these relationships have to be appropriate, especially given the shroud of secrecy that engulfs tax. Several of Hartnett's comments to our committee suggested his behaviour was not entirely appropriate. When we asked whether it was proper for him to accept lunches when doing so could be perceived as compromising his judgement and his integrity, he replied that since civil servants had to publish their hospitality engagements, 'I find other ways of doing things.' When asked what other ways, he replied: 'Well, maybe a cup of coffee in my office ... we are not required to record a cup of coffee.' This suggested that he was happy to be less than transparent in his dealings with large taxpayers. Indeed, in answer to a parliamentary question it emerged that Hartnett had met the chairman of the UK board of partners at Deloitte on forty-eight separate occasions in the five years to April 2011.

At another point in the evidence session he told us: 'I happened to know someone who I thought could unlock it [the dispute with Goldman Sachs] and that person flew in from New York.' Again indicating a cosy relationship between the company and HMRC.

When we asked whether HMRC had a note of the meeting in which the deal with Goldman Sachs was struck, he told us that no such minute existed. Hartnett said that 'there was a note prepared of the meeting – in fact, by Goldman Sachs and our people believed the note was a fair reflection of what had taken place'.

Dave Hartnett was the principal official involved in negotiating a settlement with Goldman Sachs. But he also sat on the small internal HMRC committee that vetted the resulting deal. He was a tax commissioner (a title given to four senior officials in HMRC) with responsibility for signing off the deal – the only tax commissioner in HMRC, according to Hartnett himself, who had what he called 'deep knowledge' of tax. And he was the official with responsibility for deciding whether such matters could be placed in the public domain.

Goldman Sachs was not the only settlement where HMRC had broken its own rules. The National Audit Office had identified at least three other cases, where again we were unable to examine the facts.

What emerged from Hartnett's testimony was a wholly secret process, with inappropriate authorisations, utterly inadequate accountability structures, and relationships between top officials in HMRC and powerful taxpayers that seemed far too cosy for comfort.

Despite our best efforts, Hartnett continued to refuse to discuss the details of the tax settlement with Goldman Sachs. He conceded that a mistake had been made but he would not explain why HMRC did not go back and claim from the firm all the monies due to the public coffers, although legally it could have done so.

We decided to call Anthony Inglese, head of law at HMRC, to give evidence. We simply wanted him to confirm the veracity of the minutes of the meeting that the whistleblower had given to me.

The session with Inglese was hugely frustrating. Although he was a civil servant, he claimed he owed his allegiance to his department and not to Parliament and that any advice he gave to Dave Hartnett was therefore covered by legal privilege, a worrying assertion as it undermines the accountability of civil servants to both ministers and Parliament. He also claimed that he could not discuss the details of the Goldman

Sachs deal because the network of protest groups UK Uncut was threatening to take proceedings against HMRC on the settlement. Despite our confirming with him that, as he had only received what lawyers call a letter before action, the matter was not yet sub judice and therefore could and should be examined, he persisted in refusing to answer questions. He also used the argument of confidentiality of taxpayers' interests to justify his persistent obfuscation.

I was wondering where to go next, when Richard Bacon, the Conservative MP who had served on the committee for a decade, whispered to me that I should put Mr Inglese on oath. He was feeling as frustrated as the rest of us and clearly thought that putting the witness on oath might elicit more information. I was unaware of my authority to do such a thing and turned to the clerk for advice as Inglese continued to witter away at the other end of the room. I asked him in a whisper whether I could put the witness on oath. He told me I could.

I could not consult the other members of the committee because we were in the middle of a session. So I simply said to the clerk:

'Well, go and get a Bible, then.'

It took the officials around twenty minutes to locate a Bible in the Palace of Westminster and when it was finally brought to the committee room, the committee insisted that Mr Inglese give the remainder of his evidence on oath. He had no option but to do so.

It was not meant to be a moment of high drama, but it became one. It did not throw much more light on the truth. It completely infuriated the Civil Service, who felt that we had impugned their integrity. But it made the headlines and suddenly everybody was talking about whether HMRC dealt with all taxpayers equally before the law.

I was often accused of grandstanding. Putting a civil servant on oath was an example used to justify the accusation. But the fact was that as chair of the Public Accounts Committee, my powers were limited. I had no executive authority and few effective tools to hold people to account on behalf of the taxpayer and get some purchase. Drawing the public's attention to issues that mattered was one of the few tools available and if that required moments of hyperbole, I considered that justified.

Those moments were never used to secure publicity for its own sake. We wanted to break through the conspiracy of silence. Our aim was always to attract publicity for a purpose. Our purpose here was to question whether HMRC was treating all taxpayers equally before the law; whether they were always acting in accordance with their own published guidelines for dealing fairly with tax disputes; whether there had been a sweetheart deal struck with Goldman Sachs; whether the accountability structures within HMRC were adequate to protect the public interest; and whether a senior civil servant had misled Parliament.

Our forthright sessions with HMRC officials secured some important changes. Dave Hartnett announced his retirement within a few weeks of our hearings. HMRC brought in two new tax commissioners who had a proper knowledge of tax law. The accountability structures were transformed to ensure a proper separation between those agreeing to a deal on a particular tax dispute and those responsible for approving it. A new post of tax assurance commissioner was created to oversee large tax settlements and scrutinise the governance arrangements. The tax assurance commissioner now produces an annual report and reviews all the large settlements and a random sample of other settlements of tax disputes.

All these are welcome changes. But what else did we learn from this inquiry? We never secured the transparency we sought and senior officials at HMRC continue to assert that they cannot discuss the details of taxpayers' affairs, whether it is the affairs of an individual or of a company.

The UK tax system is hugely complex with an enormous amount of room for discretion in the interpretation of our tax law. Indeed, Goldman Sachs's attempt to establish an offshore company and employee benefit trusts is evidence of both the ambiguity and complexity. So settling these disputes must sometimes be a matter of judgement, but one where substantial amounts of public money are at stake. In these circumstances it seems wrong that there is no proper, transparent mechanism for holding the people who make these decisions to account.

HMRC is different from most government departments. It is what is known as a non-ministerial department, which means that there is no minister involvement in taxpayers' cases, no minister to whom civil servants can be held to account, with the minister, in turn, being accountable to Parliament. The justification for this status is clear: it would be wrong for a politician to be able to direct HMRC to investigate the tax affairs of any individual. However, because taxpayers' details remain confidential (unless the taxpayer chooses to divulge them), there is no check on HMRC. Even the non-executives who sit on the HMRC board are not allowed to see any papers relating to individuals.

HMRC's actions and decisions cannot be called to account to give all taxpayers confidence that we are treated equally by them. The system is based on the rest of us trusting that they stick by the rules. Operating behind this thick shroud of secrecy means that when there are leaks about sweetheart deals, confidence in the integrity of the whole system is damaged.

Our suspicion that there is one set of rules for the rich and powerful and another for the small and ordinary is reinforced when we see from the published accounts of corporations how little tax they pay and when we are told about regular lunches and private dinners held between HMRC officials and large companies and their advisers. My colleague Austin Mitchell, then the MP for Grimsby, was so taken aback, he remarked ironically at one hearing: 'I just want to make it clear that in the eyes of my constituents, I am a very high taxpayer – a very high earner. My tax affairs are in their usual chaos ... and I am available for lunches on Tuesdays.'

Our ability to follow the taxpayer's pound became the Public Accounts Committee's oft-repeated mantra. If Goldman Sachs had been awarded a grant for £5 million–£8 million, the committee could have investigated that expenditure and come to a view on whether or not it represented good value for money. Because Goldman was let off tax in secret, we were unable to interrogate officials to judge whether this decision represented good value.

The committee tried hard to extract the facts. HMRC argued that they were constrained by the 2005 Revenue and Customs Act, Section 18 (1), which states: 'Revenue and Customs officials may not disclose information which is held by the Revenue and Customs in connection with a function of the Revenue and Customs.' A later section of the Act says that anybody who does reveal confidential information can be subject to criminal sanction and conviction. However, there are exceptions to this duty that are also set out in the legislation, including a clause that permits disclosure that is 'made for the purpose of a function of the Revenue and Customs'. Assisting Parliament is one such function.

HMRC argued that there were wider considerations. They thought that revealing information would have a damaging effect on the relationship of trust they have with taxpayers and would adversely affect their ability to collect tax. They argued that giving information to one body (the Public Accounts Committee) would make it impossible to resist requests from ministers and other agencies. They feared that revealing information would damage their reputation for impartiality.

We took a different view both of the law and of the policy judgement not to provide us with the facts. The law is clear that HMRC can disclose information in connection with a function of the Revenue and Customs, and as it is a function of HMRC to assist Parliament it must be lawful to provide us with the information we need to judge the efficiency and effectiveness of HMRC. We felt that HMRC were not constrained by the law, but that they had taken a policy decision not to give us the details.

We also felt that the policy argument that more openness would undermine taxpayer confidence was misplaced. On the contrary, openness might help to inspire greater confidence that HMRC treats everybody equally.

We only learned about Goldman Sachs because of thorough and tough investigative journalism and the actions of a brave whistleblower. There have been innumerable stories about preferential treatment given to other taxpayers. Surely confidence in the tax system would be better served if we had greater transparency?

A key frustration was our inability to challenge HMRC's decision on taxpayer confidentiality. HMRC kept referring to the legal opinions they had and the National Audit Office insisted that although they were able to see the papers relating to all settlements, they could not share them with us. The NAO, too, had scuttled off to get a counsel's opinion confirming this view.

Both HMRC and the National Audit Office have two sets of legal obligations: one to the taxpayer, the other to Parliament. We believed that their legal obligation to Parliament was as important as maintaining taxpayer confidentiality. We suggested that we could be given the information in confidence. We even suggested that I personally could see the papers on behalf of the committee, given that I was a Privy Counsellor, with the special privileges and obligations conferred by that status.

All our suggestions were turned down. As both the National Audit Office and HMRC had legal advice backing them, we wanted to obtain our own legal advice to challenge them. However, when I asked for this to be arranged I was told that there was no money available. The House of Commons has a £200 million budget, but the powers that be could not find the money we needed to test our view with the lawyers. That decision had, I thought, more to do with the system conspiring against us than with the finances of Parliament. If select committees are to hold the government to account effectively, we need to be able to access all the advice and support necessary to help us do our work. It is simply not on to permit public money to be used to fund advice to officials, but to deny the facility to politicians.

There are two important postscripts to this story. Senior civil servants were angered by the way we had conducted our inquiry. They strongly objected to our hearing with Anthony Inglese and our insistence that he should give evidence on oath. Gus O'Donnell was on the point of retiring as Cabinet Secretary but before he left the Civil Service at Christmas 2011, he sent me a highly critical letter. After reading it, I decided to ignore it as he was on his way out, so engaging in an argument with him seemed like a waste of time – until I discovered that he had copied the letter to everybody: all the senior civil servants, the National Audit Office and the Clerk of the House.

In the letter he said:

That is why I raise Anthony Inglese's hearing. Whilst
I acknowledge that the circumstances surrounding
this hearing were in many ways atypical, there is now
a serious issue about the way you are perceived by the
wider Civil Service, but more especially by the legal
community . . . First, when questioning him you set
out – in clear terms – a view held by your committee
that civil servants are directly accountable to Parliament.
I disagree strongly with this as a general principle. I am
sure you would agree that, to maintain their impartiality,
it is essential that civil servants remain accountable to
ministers, who are in turn accountable to Parliament . . .
only Accounting Officers are considered directly
accountable to Parliament, and they are only considered
accountable for a limited set of responsibilities . . . Second,
the Committee decided to overturn the usual conventions
on legal professional privilege, arguing that the balance
of the public interest in this case weighed in favour of
open discussion of the legal advice. However, looking
at parliamentary precedent for this, I find it difficult
to see how you could favour these [the public interest
arguments] over the very strong, long held and widely
accepted arguments for protecting legal professional
privilege.

Later, arguing against our decision to put the witness on oath,
he wrote: 'All civil servants are already bound by duties of
honesty and integrity which are now set out in legislation.'

He seemed to ignore the apparent discrepancies in the evidence we had had from the permanent secretary for tax. He
seemed unaware of present-day demands for accountability
and transparency that, in my view, must trump age-old conventions on the accountability of civil servants. He seemed

more focused on defending the civil servants than on using the experience to improve HMRC and defend the taxpayer's interest.

While O'Donnell determinedly supported his senior civil servant colleagues, neither he nor his successors showed the same concern to protect brave whistleblowers in the lower echelons of the public service.

Osita Mba was the lawyer who sent me the thick brown envelope. I deliberately never met him because I did not want to be accused of any personal bias, but I have kept in touch with him by text and email. He joined HMRC after training as a barrister in Nigeria and then completing a postgraduate degree course at Oxford. He sent incredibly detailed and meticulous evidence. It was his evidence that allowed us to expose what had happened. He demonstrated strong public service values and should have been commended for it. Instead he was hounded by HMRC who wanted to charge him with breaking the confidentiality laws. Exploiting powers under the Regulation of Investigatory Powers Act (2000) that had been brought in to tackle terrorists, HMRC gained entry to his locked office cabinet beneath his desk; they hacked into his hard drive; they looked at all his emails and traced his texts and phone calls; they even examined his wife's phone records. But they never found the evidence to charge him. However, HMRC kept him off work for a long time and when he finally came back, they made his life so intolerable that he decided to quit, and later his marriage broke down. At every possible occasion when HMRC appeared before the committee I asked whether they were treating Osita Mba properly and well. The permanent secretary, Lin Homer, always assured me they were, but this was clearly not the case. Worse still, when I sought assurances from Ms Homer that she would never employ RIPA powers against whistleblowers again, she refused to give that assurance.

My deepest regret from my time as chair of the Public Accounts Committee was a failure to protect a highly principled individual who refused to collude in a cover-up.

Whistleblowers played a vital role in many of our inquiries. Mostly they felt hounded after they had blown the whistle. When we held an evidence session on whistleblowing we could find only one individual willing to give evidence about their experience. Most felt beaten by the system. That is shameful. Senior civil servants may rush to protect their own class. Until they demonstrate equal concern for the ordinary civil servant who feels so frustrated by perceived wrongdoing and management failure to listen that he or she blows the whistle, they will not earn the confidence and respect they seek.

5

The Tax Tricks of Google, Starbucks and Amazon

Exposing the cosy relationships between HMRC and powerful companies, and identifying the loss caused to the taxpayer, was deemed a triumph. But none of us expected tax avoidance to dictate so much of the agenda for the Public Accounts Committee over the rest of the Parliament.

Our success in getting to the bottom of the Goldman Sachs affair had been made possible because of the brave and determined efforts of a whistleblower. I was pleased that we had achieved changes in the governance processes in HMRC. It was also good to see that Dave Hartnett had taken early retirement and that new people had been brought in. But I believed that this would close the chapter.

However, shortly after we published our report on Goldman Sachs, I got a call from Tom Bergin, an immensely able investigative journalist who worked for Reuters and who had seen what we had done on Goldman. He wanted to come and talk about the tax affairs of Starbucks, an American multinational company that he claimed was legally exploiting the national and international tax laws to shunt profits from one jurisdiction to another in order to avoid paying tax in the UK.

The story Bergin told astounded me. Starbucks had been operating in the UK since 1998, expanding its outlets and growing its business. Yet every year, bar one, the company filed losses in their accounts at Companies House. And while the published accounts showed these losses, Starbucks was busy telling investors that the business was highly profitable.

By declaring losses in the UK for every year except 2006, Starbucks avoided paying UK corporation tax. The Public Accounts Committee decided to invite the company to give evidence so that they could explain publicly how they ran their financial affairs and so that we could question them about why they adopted complex corporate structures that appeared to have no purpose other than to enable them to avoid paying the proper share of tax.

There had been a few stories in the press about other multinationals and their tax-avoidance strategies and I thought we would learn more if we grilled Starbucks alongside one other such company. I suspected that the Starbucks story raised bigger issues than we all had knowledge of at the time and I wanted to establish whether they were the only company behaving in this way.

My parliamentary researcher Liz Bradshaw showed me a list of a dozen companies whom the press had highlighted. I decided that Amazon would provide a good example of what was probably happening. I was a regular customer of Amazon and when the company sent me its daily emails, the term 'Amazon.co.uk' typically appeared four or five times in the message. Yet the company claimed to the UK tax authorities that it was not selling to its customers from a UK company but from a company based in Luxembourg and so they avoided UK corporation tax. They claimed the UK company was merely a service company, but by burying the information on the Luxembourg-based parent company in the small print, they hoodwinked customers like me into believing that we were dealing with a UK company. Amazon's company structures and financial arrangements seemed to demonstrate clearly the tactics that they and other companies were apparently employing to avoid tax.

The clerk to the committee rang Amazon but was told that no one was available to give evidence on the day we had pencilled in for the hearing. I was reluctant to change the date as we had a very tight schedule.

So I went back to the list Liz had provided and suggested that we call Google instead.

The clerk rang Google, but they, too, claimed that their executives were unavailable on the date we suggested. So I was left with no option but to change the date of the hearing. My staff asked which of the two companies I wanted to come and give evidence alongside Starbucks: Google or Amazon? 'Oh goodness, ask them both,' I replied. Both agreed to come. It was thus something of an accident that representatives from all three companies appeared before us on the same day, thereby collectively coming to symbolise the culture of corporate tax avoidance.

Starbucks

The Starbucks story was not unique, but it was – and is – enlightening. We took evidence from Starbucks in November 2012 and by then the company had been operating in Britain for over fourteen years. They ran 735 coffee shops and licensed a further 200 franchised stores to other operators in both the UK and Ireland.

Starbucks enjoyed over 30 per cent of the coffee shop market in the UK. Yet despite this rapid expansion and substantial presence, they claimed in their accounts that they were actually losing money.

Tom Bergin's research established that during thirteen of those fourteen years they had earned over £3 billion through sales, but had paid only £8.6 million in taxes because, despite such a large turnover, they claimed that they only made profits during one of the fourteen years. However, tapes of briefings for Starbucks' investors told a different story. Bergin found out that in those briefings executives consistently said that their UK business was extremely successful and lucrative.

In 2007, despite having filed losses for nine out of ten years, Starbucks told investors that it was the profits from the UK that were supporting their expansion overseas. In 2008, the CEO, Howard Schultz, told analysts the UK business was so successful that he planned to take the lessons learned and apply them in the USA. Shortly afterwards, he promoted the head of the UK and Europe Starbucks business, Cliff Burrows, to head up the business in the United States.

In our evidence session I asked Starbucks' representative Troy Alstead, the global chief financial officer: 'But it still seems very odd to file losses and then tell your US investors – or your global investors – that you are pleased with the performance in the UK and to promote Cliff Burrows. Why did you promote Cliff Burrows?'

To which Troy Alstead replied: 'Cliff Burrows helped us turn the UK from perpetual losses into the one year of profitability.'

In 2011, the President of Starbucks' International Division, John Culver, told analysts that 'we are very pleased with the performance in the UK', yet the company filed £33 million losses in that year. In 2012, Howard Schultz was ranked as the

354th richest person in the United States. There was one version of events for the investors, another for the UK authorities. What is so extraordinary is the sheer brazenness of this open inconsistency.

When the committee interrogated Troy Alstead he explained the contradiction by asserting: 'We are required to report our accounts in the UK under one standard. We are also required under US accounting to speak to our profitability in a different way . . .'

I said to him: 'The other thing that is odd to me is that you have made losses in the UK over fifteen years, which is what you are filing. Why on earth are you doing business here?'

He replied: 'We know that we must be in the UK to be a successful global company.'

When I came back with, 'But you are losing money here,' he replied, 'It is a critical market.'

I wanted to find out how they managed to convert the profits they made for the company in the UK into the losses they declared to the taxman. Over time and after looking at a number of multinationals, I came to understand that the tricks Starbucks used were commonplace.

Starbucks employed three specific devices to shift their profits out of the UK. First, global companies charge royalties to their businesses across the world. They locate their headquarters in a low-tax or no-tax jurisdiction and then charge subsidiaries in other jurisdictions a royalty fee, which is paid to the HQ company. Starbucks outlets in the UK had to pay a percentage of their earnings, for using the brand and for using certain business processes, to the Starbucks head office on the basis that the UK outlets are related to Starbucks HQ. This is what tax professionals call 'transfer pricing' and a huge industry of accountants, lawyers, bankers and advisers has grown up to help companies maximise brand charges paid by outlets operating in the UK to their headquarters, which are nominally located in a low-tax jurisdiction elsewhere.

In the case of Starbucks, they had chosen Amsterdam to locate their headquarters. They claimed that the HQ was in Amsterdam, even though the firm's President for Europe was actually based in London. But by doing this, they could legitimately do a deal with the Dutch tax authorities that helped them pay less tax and avoid UK tax. Starbucks told us that they were bound by obligations of confidentiality to the Dutch government, which prevented them from disclosing the details of the tax deal, thus shrouding their tax affairs in even greater secrecy. Not only were tax rates lower in the Netherlands but the deal with the Dutch allowed them to transfer money from the Netherlands to the tax haven of Bermuda where no tax was levied.

With Alstead still before the committee, I asked him: 'You are paying tax on royalties in the Netherlands, aren't you? Is there a special low-tax regime in the Netherlands on royalties?'

He replied: 'Yes, there is. We have a tax ruling that we have had since—'

MH: 'So it is less?'

Troy Alstead: 'Oh yes, it is a very low rate.'

MH: 'So there is a tax advantage to you from paying
    royalties to the Netherlands.'

Troy Alstead: 'It is a favourable tax rate that we have in the
    Netherlands on all income that comes from all over
    the—'

MH: 'That is why you put it into the Netherlands?'

Troy Alstead: 'It is not why, but it is an attractive reason to
    be there, there's no question.'

MH: 'No, it is why.'

Stephen Barclay MP: 'What is the tax rate you pay in the
    Netherlands?'

Troy Alstead: 'I am very happy to provide that to the
    committee but I am bound by confidentiality to the
    Dutch government on that.'

We then tried to find out how and why Starbucks claimed
that the value of their brand was 6 per cent of turnover. For
every £100 earned in Britain, £6 had to go to Amsterdam.
Even HMRC thought it was excessive to claim that the
uniqueness of a Starbucks cup of coffee and the intellectual
property rights associated with the design of a Starbucks coffee
shop justified 6 per cent going out of the UK in royalties for
the brand. HMRC cut the percentage to 4.7 per cent.

MH: 'Let me take you through the charges that have
    been put in the public domain. The first is that
    you charge for intellectual property. I gather
    it was originally 6 per cent, and I understand
    that somehow there has been a negotiation with
    HMRC and it is now 4.7 per cent. I have to tell
    you that I am a coffee addict, so I drink far more
    coffee than is good for my health. I cannot tell
    the difference between a Starbucks coffee and one
    from Nero, Costa or anywhere else, so perhaps
    you can enlighten me . . . I cannot understand this
    great intellectual property that we are paying for,
    whether it's 6 per cent or 4.7 per cent. I just do not
    get it. Perhaps you can explain how on earth you
    reach that figure.'
Troy Alstead: 'I will try to. Licensors . . . typically assess
    for their licensees these fees to represent goods and
    services. These are very tangible costs associated
    with product innovation, store design and trademark
    protection.'

We felt little the wiser. So we pursued the issue by asking further questions.

> MH: 'For the UK taxpayer, who forgoes the corporation tax, how much are you charging for the design of the building?'
>
> Troy Alstead: 'It is not articulated beneath that which components sit in it. It is an all—'
>
> MH: 'There must be some figures underpinning.'
>
> Troy Alstead: 'No, there are not. It is an all-in fee that we have triangulated on over the years to represent—'
>
> MH: 'There are no figures underpinning.'
>
> Troy Alstead: 'There are no detailed figures that represent which pieces of product innovation versus store design—'
>
> MH: 'So how on earth do you get that 6 per cent or 4.7 per cent is the fair and proper charge?'
>
> Troy Alstead: 'Two or perhaps three ways. One is understanding what global brands charge for those goods and services to licensees around the world. In the UK that ranges from close to 5 per cent up to a maximum of 8 per cent or so.'

After this exchange in the hearing, Starbucks wrote a letter to the committee in which they said: 'Charging a royalty payment for the right to use a global brand and for services provided is standard business practice for multinationals.'

The conclusion we drew was that the 6 per cent was not based on real costs but on what Starbucks and other companies thought they could get away with. It allowed them to export 6 per cent of their profits to a low-tax or no-tax jurisdiction and deny the UK taxpayer tax income on profits earned from cups of coffee sold in the UK.

The second device Starbucks employed to shift profits out of the UK was to buy all their coffee beans in Switzerland, another low-tax jurisdiction. Indeed, Starbucks admitted: 'Yes, around coffee trading and trading houses in general, Switzerland offers a very competitive tax rate.' All the UK Starbucks coffee shops had to buy their coffee from Starbucks in Switzerland. 'If they operate a Starbucks coffee shop, they must buy Starbucks coffee,' we were told.

Stephen Barclay MP, who was a very persistent, determined and effective interrogator on the committee, pursued this issue. 'And how many people work in the Swiss operation?' he asked.

Troy Alstead: 'I believe that our global coffee-buying operation perhaps has thirty people.'

Stephen Barclay: 'Thirty people. And what mark-up do you apply to the coffee you buy in the Swiss operation before it is transferred?'

Troy Alstead: 'The margin that Starbucks makes on coffee that is sold to the UK ... is approximately 20 per cent.'

Stephen Barclay: 'So what do the thirty people in Switzerland do to account for the 20 per cent mark-up?'

Troy Alstead: 'They run all our global buying operations, they run our sustainability programmes, and they have all the agronomy offices that we operate around the world ... They ensure that the quality of the coffee is appropriate ...'

Stephen Barclay: 'And how do you come to the figure of 20 per cent from that?'

Troy Alstead: 'That is benchmarked, based on transfer-pricing regulations in tax authorities all around the world ...'

Stephen Barclay: 'Just to confirm, the coffee does not
physically go to Switzerland, does it?'
Troy Alstead: 'The coffee is bought in Switzerland and
then shipped to our roasting facilities around the
world.'
Stephen Barclay: 'It is bought there. Does it physically go
to Switzerland?'
Troy Alstead: 'No.'

No coffee bean ever reaches Switzerland, but with the 20
per cent mark-up, another chunk of money is knocked off the
profits earned in the UK, so reducing further the corporation
tax liability in the UK.

Their third and final wheeze concerned the use of intra-
company loans. Any UK Starbucks outlet that undertook capital
investment was forced by Starbucks to borrow from Starbucks
in Bermuda or the Netherlands. Both branches of Starbucks
charged an exorbitant interest rate on the loans. Although the
deals involved one part of Starbucks lending to another part of
Starbucks, the interest charges were much higher than those
that commercial banks would demand. Again, forcing all
Starbucks businesses in the UK to borrow from Starbucks in the
Netherlands or Bermuda was simply a device to export profits
to pay for the borrowing costs and avoid tax. Money earned in
Britain was shifted abroad to pay for the excessively high interest
charges. UK Starbucks was able to both reduce its profits and
claim tax relief on the interest paid in the UK, and so offset that
against any tax due in the UK. Starbucks US never paid any tax
at all on the money it held in Bermuda.

Multinational companies are always concerned that they
may be forced to pay double taxation on their global activities – that is, both in the country where they are operating
and in the country that houses their headquarters. Many of

the international tax rules that exist today were designed in the 1920s to prevent that from happening. But I don't think any government that signed up to those rules wanted multinationals to engage in double non-taxation. Yet that is precisely what this particular artificial device facilitates: tax relief on contrived interest payments against profits in the UK and no tax in the tax-free tax haven.

By adopting these three strategies, UK profits were turned into UK losses simply to avoid paying a fair amount of tax on the activity and profits Starbucks earned from selling coffee in Britain. Our hearing opened these practices to the public gaze. The public's response was fierce and instant. Even before the hearing the media coverage of the issue had converted the three-point positive Starbucks once had on the YouGov brand index into a twenty-six-point negative.

After the hearing the boycott of Starbucks coffee shops gathered apace and it seemed obvious – though we were never able to see the figures – that the company's market share had plummeted. Probably as a result, I received a phone call from Kris Engskov, the managing director of Starbucks UK. He wanted to see me. Over a cup of ordinary House of Commons coffee, he sought to justify the company's financial arrangements and then said that Starbucks would voluntarily pay £20 million in corporation tax to the Exchequer.

This extraordinary offer simply confirmed my view that the system was broken and open to manipulation by corporations. How could the company be allowed to choose the amount of tax it paid? Surely tax had to be assessed by the tax authorities, not decided on the whims and assessments of the companies themselves? If the companies could simply choose, it showed that the corporation tax system was not working in the way Parliament had intended and the general public expected. It remains difficult to discover the impact the row over tax has had on Starbucks' market share, but I know that many people boycott the coffee shops. I will continue to do so until I know for certain that Starbucks is contributing a fair share to the Exchequer based on the profits it enjoys from the economic activity it undertakes here in this country.

Amazon

Inquiring into Amazon's tax arrangements was also mind-boggling. Amazon's strategy was to create a complex web of companies to convince HMRC that they were not selling goods in the UK, but selling goods from Luxembourg into the UK. The company gave evidence alongside Starbucks and Google. They had clearly decided to deal with the public evidence session by sending a witness who could not answer our questions because his knowledge of the company's financial arrangements was woefully limited. Andrew Cecil was Director, Public Policy at Amazon. He acted like a nervous rabbit, hesitating with his answers and stumbling over his words. But his tactic of pleading ignorance backfired badly as his inability (or deliberate refusal) to answer questions simply irritated us all.

When asked how much of Amazon's Luxembourg business was sales in the UK, he limply said: 'Unfortunately we have never broken our revenue on a country or website basis.' When asked who owned the holding company in Luxembourg, he answered: 'I will need to come back to the committee on that.'

He made us all more convinced that Amazon had something to hide and simply damaged the reputation of the company. To the extent that, when he went so far as to claim he did not know the company's UK sales figures, Amyas Morse, the Comptroller and Auditor General, was moved to observe: 'You cannot possibly pretend – and it is really quite annoy-ing to listen to – that you can possibly be running a strategy in Europe and not know your territorial profitability. You are doing advertising. You are putting up warehouses on the assumption of sales volumes. Come on, it is actually quite insulting to everybody's intelligence to say that you don't know what sales volumes are going to be in the territory. That is just not feasible as an argument. You cannot possibly advance that. I don't think anybody who knows anything about business would accept that line.'

At the time of our hearing in 2012, one in four books sold in the UK was purchased from Amazon. Cecil claimed that 'Amazon.co.uk is merely a service company in the UK providing services to Amazon EU Sarl, for which it receives payment.' He claimed that all the books and other goods were bought from Amazon's company in Luxembourg so the revenue earned had to be assessed and taxed in Luxembourg. The server for their computer is still held in Luxembourg and so they are not selling in Britain but into Britain from Luxembourg.

This exchange during the committee session with Andrew Cecil clearly demonstrated the artificiality of the whole set-up.

MH: 'Amazon, when I buy a book from you – I do it
     online and I am a regular buyer – I get "Amazon.
     co.uk." That is what I am told. Is that correct? I can
     show you. In fact, I think you write to me every day
     with new offers. It is from Amazon.co.uk. Do you
     accept that?'
Andrew Cecil: 'Chair, maybe I can explain how we are set
     up as a single European company, because I think it
     is very useful background for the committee.'
MH: 'Let me ask you the questions, because I am asking
     from a UK perspective. It is the UK where we
     seek taxes in these troubling times and we want

everybody to give their fair share – all in it together. I just want you to explain to me. I buy from Amazon.co.uk – that is where I buy from.'

Andrew Cecil: 'Amazon.co.uk is the trading name for Amazon EU Sarl, and we operate—'

MH: 'But you are saying to me that it is a UK company that I am buying from.'

Andrew Cecil: 'No, you are purchasing from a single European company. We operate a single European company.'

MH: 'I then agree to purchase something and I get an email from you telling me that it is being delivered from a UK warehouse. That is correct too?'

Andrew Cecil: 'Yes, we have eight warehouses in the UK.'

MH: 'And I am told how much I am going to have to pay for the Royal Mail to deliver the books, or the toys, or the kettles to my home.'

Andrew Cecil: 'You will be charged the postage as a UK customer, but actually we may be delivering that product from any of our in excess of twenty fulfilment centres [warehouses] across Europe.'

MH: 'Do you have books in Luxembourg?'

Andrew Cecil: 'No, we do not have a fulfilment centre in Luxembourg. We have our European headquarters in Luxembourg.'

MH: 'So I buy I think from a UK company; I am billed by the UK company; I am billed from the UK—'

Andrew Cecil: 'No. I think that you will see that Amazon. co.uk is a trading name for a Luxembourg company, Amazon EU Sarl . . . you will be billed by a Luxembourg company . . .'

MH: 'You are telling me that the bills are printed in Luxembourg?'

Andrew Cecil: 'The bills themselves may be printed in one
      of our fulfilment centres ...'

MH: 'What business is conducted in Luxembourg?'

Andrew Cecil: 'To give the committee a sense, we have in
      excess of five hundred people working there. In fact,
      we are still recruiting heavily ...'

MH: 'And how many people do you have in the UK?'

Andrew Cecil: 'Across the UK today we have about fifteen
      thousand employees.'

MH: 'We are delighted that you have business in the UK. I
      was delighted that I thought I was buying from a UK
      company, which delivered from a UK warehouse,
      books that have never appeared in any other
      jurisdiction. Why are you not paying tax in the UK?'

What emerged from this exchange was a bogus arrangement that appears to be admissible under current international tax rules. Amazon had created a web of companies to claim no sales took place in the UK; they were all accounted for in Luxembourg.

In 2010, the company showed an income of €7.5 billion in Luxembourg. However, in written evidence submitted after the oral hearing, Amazon admitted that of the €7.5 billion, £2.36 billion represented the net sales in the UK for 2010 (about €2.7 billion). Yet the 2010 UK company accounts showed a mere £147 million of revenues earned in the UK. A year later, in 2011, in their written evidence, Amazon told us that net sales earned from the UK, but accounted for in Luxembourg, were £2.91 billion, yet the income shown in the UK accounts was just £208 million.

In 2012, Amazon's accounts showed that they had paid a very modest corporation tax contribution of £2.4 million. In the same year they received a regional grant from the UK government for the higher sum of £2.5 million to build one of their warehouses, funded, of course, by the UK taxpayer.

As far as we could deduce from very opaque figures, from 2003 to 2011 Amazon paid only £3 million in UK corporation tax.

During the same time period, the €7.5 billion revenue they filed in Luxembourg didn't bring much benefit to the people of Luxembourg. Amazon claimed their administrative expenses amounted to €7.4 billion, leaving them with a minuscule profit. So not only were they telling us that they were not selling books and other goods in the UK, Amazon appeared to be manipulating their accounts in Luxembourg too.

A similar story was told by Andrew Cecil on the 2011 Luxembourg figures. 'Our net profit after tax was €20 million, on revenues of €9.1 billion,' he said.

This staggering admission led to the following exchange between a number of committee members and Cecil.

Stephen Barclay: 'What I am interested in is how you are stripping out the profits in Luxembourg, because that is the impression. If it is €9.1 billion going down to €20 million that suggests you are stripping out the profit in Luxembourg. Who owns the holding company?'

Andrew Cecil: 'I will need to come back to the committee on that.'

Stephen Barclay: 'So the profit is going into a company, and is then going into a holding company. What about the title and goods from affiliates or third parties—'

Ian Swales MP: 'Sorry, there is another unacceptable answer. You are telling us you don't know the corporate structure of your company. Really?'

Andrew Cecil: 'I do know the corporate structure of
the European company. I work for the European
company. I would be happy to come back.'

Ian Swales: 'All we need to know is who owns the holding
company.'

Richard Bacon MP: 'You are the director of public policy.
It is incredible that you wouldn't know who owns
the holding company. It is just not credible.'

Andrew Cecil: 'I am very happy to come back to the
committee.'

Richard Bacon: 'Well, you can tell that we are not happy.'

Amazon's claim that they made such limited profits in Luxembourg was unbelievable. Their further claim that the UK operation was simply a delivery service was equally unbelievable.

The company also said that no research and development took place in the UK. It was important for Amazon to assert that because a UK research and development presence would have undermined their story that the UK entity was simply providing delivery services to the Luxembourg company. However, one of our committee members, Fiona Mactaggart, happened to be the MP for Slough, where Amazon's UK headquarters are based. She had visited the premises in Slough and had been told that they were developing new products there. Andrew Cecil simply skirted around the issue when she asked him about this, saying: 'I am sure Brian would never have misled you. As I said, we are operating on a single European company basis.' Just like Starbucks, Amazon was quite relaxed about telling different stories to different people.

At one point, we questioned Cecil as to why Amazon.co.uk was not a branch of Amazon EU Sarl. He replied, 'I am not a detailed tax expert,' which gave the game away. The structure

Amazon had devised, the complex web of companies they controlled, was all about tax and avoiding it; there was no other commercial purpose.

Since our hearing, the European Union has challenged Amazon's tax deal with Luxembourg, and Amazon is changing its structure and may start to pay some tax. Another recent EU ruling means that the UK will now receive income from the VAT charged on eBooks. Prior to this ruling VAT was collected by the country where the seller resided (Luxembourg) rather than the country where the purchaser resided (UK). But the company will still hide most of its profits by charging exorbitant fees to the branches in countries like the UK for the right to use Amazon patents. The UK is unlikely to get a proper contribution through tax for the profits made from sales in the UK. Indeed, in 2014, Amazon paid only £11.9 million in corporation tax, even though the Luxembourg company took £5.3 billion from Internet sales in the UK.

And what has the UK government done about this? They have appointed an Amazon senior executive, Doug Gurr, to the board of the Department for Work and Pensions. Is that really the best the UK government can do? Reward a company that intentionally avoids tax with a prestigious government job as a non-executive director. No wonder people get angry; no wonder they feel that there is one set of rules for the rich and powerful and another set of rules for everybody else.

Google

The same is true of the all-powerful Google. Google was the third company to give us evidence alongside Starbucks and Amazon. Their representative, Matt Brittin, who was in charge of sales and operations in northern and central Europe, openly admitted that the complex web of companies through which they operated was designed to avoid paying tax. Brittin appeared before the committee dressed in an open shirt and wore no tie. He gave a confident, indeed somewhat arrogant performance. A man who had moved seamlessly from success to success – rowing for Cambridge University in the Boat Race and for Great Britain in the Seoul Olympics, to becoming a senior executive with Google – he left us with the impression that Google was doing the UK a favour and he had absolutely no intention of expressing any humility or regret about their aggressive tax-avoidance practices.

Like Amazon, Google claimed that they were not selling in Britain. The company placed their server in Ireland and alleged that they were selling into Britain. In fact, 92 per cent of Google's sales outside the USA were billed in Ireland. We looked at their figures for the financial year ending December 2011. In that year sales to customers with a UK address amounted to $4.06 billion. The accounts Google filed in America demonstrated that the UK was their biggest market outside the USA, accounting for 11 per cent of their worldwide business. But they told the UK tax authorities that their sales in Britain were not $4.06 billion but a mere $396 million, because they claimed that the sales transactions were closed in Ireland.

Google achieved this sleight of hand by making use of highly artificial structures, the sole purpose of which was tax avoidance. I tried to understand how monies were moved across national boundaries and the only way I could get my head around how it was done was by having a picture of the structure. Such a picture was provided by a talented intern in my office, Michael Lillis, who drew a diagram that helped me to unravel the complex financial structures of a global corporate giant.

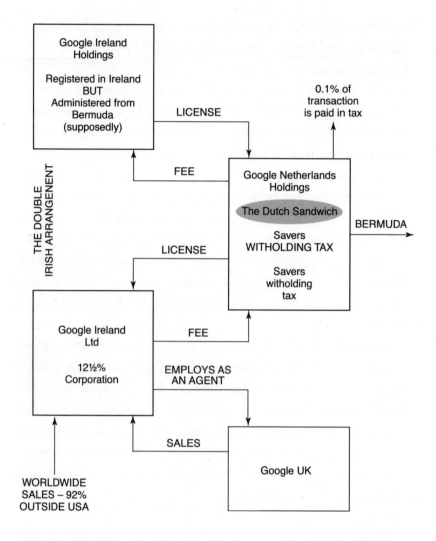

As the attached figure shows, cash from sales in the UK was received in Ireland by a subsidiary of the American-based corporation. Google did this by granting a licence for its advertising software and technology (the principal way in which the company earns revenue) to Google Ireland. From there, the money went to Google in the Netherlands through the device of Google Ireland Ltd paying a fee for a licence held by Google Netherlands Holdings. Google in the Netherlands then passed 99.8 per cent of the monies back by paying another fee to another entity in Ireland, called Google Ireland Holdings, which is registered in Ireland, but administered in Bermuda. Confused? Of course. And it is precisely this confusing complexity that has enabled companies like Google, Amazon and Starbucks to remain unchallenged on their failure to pay a fair share of tax on the profits they earn, while at the same time parading themselves as good corporate citizens to their worldwide customers.

Google's tactics were known in the tax industry as the 'Dutch sandwich' because they enabled Google to avoid both UK corporation tax and Dutch withholding tax. Eric Schmidt, Google's executive chairman, openly proclaimed to Bloomberg News that he was 'very proud' of the structure. 'It's called capitalism,' he said. 'We are proudly capitalistic. I'm not confused about this.'

What did this version of capitalism mean for the British taxpayer? In the financial year ending December 2011, Google reported a turnover of €12.5 billion in Ireland, of which nearly €4.06 billion came from UK addresses. Yet in the UK they filed losses of £24 million. In Ireland they said their gross profit on the €12.5 billion was over €9 billion, €9.08 billion to be precise. But Google then declared that administrative costs, including royalties, were €9.054 billion, leaving a net profit of €24 million, on which they then paid company taxes in Ireland.

What this all showed was that there was no relationship between where money was made and tax was paid. Google's assertions lacked credibility, but we had nothing tangible with which to challenge the company. I thought we had hit a brick wall.

The breakthrough in the Google inquiry was once again down to the bravery of whistleblowers. In the days following Matt Brittin's appearance, I received a raft of emails from a large number of whistleblowers, both current and past employees and clients of Google who were infuriated by what they felt was misleading evidence given by Google to the committee.

The evidence was overwhelming, so I asked two of the whistleblowers to come and talk to both me and the Comptroller and Auditor General in a private meeting. The allegations were serious and if they were true, they suggested that Brittin had misled the committee and the company was misleading our tax authorities. Having questioned the individuals in detail, both of us were convinced by the evidence we were given. The witnesses were genuine whistleblowers who had a credible story to tell. On the basis of their evidence, I suggested to the committee, and they agreed, to recall Google together with their accountants, Ernst and Young.

All the whistleblower evidence had to do with whether or not Google was selling *in* the UK rather than selling *into* the UK as they claimed. If they had been selling in the UK they were liable for tax on the profits earned from this economic activity here. Google's claim, underwritten by their auditors Ernst and Young, was that because the server was in Ireland, their 'permanent establishment' was in Ireland and they were not selling in the UK.

One of the whistleblowers was a young man called Barney Jones, who had been employed by Google for four years from March 2002 to March 2006. From offices in Soho, he had led a small sales team and had worked with the larger UK companies, who spent considerable sums on advertising. When he left the company he downloaded all his files and they formed the basis of his evidence to us.

Barney Jones was clearly motivated by a sense of moral outrage. He felt ashamed that the company for which he had worked for four years was operating through an artificial structure to avoid tax. He told the Comptroller and Auditor

General and me that he was about to start a career in the Church and that his motivation to blow the whistle came from his ethical and religious values.

He was in possession of tens of thousands of documents from his time at Google. He was absolutely clear that he and his team had been selling in the UK. While Matt Brittin, on behalf of Google, claimed that sales were 'closed' in Ireland, Barney Jones said that he was closing deals in Britain. At our meeting he claimed that they were signing up clients to spend money with Google in the UK: 'No normal understanding of the words "sale" or "closing a deal" could be associated with what was going on in Ireland. That was all happening in the UK,' he said.

Jones produced documents which showed that UK-based staff were selling to major clients such as BT, Lloyds TSB, Amazon, Halifax, British Airways and Land Rover. They met the clients and their agencies in the UK. UK-based staff designed the advertisements. The key words that determined the ranking of the advertisements were suggested by UK-based staff. In Google's early days, the actual accounts were established in the UK and we saw copies of invoices sent out to clients from the London offices. Even if Google later transferred the accounts to Ireland, both the original sales and the original billing took place in the UK.

Barney Jones's evidence was reinforced by another whistle-blower who was still working for Google when he met us. He was a senior salesman working from Google's office in Centre Point in London. He brought his monthly salary slips, which showed he earned a relatively modest basic salary, but received a success bonus of between three and four times his basic wage for selling and agreeing deals. He told us that the commission he received was relatively small for achieving the minimum sales target he had been set, but that he was more generously

rewarded as he exceeded his target. His clients were signing
off on deals in the UK, agreeing to media plans and spending
money; it was just the administrative billing that took place
in Ireland.

This whistleblower showed us detailed sales documents
that Google called 'display documents'. These focused on
particular sectors and set ambitious targets for the UK staff to
grow sales. I saw one that covered the ten biggest companies
in one sector and spelled out the revenue earned in 2010 and
the growth targets for UK staff for the two ensuing years until
the end of 2012. The total revenue growth target for UK-based
staff was 100 per cent in those two years.

The documents laid out the objectives for UK-based sales
staff and contained detailed sales plans. These covered the
number of sales pitches staff were expected to make, the
number of meetings they were expected to fix with both clients and agencies, the media plans they were expected to agree
on, and so on. Again, any common-sense view would regard
these activities as evidence of sales taking place in the UK.

While we were talking to whistleblowers, Reuters undertook further investigative digging. The journalists looked at
dozens of Google job advertisements which gave job specifications that included 'negotiating deals' and achieving 'quarterly
sales targets'.

They looked at the LinkedIn profiles of 150 UK-based Google
staff. Again, the way these individuals described their work
seemed to confirm that selling was taking place in the UK. One
strategic partner described his role on the LinkedIn profile as
'selling Media Platform solutions to existing Publishers, Agencies
and Marketers' and boasted that he 'constantly exceeded his
target'. Another account manager described her role thus: 'From
the initial first call to establish the right contact, I pitch clients
over the phone and face to face. Once the client is on board I

manage and grow the account and client relationship.' Here was further evidence that the staff employed by Google working in the UK believed that their jobs involved selling Google products in the UK.

A similar picture emerged from Google's customers. A whistleblower who was a client of Google gave evidence that had convinced him that he was doing business with Google in the UK; he was asked to settle his account with Citibank in the Strand and pay in sterling. A survey of advertising agencies, who were Google's principal clients, carried out by *The Drum*, an advertising industry publication, reported that: 'Almost 80 per cent of respondents said they dealt with London when buying Google advertising. Around 14 per cent said they used Dublin, the remainder said they did not know. When asked what they considered was the primary role of Google's London advertising team 80 per cent said it was sales. 17 per cent said it was support. When asked what they considered they were doing when dealing with Google's London team 76 per cent said they considered they were buying from them. 17 per cent said they were receiving general advice ... When asked whether they believed Google should pay more tax in the UK 83 per cent said they should.'

We were now armed with this strong body of evidence and wondered how Google would react when appearing before us for a second time. At the initial hearing Brittin had claimed: 'Anybody who buys advertising from us in Europe buys from Google in Ireland, from our expert team.'

At the second hearing he stood by those words, despite all the evidence to the contrary. In the course of one exchange he told us: 'The UK team – people in Google UK Ltd – are promoting our properties and encouraging people to spend money with Google. Clients may well feel that they are selling; we hire people with sales skills and they are encouraging people to spend money and showing them the business case, but what is very clear is that no one in the UK team can execute a transaction – no money changes hands.'

Later he said: 'We could debate sales all day – what is and what is not sales – but the fact of the matter is that calling somebody a sales rep or saying it is part of the sales process is not the issue here. It does not alter our tax bill.'

And later still he specifically argued: 'These people are called salespeople and they have sales skills, but for the purposes of the rules for taxation . . . it is what people actually do and what actually happens that is important here. What actually happens is that when people spend money with Google, they spend it on a technology platform that is built globally and that is owned in Ireland. The transactions are closed with Ireland, the billing is with Ireland and the technology is owned there, so the people in the UK cannot sell, because they do not own the property.'

As Austin Mitchell observed: this was a 'scheme for saying that sales people were not sales people but marriage counsellors, thereby avoiding taxes'.

During the hearing, Brittin tried to claim that when face-to-face meetings and negotiations did take place with clients, they involved only 1 per cent of the client base and that '99 per cent of the UK companies that spend money with Google spend it without seeing or talking to anybody who is in Google because they do it online'. But a little later Brittin was forced to admit that the 1 per cent of clients to whom UK-based staff were selling advertising accounted for between 60 per cent and 70 per cent of the revenue earned by Google in the UK.

Brittin was also dancing on the head of a pin when he tried to assert that there was no substantive research and development activity taking place in the UK, activity that might have undermined the firm's basic claim of there being no substantive economic value-adding activity happening in the UK. In the first evidence session Brittin had told us: 'The people in the UK are not doing the innovation ... they are not doing product development.'

However, we learned from our whistleblowers that one of their premises in Buckingham Palace Road was occupied by many hundreds of systems developers who, among other things, were developing the new Android telephone management system. Again, Brittin refused to accept that he had misled the committee. 'They are contributing to the development of products, absolutely ... but the leadership of the products that are being built is in California.'

At the end of the day, whether Google is doing what they say they are doing is a matter of judgement. Our committee unanimously believed that Google was selling in Britain and should pay taxes in the UK. We looked at what they said and then what they did, putting together all the evidence we had obtained from whistleblowers, investigative journalists and our own research.

We looked at the guidance published by HMRC, where it said: 'In the case of selling goods in the UK, there is likely to be trading here if in substance the selling takes place even if the formal conclusion of contracts takes place abroad.'

We looked at case law and judgements which had established that the place of sale is the place where the customer is, not where the technology platform is.

We questioned Google's accountants, who said they did look at whether clients like Google 'get so close to the point of sale that in substance the sale is being made in the UK'. When Stephen Barclay asked Ernst and Young whether 'there is a grey area in tax law between what is promotional activity and what is concluding a sale?', John Dixon from Ernst and Young replied: 'Yes.'

Yet Google would not admit anything. And unlike their French counterparts, where action against Google has been launched by the tax authorities, as far as we know, HMRC is not challenging the Google structure.

Chris Heaton-Harris MP, a strong member of the committee who saw his role as keeping me in check, had warned me in our pre-hearing preparation meeting to keep my cool. However, at the end of a long and frustrating session I could no longer resist. When preparing for the session, I had come across Google's own company motto, which read: 'Don't be evil.' Observing the arrogant attitude of Matt Brittin at our hearing and angered by the difficulties in his evidence, I concluded the session by saying: 'You are a company that says you "do no evil", but I think you do do evil, in that you use smoke and mirrors to avoid paying tax.' That became the headlines on the news that evening.

As always happens, the publicity died down.

But it was reignited in January 2016 in the most bizarre manner. At 10 p.m. on a Friday night, Matt Brittin announced from the World Economic Forum in Davos that Google would pay the UK Exchequer £130 million in tax for the ten years from 2005 to 2015. George Osborne, also speaking from Davos, welcomed the announcement as 'a major success of our tax policy. We have got Google to pay taxes . . . It is a big step forward and a victory for the government.'

Both men, ensconced in the exclusive and closed environment that is Davos, thought they had secured a remarkable PR coup designed to restore the reputation of the powerful corporation and enhance that of the government. Within forty-eight hours their plan had unravelled and the announcement had backfired. Google found itself back in the headlines, criticised for failing to pay a fair share of tax on profits earned in the UK, and the government was widely seen to have signed another sweetheart deal with a rich and powerful company. Google's offer amounted to £13 million a year over ten years and was described by the Conservative Mayor of London as being 'derisory'. By parading as a victory what experts calculated was an effective tax rate of 3 per cent, when every small and medium-sized business was paying 20 per cent in corporation tax, the government managed to simply highlight the seeming unfairness in the tax system.

Google published their annual accounts the following week. They showed that Google had earned $6.4 billion in that year from UK sales declared in Ireland. They showed that a sub-stantial part of the £130 million tax deal had nothing at all to do with corporation tax, but was being paid to settle another dispute with HMRC around tax due on shares that had been issued to Google staff. The same accounts also revealed that Eric Schmidt – the man at the top of Google – was personally paid the equivalent of nearly £76 million in 2014 alone; that is, well over half of the £130 million tax paid to the Exchequer for all the profits made by Google in the UK over ten years. Indeed, Schmidt was paid the equivalent of £166 million for just four years – more than Google paid in tax to the UK government for ten years. The episode confirmed the smug and contemp-tuous attitude too many multinational businesses have towards the British people and British taxpayers. There was no way the British public would see this as Google paying their fair share.

Pro-fairness or anti-business?

Throughout this period, there were those who tried to argue that our action in exposing the behaviour of big corporations was anti-business. They were simply wrong. My purpose – and that of all the other members of the Public Accounts Committee – was to encourage fairness in the tax system.

Indeed, our pro-fairness agenda aimed to support British businesses. All the companies we saw were able to undercut British companies and undermine British jobs, in part because they avoided tax.

Global corporations seek to justify their actions by talking about the other taxes they pay to the British Exchequer. For example, they mostly pay their employers' contributions to National Insurance and they mostly pay business rates. But that in no way dents the argument on corporation tax.

We all pay a variety of taxes in our daily lives – we pay council taxes and VAT but we do not think that excuses us from paying our income tax. Similarly, just because companies contribute to other tax streams does not justify action to avoid paying corporation tax. If global corporations contribute less in taxation, others will have to contribute more, or services will need to be cut to balance the books.

Furthermore, the public services provided through taxation are important to the corporations that depend on them. They need a good transport infrastructure and a fast communications network. They want their workforce to have the skills on which their businesses depend and they need a healthy workforce to keep their businesses profitable. All of this requires investment in public services and they should help to pay for these services.

There are those who argue that competition on tax between countries is a key way of attracting inward investment, growth and jobs. My own view is that accepting that proposition is too simplistic and short term. First, if countries do try to compete on tax, they can quickly get locked into a race to the bottom as other countries undercut them, and this creates more damage than benefit in the longer term because the tax base is eroded.

Second, companies consider a range of issues when they decide where to locate and do business. It may be true that capital is pretty promiscuous and global companies are happy to transfer headquarters and show little loyalty to any particular country. But they will look at other factors as well as tax when taking these decisions, like the size of the market, the skills of the workforce, the language, the infrastructure and whether the country is a pleasant place in which to live and work.

When Eric Schmidt, formerly chief executive and then chairman of Google, was interviewed on Channel 4 after our second hearing with the company, he was asked whether Google would leave the UK if they were made to pay company taxes. He replied: 'Google will invest in the UK no matter what you guys do, because the UK is just too important for us. The citizens are too important for us and in our view we provide too much good. My guess is we will continue investing in Britain no matter what.' When Starbucks gave evidence to the committee, they too said that they had to be in the UK to be a successful global company.

But the argument goes beyond naked self-interest. Over the last twenty years or so, corporations have recognised the need to adopt an ethical code of behaviour to maintain and enhance their reputations and hence their profitability.

So while avoiding tax may have been seen as cool and clever in the past, that approach now has to change and paying tax should simply be another component of the corporate social responsibility agenda.

I remember one day when I bumped into David Gauke in the House of Commons lobby. He was the Treasury minister with day-to-day responsibility for taxation. He told me he was receiving representations from a number of global companies telling him that they would not locate in the UK because of the possibility that they might be grilled by the Public Accounts Committee about their tax. I laughed, but then saw that he was taking the threat seriously. I was taken aback. It seemed so obvious that at any time companies would use such ploys in negotiations to secure a tax advantage from the government, whether they meant it or not. It was part of the negotiating game. And if their threats were serious, they were clearly primarily engaged in aggressive tax avoidance and shifting their headquarters to the UK would bring little money into our coffers and few jobs to our country. The scary thing for me was that government ministers were taking such threats seriously.

This is not an anti-business tirade. I very quickly learned from the huge number of letters and emails I received and from the way in which I was warmly greeted by strangers in the street that our investigations had unleashed a colossal anger among people of all ages, from all backgrounds and living in all areas. People just thought it was unfair and unjust.

David Cameron understood that quite quickly. In his speech to the World Economic Forum in Davos in January 2013, he used the Starbucks case to say: 'There are some forms of avoidance that have become so aggressive that I think it is right to say these raise ethical issues and it is time to call for more responsibility and for governments to act accordingly . . . Individuals and businesses must pay their fair share. And businesses who think they can carry on dodging that fair share, or that they can keep on selling to the UK and setting up ever more complex tax arrangements abroad to squeeze their tax bills right down, well they need to wake up and smell the coffee, because the public who buy from them have had enough.'

Of course actions speak louder than words, but I could not even extract the right words from either Ed Balls or Ed Miliband. Following our hearing with Starbucks, Amazon and Google, and in the run-up to the G8 summit in June 2013, I was keen for the Labour Party to take up the mantle and lead the campaign against aggressive tax avoidance in the same way that Ed Miliband had led the way on phone hacking. Of course,

I wanted the government to act, but I wanted Labour to champion an agenda that was so strongly aligned with our values. Yet with the honourable exception of Tim Livesey, the leader's chief of staff, who instinctively understood that this was both a moral issue and an opportunity to demonstrate what Labour actually meant by the mantra of 'responsible capitalism', it became clear that neither of the Eds or their aides wanted to know.

I sought and held meetings with frontbench Treasury shadow ministers and people working in both the Opposition leader's office and the Shadow Chancellor's office. My staff talked to the staff working in their offices. I went through what we were discovering and suggested appropriate policies that I believed Labour should champion to promote fairness in the tax system.

I kept emphasising that I believed this agenda struck such a strong chord with the public and that we should drive it. I couldn't get a response. I suspected that because both the Eds had worked in the Treasury under Gordon Brown, they were worried that anything they said would shine a spotlight on their complicit failure to act to stamp out aggressive tax avoidance when they had the power to do so. I felt I was banging my head against a brick wall.

On one occasion at a meeting with my researcher, a representative from Ed Miliband's office argued that the agenda was 'anti-business', 'too complicated' and 'not an agenda that was going anywhere any time soon'.

By the time they grasped how important and popular the issue was, the government was acting and Labour's efforts in this space were indeed seen to be anti-business and punitive, rather than pro-fairness and just.

6

The Big Four – Vested Interests and Undue Influence

After our inquiry into Google, Amazon and Starbucks, I was inundated with emails, letters and phone calls from members of the public, journalists and the media asking us to hold hearings with other companies. Requests poured in for us to enquire into companies in the oil sector, the extractive industry sector, the energy sector, the financial services sector and the retail sector. From Thames Water to Boots and from RTZ to Accenture, similar stories began to emerge. The allegations were always the same – that these companies had set up complex financial structures and a web of subsidiaries in order to exploit the transfer-pricing rules and export their profits to low-tax or no-tax jurisdictions. The sole purpose appeared to be tax avoidance.

Hauling individual companies before the committee to expose what they were doing might make for good headlines, but would not move the agenda forward. I wanted to take a more systematic approach.

The companies did not dream up the tax-avoidance strategies on their own. They were advised by accountants, lawyers, banks and financial advisers. We needed to move the conversation on to the advisers. They needed to explain themselves in a public forum.

In January 2013, the Public Accounts Committee decided to ask the four big accountancy firms to give evidence on the tax advice they gave to businesses. Between them in the financial year 2011–12, KPMG, Ernst and Young, PricewaterhouseCoopers and Deloitte earned £2 billion in the UK from their tax business. Globally the companies earned around $25 billion from the support and advice they gave on tax. In the UK, the four big accountancy firms employed nearly nine thousand people in their tax businesses. Some of the earnings came from straightforward processing and compliance work relating to the traditional auditing function. But most derived from the giving of advice. PricewaterhouseCoopers told us that only £110 million of the £659 million that they earned through their UK tax practice came from compliance and processing work; not even 20 per cent.

The companies also told us that while their tax practices represented on average 22 per cent of UK partnership revenues, they accounted for more in terms of profits. At the hearing, John Dixon of Ernst and Young, when asked about the profitability of the tax business, replied somewhat modestly: 'At a marginal level, tax is a profitable part of the business in the UK for Ernst and Young.'

In written evidence submitted after the hearing, Deloitte revealed that, although tax represented 19 per cent of the revenues earned in the UK, it accounted for 29 per cent of the operating profit. In a similar vein, PricewaterhouseCoopers told us that tax represented 25 per cent of their revenues in the UK, but 32 per cent of profits.

Unsurprisingly the firms' substantial earnings were then reflected in the remuneration enjoyed by the four individuals who gave evidence to the committee. They each headed up their firm's tax practices in the UK. Two told us that they earned seven-figure sums – that is over £1 million a year – and two said they enjoyed six-figure earnings.

At the same time, their business clients were not overly concerned by the fees charged by the accountants because, of course, they could set those off against their tax bill.

The Big Four accountants worked internationally. The fees they earned in the UK were more transparent. It was harder to nail down the earnings they secured through work carried out by their firms in Luxembourg, Holland or Switzerland and in other low-tax jurisdictions and tax havens.

Action Aid, the development charity, had published a report in May 2013 alleging that ninety-eight of the FTSE top 100 companies had subsidiaries in tax havens. (They included places like Delaware in that definition. The US state is often referred to as a 'corporate haven' as it has developed a very secretive tax regime that, with little transparency on ownership, allows companies to shift profits there to avoid tax.) Regrettably, during that first evidence session with the Big Four in January 2013, we did not get far in shining a light on activities in tax havens and their implications for UK companies and the tax they paid.

We did ask Deloitte about their presence in the Cayman Islands. While only 56,000 people lived in the Cayman Islands at the time, by simply searching the Internet we found that Deloitte had 160 staff working there. One hundred and sixty highly paid staff serving a community of 56,000.

'What are the 160 staff doing there?' I asked.

Bill Dodwell (head of tax policy, Deloitte LLP): 'They won't be doing tax work, will they? It will be auditing.'

MH: 'Auditing what? The hotels?'

Bill Dodwell: 'The financial institutions there and the
        funds that have their top structure there. Many hedge
        funds, as you may know, have a Cayman Island
        company at the top of the hedge fund.'

Fast forward two years to Christmas 2014, and we had much
more information and ammunition at our disposal. Documents
from a PwC whistleblower on the company's dealings with the
Luxembourg tax authorities, together with a set of documents
revealing information about HSBC's Swiss bank accounts –
leaked by a Swiss HSBC employee, Hervé Falciani, to the
French tax authorities – would help us open to public account
the role that accountancy firms and banks played in aggressive
tax avoidance by using tax havens and low-tax jurisdictions.

In our first hearing in 2013, we wanted the firms to
talk about the work they did. That proved difficult. Kevin
Nicholson, head of tax at PwC, was probably the most open,
but only when he returned for a second time at the end of 2014
to explain the Luxembourg operation. 'Tax is a commercial
cost,' he said. Later in the hearing he was more explicit. 'Tax
is a commercial cost to the business, so yes, one of the things
we would do was to work with clients to say, "If you do it this
way, it would reduce the tax cost." Absolutely.'

Those remarks highlighted the difference in attitude
between those tax professionals and the average UK taxpayer.
The accountants see tax as a cost to a business, not a societal
obligation. They believe it is legitimate to minimise that cost,
even if that involves creating completely artificial structures
that have no commercial purpose other than to avoid tax.
Others, like me and most UK taxpayers, think that there is a
difference between sensible and legitimate tax planning and
illegitimate aggressive tax avoidance.

The Big Four made their money by exploiting the inevitable

ambiguities in both national and international tax law. As I observed in the chapter describing the start of our journey on tax, Jane McCormick acknowledged the ambiguities when she said: 'There is this grey area. We have difficulty in definitions. The Oxford University Centre for Business Taxation wrote a paper that was published last month that talks about how difficult it is to define this.'

Having accepted that the law is ambiguous and open to interpretation, one might have expected to find that the Big Four would be cautious in their judgements and in the advice they gave to businesses. But no. They did not just recommend copper-bottomed, legitimate schemes to clients. They were content to advise companies on the basis of a scheme having only a 50 per cent chance of not being challenged by HMRC. Bill Dodwell, Deloitte LLP: 'I cannot think of any case where we would set out to indemnify a client in any scenario. Our advice . . . is that one is only allowed to file a tax return claiming a tax position if one has a more than 50 per cent view it will succeed.'

So conversely there was up to a 50 per cent probability that a tax scheme would be challenged. The advice is a one-way bet for the accountancy firms, because they generally do not offer any indemnity in the event that things go wrong.

They make a lot of money and they give chancy advice. On top of that the power of the accountants when set against that of HMRC resembles a David and Goliath encounter. And from the evidence we saw, not one that David can often win. The people working for the accountancy firms are paid much more than HMRC tax officials and there are many more of them. The Big Four told us they employed 250 specialists on transfer pricing alone. HMRC at the time of our hearing in May 2013 had sixty-five transfer-pricing specialists and they had to deal with all accountants, advisers and businesses, not just those working for the Big Four. By May 2014, HMRC had only increased the number of transfer-pricing specialists to eighty, and that remains the number in 2016.

With fewer people, who are paid much less, HMRC is always going to be behind the game. Some structures proposed by the accountants go unchallenged. Other cases can take well over ten years to reach a tax tribunal. In this uneven contest, the loser will always be the law-abiding taxpayer who will either have to pay more or get less. Furthermore, the Big Four enjoy another huge advantage. They work for a number of companies. They can take the knowledge of negotiating one deal with one firm into the negotiations for another deal with another business. In the meantime, small businesses and the general public have no such inside knowledge because of the confidentiality of taxpayers' interests.

The Big Four were very sensitive to our accusations that the schemes they had invented were unlawful. They clearly did not like to be tarred with the brush of any illegality. Such as when Richard Bacon put it to Bill Dodwell of Deloitte in relation to the Goldman Sachs tax dodge: 'At the point that the court rules against you, it shows that what you are doing is unlawful, does it not?'

Bill Dodwell: 'No, it doesn't. What it shows is that the interpretation of the tax law proved to be wrong.'

MH: 'You lost in the tribunal. Are you saying that the tribunal does not find whether it is lawful or unlawful? You lost. You don't need to pussyfoot with words. You lost.'

Bill Dodwell: 'There is a difference between committing a criminal offence—'

Richard Bacon: 'That is indeed true, but that is not what

I asked. What I asked was, at the point at which you
lose in the courts, the courts have found that what
you were doing was unlawful. Yes or no?'
Bill Dodwell: 'Yes.'
Richard Bacon: 'Right.'
Bill Dodwell: 'That interpretation was wrong.'
MH: 'No. It was unlawful.'

Another important finding that emerged during our inquiry
was discovering both the cosy relationships and the revolving-
door appointments that are commonplace in the world of tax.
Both phenomena are closely related and significant. Tax policy
and how it is administered is dominated by a charmed circle
of tax professionals and their powerful clients. Their influence
is disproportionate and their advice to government is biased
towards the interests of big businesses at the expense of the
wider public interest.

I understand from my work as a minister during the Blair/
Brown years how important it is to work closely with your
stakeholders in developing new ideas and policies. Talking
to experts and taking full advantage of their knowledge and
experience improves the quality of what you do. But you
always have to guard against capture by an elite group of
powerful interests. I think government has been captured by
such a group on tax, a group who exert undue influence and
enjoy preferential treatment.

The examples we came across seemed endless. I have already
described the way one of KPMG's senior partners, Jonathan
Bridges, provided technical advice to government on the Patent
Box tax relief, and how he then immediately returned to his
firm and marketed the relief as a vehicle for tax avoidance.

KPMG appeared to act in a similar way when brought
into the Treasury to help rewrite some other technical rules,

known as the Controlled Foreign Companies rules. Again, the idea here was to ensure that global companies paid a fair share of tax on their UK activities and profits. Robert Edwards, a senior manager working on corporate tax for KPMG, was seconded for two years from April 2010 to 2012 to give technical advice to the Treasury, particularly around new exemptions for the finance function of global companies. He went back to KPMG after his secondment and became part of a team advising companies on how the new rules could help companies cut their tax bills.

A document produced by KPMG, which I saw, said specifically: 'The Finance Company regime is an opportunity for additional tax efficiency that is set out in legislation and therefore should not add UK tax risk to your group.' Again, KPMG – the poacher – seemed to have turned gamekeeper and become a poacher again. KPMG had helped to design the laws and was then helping companies to interpret them to cut their tax bills.

The unhealthy chumminess was evident in other ways. The Exchequer Secretary, David Gauke, said in a speech in December 2011: 'Making the right decisions on tax policy is critical. But a competitive tax system is not only about the level of taxation and the policy choices that determine its incidence, it is also about the quality of tax law and the way we make tax policy.'

To support him in improving the quality of the legislation, he established a Tax Professionals Forum to advise him. All fine and sensible until one looked closely at the membership of the advisory group. Senior people from KPMG, Ernst and Young, BDO LLP, Grant Thornton, Travers Smith and Gray's Inn Tax Chambers were there. Nobody with a different perspective, like fair tax campaigners, development charities for whom tax was hugely important, or academics with a different analysis and viewpoint. Hardly what anyone would call balanced advice.

At tax conferences, speakers from the big accountancy firms regularly parade their special relationship with the Treasury, HMRC and ministers. A partner from Grant Thornton boasted, as though it were something to be proud of, that HMRC had 'entered into a fairly narrow conversation with a small number of people and have deliberately sought to keep it within a small number of firms'. A senior PwC partner told an audience: 'Senior people in our firm in London speak to senior people in the Revenue on a regular basis so that we get the benefit of that filtering through.'

Even more worrying, one of the individuals appointed to the newly created General Anti Avoidance Rule (GAAR) in the summer of 2013, the mechanism established to tackle tax avoidance and close tax loopholes, was a man called David Heaton, who worked for the accountants Baker Tilly. His responsibilities on the GAAR were to assess whether tax schemes constituted aggressive avoidance or were reasonable. The same man was filmed at a tax conference around the time of his appointment, describing ways to keep 'the money out of the Chancellor's grubby mitts'. He had to resign when this was revealed by *Private Eye*, but should we really rely on *Private Eye* to conduct due diligence on individuals who are given public appointments?

The revolving door extends to employees of HMRC. Many individuals are trained by HMRC and then leave to join one of the big accountants. That is inevitable, but unlike the private sector, the clauses civil servants have in their contracts that control how and when they take their expertise and contacts to serve another master are far too weak. Dave Hartnett, who resigned as permanent secretary for tax at HMRC in the wake of our inquiry into Goldman Sachs, took up a job with HSBC six months later and three months after that was cleared by the Civil Service to take up an appointment with Deloitte.

At the same time Edward Troup, who succeeded Hartnett in HMRC as tax assurance commissioner and second permanent secretary in the department, had previously headed tax strategy at the City law firm Simmons and Simmons. While there he wrote an article in 1999 for the *Financial Times* setting out his view:

> Tax avoidance is a normal market reaction. Faced with the opportunity to devote resources to increasing sales or minimising tax bills, business will make a risk/return evaluation ... This judgement is not immoral, it is inevitable in a market economy ...
>
> Taxation is legalised extortion and is valid only to the extent of the law. Tax avoidance is not paying less than you 'should'. Tax avoidance is paying less than Parliament would have wanted.

Later in the same article, which attacked the concept of the GAAR, he said of the anti-avoidance measure: 'The taxpayer would be laid at the mercy of the bureaucrat.' He then went on to write: 'The determination of what Parliament might have intended would be shifted further from the hands of the courts ... and further into the hands of the executive. Hardly the outcome a good constitutionalist would wish.'

Are these really the attitudes we want from top officials in HMRC?

I set out these examples, not to impugn the integrity of any individual, but to show that the system is at fault and to enable us all to know a bit more about the sort of people who are in charge of tax in the UK. And to question whether this cosy circle of experts, with what seem to be clearly partial and predisposed views on tax, are really the best people to protect and promote the wider public interest.

It's another instance of the way in which vested interests and powerful institutions control our lives. The Big Four hold undue influence over how tax policy is framed and how it is delivered. It is this that undermines public confidence in the fairness of the tax system. Are we really all treated equally before the law?

So far, I have described how the big accountancy firms identified tax-avoidance loopholes and the privileged relationships they enjoyed and exploited. But what was so shocking was the industrial scale of these avoidance activities. Once the accountants had identified a loophole, they marketed it as widely as they could across a vast array of businesses. The accountants vigorously denied that this was the case.

At the first hearing in January 2013, Kevin Nicholson of PricewaterhouseCoopers was adamant: 'I don't recognise that statement,' he said, when I suggested the accountancy firms were offering schemes to their clients. 'We do not mass-market tax products, we do not produce tax products, we do not promote tax products.' Later he insisted: 'We are not in the business of selling schemes.'

Although I had been given details of a presentation of a tax-avoidance scheme that PwC had made to Heineken, in which PwC used examples of financial structures they had established for other global companies, Nicholson denied that PwC marketed tax products. When we presented him with evidence of a concept called the Swiss Principal model that PwC sold to global companies, through which those companies centralised their purchasing in the low-tax jurisdiction of Switzerland, he again insisted that this did not constitute selling a tax product. 'Very few of these global businesses mirror each other. They are incredibly complicated with incredibly different commercial—'

At this point Stewart Jackson MP interrupted to say: 'But there are enough issues of commonality between them for you to be able to ... use them as exemplars for other large multinational organisations.' Yet Kevin Nicholson continued to deny that PwC was selling schemes to companies.

During our hearing in January 2013, we had only limited evidence to prove that the accountants were being economical with the truth. By December 2014 that had changed. More than eighty journalists from twenty-six countries had worked together for six months to unravel what PwC was actually doing on behalf of its clients in Luxembourg. Working together via the International Consortium of Investigative Journalists, the journalists had used documents leaked by a whistleblower from PwC to uncover what I can only describe as the mass-marketing of tax-avoidance products to global companies. In the UK, both the *Guardian* and the tax expert Richard Brooks, from *Private Eye*, had been involved in the investigation. PwC's only reaction when these revelations were made public was to sue the whistleblower in the courts.

The journalists let me see many of the documents. They comprised 548 letters that had been written to the Luxembourg tax authorities on behalf of 343 global companies on PwC-headed notepaper, seeking clearance by a tax ruling from Luxembourg for an organisational structure that would facilitate tax avoidance. Of these companies, 122 were customers of the Large Businesses unit in HMRC. They included household names such as Dyson, Burberry, Amazon, IKEA, Vodafone, Apple, Accenture, HSBC and the Guardian Media Group. Between them avoiding billions of pounds of tax.

The evidence suggested that PwC did not simply advise their clients. They designed the schemes, they brokered the schemes and they got them signed off on their clients' behalf with the Luxembourg tax authorities. While PwC continued to claim that the advice was bespoke, it was clear that the template was identical.

In the words of the Harvard professor Stephen Shay, who has held senior tax roles in the US Treasury and who in 2015 gave expert testimony on Apple's tax-avoidance structures to a Senate investigation: 'Clearly the database is evidencing a pervasive enabling by Luxembourg of multinationals' avoidance.' He described Luxembourg as being 'like a magical fairyland'.

PwC invented and created hundreds of complex company structures. They helped global companies set up shell companies in Luxembourg; these Luxembourg companies were simply vehicles that lent money through artificial loans to other sister companies in the same group. The only purpose of the loan was to transfer money out of one tax jurisdiction to Luxembourg. The Luxembourg branch of the group charged exorbitant interest on these intra-company loans to the sister companies, located in places like the UK. In this way, profits were shifted to Luxembourg where little or no tax was paid. PwC negotiated the deals on behalf of the companies. The letters to the tax authorities in Luxembourg were on PwC-headed notepaper. The letters showed that 95 per cent of the tax rulings were made between 2008 and 2010 – in what can only be described as a mass-marketing exercise.

Of course we had to recall PwC, which we did just before Christmas 2014. I thought we should also hear directly from one of the companies. Dyson would have been an obvious exemplar – a household name in Britain and a successful British company. However, Sir James Dyson was closely linked to the Conservative Party and it was clear that the Conservatives on the committee would shy away from asking the Dyson company to give evidence, particularly as we were months away from the 2015 General Election. I wanted to maintain unity among committee members so we settled for asking Shire Pharmaceuticals, a less well-known company, to give evidence alongside PwC.

Shire is a successful global pharmaceutical company selling drugs for ADHD, Alzheimer's, chronic kidney disease, and a number of other rare and life-threatening diseases. The company employed around six thousand people globally; only two worked in Luxembourg. Shire had until recently been domiciled in the UK but moved their headquarters to Ireland in 2008 – for tax reasons – when the then Labour government started to pursue companies for tax. They had companies around the world and, of course, some shell companies based in Luxembourg. The board remained pretty British, with one member, Anne Minto, given an MBE; another, David Kappler, was a Fellow of the Chartered Institute of Management Accountants; and a third, Dominic Blakemore, had worked for PricewaterhouseCoopers and given advice to pharmaceutical sector clients.

The company, at the time of our hearing in December 2014, was borrowing $800 million externally for investment. However, its Luxembourg-based shell companies were lending $10 billion in intra-company loans to other companies in the group. Over five years, Shire made $1.87 billion profit in Luxembourg from this intra-group lending, but following the agreement made on their behalf by PwC with the Luxembourg tax authorities, they paid around $2 million in tax – an effective tax rate of 0.107 per cent.

The idea that Luxembourg, with its population of just over half a million citizens, housed anything other than a shell company created to facilitate tax avoidance was exposed during our questioning. Shire admitted to us that they had only two employees in Luxembourg and that they spent just €135,000 on staffing costs there. One of the two employees held forty-one other directorships with other companies in the Grand Duchy, so he could hardly be described as full-time, yet the employees were nominally responsible for lending $10 billion across the world to other companies in the group.

Fearghas Carruthers (head of tax for Shire Pharmaceuticals) claimed that the staffing was 'entirely appropriate to the operation we have in Luxembourg. If it were anywhere else doing these activities, that would be the level of staffing we would use.'

Stephen Phillips MP, a ferocious interrogator at our committee, remarked:

'It is extraordinary: you are a Jersey company, domiciled for tax purposes in Ireland, with your major operations in the United States, a legacy in the United Kingdom and a treasury operation of gargantuan proportions operated by two middle-ranking employees in Luxembourg, whom you visit a few times a year.'

Fearghas Carruthers was anxious to tell us about the vital work his company undertook in the pharmaceutical world. But I was cross. I cut short his attempts to justify the company by saying: 'It is because what you do is so important that we are so offended by the way in which you do it. It is because these medicines are so important that we feel such huge offence at the way in which you have scammed the British public . . . You are trying to tell us that what you do is important. We know that – those medicines are very important to lots of people – but the way in which you conduct your business is outrageous.'

Opening up these arrangements to public account was hugely important and, yet again, we were only able to do so, and do so effectively, because of the actions of a whistleblower and the investigations of some dedicated journalists.

Yet there were those who, even in the face of this overwhelming evidence and widespread public disapproval, remained in

my view stalwart in their arrogance and shameless lack of respect
for the process. Kevin Nicholson from PricewaterhouseCoopers
was one such person. He had appeared before our committee
in January 2013 and said in his evidence that PwC did not sell
or mass-market schemes. He had gone further and led us to
believe that such schemes were not possible. At the first hearing
he asserted: 'If there is no substance there, that planning – that
particular structure – would not work. There has to be substance there. If you have a finance company in Luxembourg, the
Cayman Islands or Bermuda, and you haven't got the people,
the loans and the agreements there, I do not understand how
that would work … If there is no substance – we would always
advise that whatever it is that you say you are doing, you have
to be doing there.'

Yet all the time PwC was selling arrangements which
bore all the same hallmarks of standard schemes and which
they knew worked for all their clients. At the 2015 hearing
Nicholson might at the very least have apologised for misleading the committee in 2013. However, he simply said:
'I stand by what I said in that meeting (our previous hearing).' And then he tried to squirm his way out of a hole in
a number of ways. He said that when he had told us PwC
did not mass-market schemes, he was referring to 'HMRC's
definition under DOTAS [the government's Disclosure of
Tax Avoidance Schemes]. It's all around secrecy, not wanting
HMRC to know. This is nothing like that; this is going to
a revenue authority.' He used an interpretation of one set of
rules about disclosure to obfuscate. Somehow clinging to
that particular straw allowed him to tell us that PwC did not
mass-market schemes when it seemed clear to us that they did.

He argued that when he had said there had to be substance
in Luxembourg for the scheme to work, he was referring to
'the latest Treasury and HMRC guidance on what substance is

required, they actually say not much substance is required . . . [it is] the correct amount of substance'. I wondered what he thought the correct amount of substance was.

Barefaced lack of respect for Parliament and the public was certainly what it felt like. No doubt he was encouraged by the lack of consequences for his actions. HMRC appeared to know what was going on and was doing nothing to challenge the artificial arrangements PricewaterhouseCoopers was putting in place. Obviously, the international rules need to be rewritten, but even under the present rules what happened in practice – and no doubt continues to happen – was so far removed from what people claimed was happening, that surely that should have been challenged openly in the courts. The accountants verified that there was genuine business activity taking place in Luxembourg. The reality on any common-sense interpretation implied that that was not true. HMRC, however, always seems to lie down and accept the interpretation put forward by the vested interests in the tax world.

Politicians and civil servants in Luxembourg were not just colluding with the accountants and others, they were encouraging them to create artificial structures to avoid tax. Pascal Saint-Amans, Director of the Centre for Tax Policy and Administration at the OECD, which has been leading the work to rewrite the international tax rules, said of the country: 'Luxembourg's wealth comes from helping companies not pay taxes in the countries where the value was created . . . Instead of creating value they create tax advice.'

The half a million people who live in Luxembourg don't consume greater amounts of the drugs produced by Shire or buy more of the vacuum cleaners produced by Dyson. However, over $215 billion of loans and investments found their way through Luxembourg between 2002 and 2010.

The key official to whom PwC regularly wrote was Marius

Kohl, known as 'Monsieur Ruling', who for twenty-two years had sole authority to approve or reject such tax deals. In an interview with the *Wall Street Journal*, when asked how he determined whether a company's pricing information was accurate, Mr Kohl licked his thumb and held it in the air.

But Jean-Claude Juncker ran the finance ministry and was Prime Minister of Luxembourg from 1995 to 2013. He must have at least endorsed Luxembourg in its tax haven policies. Yet he is now President of the European Commission, charged with stamping out aggressive tax avoidance. In my view his record at the helm in Luxembourg renders him unfit to hold the office in Europe. Somewhere, sometime people have to be held to account for their actions. He may have helped Luxembourg financially, but in the process he damaged many other countries and tarnished the reputation of the country he served as Prime Minister. We deserve better for Europe.

As we were preparing to publish the report on our inquiry into PricewaterhouseCoopers and the Luxembourg leaks, it was clear that the committee would be hugely critical of their role. Indeed, in the press release I said: 'We believe that PricewaterhouseCoopers' activities represent nothing short of the promotion of tax avoidance on an industrial scale.'

I had spent a short time working for PwC in the early 1990s but my work had been in the public sector consultancy division and I had always acknowledged that aspect of my past. It didn't cause me a problem. However, I was also aware of the fact that a number of my Labour frontbench colleagues accepted money in kind from PwC in the form of secondees to work in the MPs' offices. PwC was supporting Labour in Opposition, another clever move by the partnership, because that helped their accountants create relationships with possible future ministers and develop an understanding of Labour Party thinking on matters that affected them and their clients.

I always thought taking money from PwC in this way was unwise. Indeed, I had turned down an offer of help from a PwC partner whom I knew when I was first elected as chair of the Public Accounts Committee.

I realised that when doing media interviews on our report I would be asked questions about PwC funding Labour front-benchers. I did not want to cause trouble for my colleagues, but I was not about to shy away from being robust in what I said. I had to think hard about how to handle the questions. The funding of political parties has always been contentious but if politics, parties and in particular Opposition parties were properly funded by the state, they would not need to turn to people like PwC for financial help or support in kind.

I discussed with my researcher how to handle the questions. We decided that first I would argue that all political parties took funding from PwC and that the need to accept such monies came from the underfunding of politics. If Britain wanted a strong democracy with an effective Opposition it should fund political parties properly so that they did not have to seek support from companies like PwC.

However, I knew the interviewers would push me on the issue. We decided that if that happened, I would have to say that I thought it was 'inappropriate' for MPs to accept funding from PwC. That was the most gentle word we felt was consistent with my views and our criticism of the firm.

We released our report on a Friday, 5 February 2015, and I was interviewed by *The World at One*. The inevitable happened and I couldn't stave off questions on the topic by making generalised comments on political party funding. So I ended up saying that I thought Labour's accepting money in kind was 'inappropriate'.

I hate attacking colleagues in public, but I felt that I had no alternative, given what we had uncovered. That night I was playing bridge with a group of friends. It was just after

11.30 p.m. and we were packing up to go home when my mobile rang. It was Ed Miliband. He hadn't rung me for months. He was furious and subjected me to a stream of abuse for my criticism of fellow Labour MPs.

The episode was bizarre: the leader of the Labour Party, of all parties, ringing me at nearly midnight on a Friday to tell me off. No consideration of what we had uncovered, no thought as to how the public, our voters, might react to the report, no discussion of the rights and wrongs associated with Labour accepting money from companies like PwC. But that is modern politics and I suppose that I should be grateful that at least I wasn't tucked up in bed, sound asleep.

7

Boutique Advisers and 'Scams for Scumbags'

We thought that what the accountancy firms got up to was pretty awful. But we had yet to meet the 'boutique advisers', the small band of consultants who designed or promoted the riskiest of tax-avoidance schemes. Their clients were mostly very rich individuals, often household names, who used these aggressive tax-avoidance schemes to avoid paying their taxes. The comedian Jimmy Carr; radio DJ Chris Moyles; footballers David Beckham and Steven Gerrard; singers Robbie Williams and Annie Lennox; TV presenters Jeremy Paxman and Anne Robinson. All named in the media as being involved in artificial schemes to avoid tax.

Yet again, the impetus for this investigation arose from the excellent investigative work of a journalist, this time Alexi Mostrous of *The Times*. He contacted me and told me the details of the stories he had uncovered. *The Times* was running a campaign against tax avoidance and had published a number of stories in the summer of 2012. It was obvious to me that this was another scarcely known and little understood scandal that should be opened to public view and debate.

Some of the clients who benefited from the schemes worked hard to keep their names out of the press. DJ Chris Moyles, for example, sought anonymity when he brought an appeal against HMRC in a tax tribunal convened to pass judgement on one of these dodgy schemes. A judge threw out his plea for anonymity saying: 'The fact that a taxpayer is rich, or that he is in the public eye does not seem to me to dictate a different approach. On the contrary, it may be that hearing the appeal of such a person in private would give rise to the suspicion that riches or fame can buy anonymity and protection from scrutiny which others cannot avoid.' Other household names employed other means to avoid adverse publicity. Many of the high-profile individuals involved invested their money through Jersey, where anonymity was offered.

The sums of money involved were immense. Between 2010 and 2012, according to HMRC's own assessment, over £10.2 billion of tax was at risk from avoidance by individuals and small companies. That sum was almost certainly, like most of HMRC's estimates, on the conservative side. HMRC knew of 324 different schemes that were being used at that time. They thought that there were around ten thousand cases of people taking advantage of these egregious schemes.

Under DOTAS (Disclosure of Tax Avoidance Schemes), advisers or individual taxpayers who use schemes that avoid tax are required to disclose the schemes and inform HMRC and they face fines if they fail to do so. The idea is that being told about new tax-avoidance schemes allows HMRC to assess whether or not such schemes are lawful. In evidence to the Public Accounts Committee, the tax authorities told us that around a hundred new schemes were disclosed each year. But they thought that less than half of the tax at risk from avoidance was captured by DOTAS; they were simply not being told about all the tax-avoidance schemes that could potentially be deemed unlawful. HMRC could obviously try to detect their existence in other ways, but it was clear from the fact that by 2012 they had only obtained fines for non-disclosure in eleven cases, that DOTAS was pretty toothless and HMRC lacked the capacity to police the system properly.

It was also obvious that HMRC was not using the full force of the law efficiently. By August 2012, nearly half of the cases being fought through tax tribunals by HMRC were more than three years old. When HMRC takes cases to court, they mostly succeed. They just don't do it often enough or quickly enough. And if they succeed in getting a particular scheme deemed unlawful, they have to pursue every person individually through the tribunal system; HMRC cannot take one class action against all the individuals who have used the same scheme to avoid tax.

The schemes the boutique advisers devised were complicated and devious, as this one example shows. The Liberty tax-avoidance scheme was marketed for four years between 2005 and 2009. The scheme involved 1600 people, including George Michael, Anne Robinson and Sir Michael Caine, and, had it not been successfully challenged by HMRC in the courts, could have led to the loss of some £1.2 billion in tax.

Investors typically formed an offshore partnership or syndicate with £100 million. That partnership or syndicate also set up an offshore parent company and an offshore subsidiary company. The investors only put in £7 million of their own money; they borrowed the other £93 million from banks. They then claimed tax relief on the money they borrowed and that tax relief was offset against any tax they owed to the UK Exchequer on their other income, so they got rid of their tax liability and avoided tax. The offshore subsidiary company then declared a dividend of £100 million and the parent company sold the right to that dividend to the partnership or syndicate. The syndicate had already claimed tax relief on the money they borrowed from the bank and a tax loophole enabled them to escape any tax liability on the dividend. The partnership or syndicate used the £100 million dividend to pay back the bank. The scheme had wiped out their tax liability on their other income.

Who were the characters that made a living out of promoting and selling this sort of tax avoidance to rich people? Alexi Mostrous suggested some boutique advisers we should invite to give evidence at a session we held just before Christmas in 2012. The committee took evidence from three people from three firms. Our first witness was Aiden James, the managing director of Tax Trade. He was amazingly and refreshingly open about what he did. I had thought long and hard about how to draw out the truth about his business and decided to start the evidence session with a general question, asking him simply to describe the purpose of his business.

He was surprisingly direct in his reply.

Aiden James: 'My business is essentially set up to provide an independent review of tax-avoidance structures in the market. We particularly specialise in income tax avoidance.'

MH: 'So you market yourselves as a tax-avoidance business. That is your business model. You are in the business of avoiding tax?'

Aiden James: 'Yes.'

He evidently found the next question harder to answer. I had to ask him the same question six times before finally getting an answer: 'Do you think that your schemes use the law to get a tax advantage that Parliament never intended?'

Eventually he came clean: 'So, in answer to your question, yes, but it is not exclusive to tax schemes.'

Aiden James was straight with us about how he ran his business. He had been going for about six years. He did not develop new schemes but took those that had been invented by others and marketed them. In his six years he had sold six schemes to hundreds of clients; he made his money by taking a commission every time he sold a scheme to a client. All six schemes had been challenged by HMRC and all had been closed down. But he did not lose his commission. He was able to carry on making money from selling schemes that he knew were dodgy because he had secured a barrister's opinion, giving him legal cover that enabled him to claim that he was acting within the law even if the schemes were clearly designed to avoid tax. (What were the lawyers up to? one might well ask.) He also took advantage of the invariable time delays in HMRC both challenging schemes and then pulling the plug.

'These structures take quite a few years before they reach their conclusion,' he told us.

'They say that they are going to challenge it,' I said. 'At that point, do you carry on selling it?'

'Yes. Why not?' he replied. 'The law hasn't changed.'

James's openness to the committee simply confirmed the absolute confidence that he and others had that their continuing business was secure; they did not feel threatened. He told us that some scheme advisers, whether they developed or marketed schemes, charged as much as 20 per cent commission. I had been given a copy of an agreement between an individual client and Aiden James's company that had been signed and said: 'Please accept this as my instruction to create gross tax relief of £250,000 through the Rushmore income tax and chargeable gains tax mitigation arrangement developed by NT (Jersey) Ltd.' The client's sole aim was to create tax relief to offset against his tax liability. When I put it to Aiden James that the public would 'consider [him] to be completely, utterly and totally immoral in the work that you are doing', he came back with: 'The product has been settled by an eminent QC. Perhaps the week before he settled that opinion, he was working for HMRC.' That remark showed not only the important role played by lawyers but the incestuous nature of the tax advisers' world, with individuals working for HMRC one week and the dodgiest of dodgy tax advisers the next. It also suggested collusion between all involved in facilitating and enabling aggressive tax avoidance.

The scheme sold by Aiden James's company that caught our eye was Working Wheels. My colleague Nick Smith MP described it as a 'dodgy second-hand car deal'. Working Wheels was based on fictitious trading in second-hand cars, and 450 people used the scheme, including Chris Moyles. These people claimed on their tax returns that they were engaged in self-employment as used-car traders. In fact, they never saw a used car or had one sitting in their driveway. Under the scheme they registered huge losses from fictitious trading that they could then offset against tax liabilities arising from their other income. In the case of Chris Moyles, he claimed to have sold second-hand cars worth £3731 but to have incurred losses totalling £1 million. Those losses were set against the tax he should have paid on the £700,000 he earned from the BBC (funded by the taxpayer through the licence fee).

When we asked Aiden James to describe how it worked, he said he couldn't because he was bound by confidentiality agreements he had signed with the developer of this product. Fortunately, I had been leaked details of the company's sales pitch. So I was able to quote to him from the leaked papers. The scheme was described as follows: 'The taxpayer will pay an irregular manufactured dividend under certain loan and security arrangements such that the manufactured payment represents an allowable tax deduction.'

'So,' I commented, 'the scheme purports to trade in second-hand cars, but in effect is a device that allows investors to avoid tax.'

To which Aiden James responded: 'I think that is a fair summary.'

HMRC did take users of this scheme to the tax tribunal. The three taxpayers they named – including Chris Moyles – had claimed losses of £20 million, which was worth £8 million in tax at the 40 per cent tax rate, the top rate in place at that time. But HMRC can only take cases against individuals to the tax tribunal. The cases we saw related to only three of the 450 people who took advantage of the second-hand car scheme and claimed they were trading in second-hand cars. When the judge issued his judgement he said: 'A realistic view of the facts shows that the aim was that appellants "as though by magic" should appear to have incurred vast fees as a condition of borrowing modest amounts of money they did not need in order to invest in a "trade" they had no desire to pursue. The supposed fee for the loan bore no relation to the loan, but was merely the amount of the artificial loss the user wished to generate.' Although the scheme used by all 450 taxpayers was the same, HMRC still had to pursue each person individually.

Our two other witnesses had been particularly active in the film industry. I was especially angered to discover that Ingenious Media was embroiled in aggressive tax avoidance because I had worked with them when I was Culture Minister. Their chief executive was the urbane Patrick McKenna, who founded the group in 1998 and who had emerged from being the son of an

Essex builder to become an extremely wealthy financier, now living in a multi-million-pound Essex mansion. He portrayed himself as an important and innovative player in the creative industries sector and held a number of prestigious positions on the board of the Young Vic Theatre, the National Film and Television School, and the National Endowment for Science Technology and the Arts (NESTA). All the while, he was making millions by exploiting a new film tax relief to help his clients avoid tax as an integral part of his financial services business. He denied any wrongdoing but he clearly sought to run rings around HMRC. Indeed, he had so enraged HMRC that in an off-the-record briefing that HMRC held for the press, Dave Hartnett, Permanent Secretary for Tax, said: 'You won't find anybody here at all, even the most pro wealthy people, who think film schemes are anything other than scams for scumbags.'

McKenna for his part was so infuriated by Hartnett's comments that he took action against HMRC, claiming that by briefing the press they had breached the law on confidentiality of his interests as a taxpayer. However, the judge found in HMRC's favour, acquitting Dave Hartnett of any breach of taxpayer confidentiality on the grounds that it was 'legitimate for HMRC to seek to maintain good and co-operative relationships with the press'. I only wish Dave Hartnett had been as open with us over Goldman Sachs as he was with the press over Ingenious Media.

Like Dave Hartnett, however, I was angry with Patrick McKenna. I had been Minister for Culture under Gordon Brown and spent a great deal of my time supporting the creative industries. Part of the work involved working with the film industry and promoting its growth in the UK. One of Gordon Brown's initiatives, in response to pleas from the film sector, was to introduce a tax relief to encourage filmmakers to make more films in the UK, a move that commanded wide political

support. As Culture Minister I had to oversee the implementation of the relief. Early on in the job, I was introduced to Patrick
McKenna and told that he was an important stakeholder in the
UK film industry and the wider creative industries sector. I
arranged a meeting with him at his offices. Most of the people
working in the creative sector were struggling to make ends
meet. However, McKenna's workplace was different. I was
taken aback by the opulence of his offices and the quality of the
original art on his walls. I remember wondering how on earth
he appeared to be making so much money, while the rest of
the sector was struggling to survive. I should have asked more
questions then and I still kick myself for simply taking him at
face value. It seemed to us that he made money by exploiting
the ambiguities in the small print of the film tax relief legislation
in order to help rich people avoid tax. We began to suspect the
abuse of this well-intentioned tax relief when I was minister.
But as I write this, we are still waiting, a decade later, for the
final judgement of the tax tribunal on some of the outlandish
schemes sponsored by Ingenious Media and others.

Unlike Aiden James, McKenna doggedly denied any involvement in tax avoidance. 'There is no question of tax avoidance
here,' he insisted. 'It is simply an issue of getting capital allowances when you invest in a film.'

Ingenious Media and our third witness, Future Capital
Partners, set up partnerships they claimed existed to finance
films. Their schemes often involved very successful films like
Avatar, Life of Pi and *The Best Exotic Marigold Hotel*. Some of the
investments did support the making of new films, but even in
these cases we suspected the schemes were primarily constructed
to avoid tax. Like the dodgy second-hand car trading scheme,
investors might invest £1 million of which a small amount
was cash and the rest was borrowed from a bank, creating a
debt with interest charges that could be offset against other tax

liabilities. Investors also took advantage of the losses always incurred in the early years of making a new film to offset further tax and most investors exited the schemes before the film started to make a profit. It seemed to us that other film schemes were established purely as tax-avoidance vehicles, often using completed films that were sold to the investors and leased back to the film studios, creating debt for investors in buying the schemes, which they could offset against their tax liabilities. These schemes were promoted by companies like Ingenious Media and Future Capital Partners and used by celebrities like Robbie Williams, Jeremy Paxman and David Beckham.

Future Capital Partners told us that from 1997 to 2012 they had completed transactions involving £6.5 billion. Future Capital also told us that they thought the market in partnerships to take advantage of the tax reliefs grew to over £2 billion a year by 2002. Patrick McKenna of Ingenious was a bit more reticent, but told us that one type of these schemes, when film companies sold and then leased back their films, had involved Ingenious in some £1.5 billion or more.

It emerged that although the tax relief was supposed to support the UK film industry, much of the investment went into American films. One of the witnesses started by saying that only 10 per cent of the films were US films, but later was reluctantly forced to admit that, in terms of value, 50 per cent of the investment by clients in the UK that attracted UK tax relief was 'possibly' used on American films.

The schemes are difficult to understand, which is one reason why the public know so little about this sort of tax practice. Future Capital Partners told us that of the 255 investments they had made, 127 had been challenged by HMRC and thirteen were being litigated in the courts. They also proudly told us that they had won two cases in the Court of Appeal.

Not only did the schemes help wealthy individuals cut

their tax liabilities, they were very lucrative for Ingenious and Future Capital Partners. In one letter we were given, which had been sent by Future Capital Partners to a client setting out the terms for exiting the scheme before he was faced with a tax bill, the advisers wrote: 'As you are aware, your projected share of partnership profits for the tax year 2012–2013 could be in excess of £520,000 on which, assuming you are a higher rate taxpayer, you would face an income tax liability of approximately £260,000. If you were to retire from the partnerships effectively from 6 April 2011, the tax arising on these profits and the future risks pertaining to this will fall due to the company.' The company that took over the interests was, of course, not located in the UK but in Luxembourg, so UK tax would never be paid, although the UK tax relief had been claimed.

Future Capital Partners set out their charges for facilitating the exit scheme: 'With regard to the cost in respect of which the company has proposed in order to assume your interest and liabilities in the partnership, (that) amounts to £60,000.'

To get rid of a £260,000 tax liability, Future Capital charged £60,000.

In his evidence to the committee, Patrick McKenna refused even to accept that he was involved in exit schemes. I was taken aback by this bare-faced denial and so turned to the more open Aiden James, which really infuriated Patrick McKenna.

> Patrick McKenna: 'It is not an exit scheme . . . I am sorry
>   but we do not have exit schemes . . . It is not an exit
>   scheme . . . They did not exit in from anywhere to
>   anywhere else . . . There is no tax avoidance here. It
>   is simply an issue of getting capital allowances when
>   you invest in a film.'

This went on and on, so I turned to Aiden James again:

MH: 'To offset tax. Mr James, what is he talking about? It
　　is an offsetting of tax, isn't it?'

Patrick McKenna: 'Excuse me, can I answer?'

MH: 'Isn't it, Mr James?'

Aiden James: 'Semantics, isn't it?'

MH: 'What do you mean by semantics?'

Patrick McKenna: 'It is not semantics.'

MH: 'Let Mr James just answer that.'

Patrick McKenna: 'He shouldn't be commenting on my
　　arrangements.'

MH: 'Yes, he can. Why not?'

Aiden James: 'An exit obviously. I have seen a number of these
　　structures over the years ... Mr McKenna is absolutely
　　right in what he is saying, but by the same token,
　　you could say that a client could engage in a different
　　tax-avoidance structure to *exit* a scheme. They may not
　　have left the old partnership. Is that an exit?'

What Aiden James appeared to be saying was that McKenna
was simply using language to obfuscate what was really happening; his clients were exiting one scheme to avoid tax, but
he did not like the use of the word *exit*.

The complexity of the schemes, the exploitation of apparent
ambiguities, and a highly semantic and imaginative use of words,
I feel these were all part of an attempt to conceal and confuse.

But the advisers did not operate alone. The schemes all
involved clients borrowing monies to create a debt on which
they could claim tax relief. The major banks appear to have
been involved in structuring these products and lending
money to the individual clients. Barclays, RBS (the majority
of which is owned by the taxpayer), HSBC and the Bank of
Ireland were all cited in our evidence sessions. The banks
seemed happy to put their money into products where the

main purpose appeared to be tax avoidance. They made 1 per cent to 2 per cent on each loan, but did we really intend that to be the way in which quantitative easing should be used?

The part played by law firms and successful QCs was equally alarming. Promoters of schemes relied absolutely on the sign-off they obtained from lawyers. Armed with an opinion from a QC, advisers were absolved of any personal liability should the scheme they had devised or promoted be struck down by HMRC. Our witnesses insisted that the schemes they promoted had the blessing of lawyers. They would not promote the schemes without that legal endorsement.

Aiden James told us in evidence: 'We prefer not to promote a structure that we feel is not robust.'

MH: 'What do you mean by "robust"?'
Aiden James: 'Able to achieve its means.'
MH: 'How do you judge that?'
Aiden James: 'We look at an eminent QC's opinion and take a technical view.'

Later, the representative from Future Capital Partners told us that his firm had engaged with all the 'magic circle' law firms at some point. It was obvious what was happening here. There was a small cohort of QCs who were willing to put their names on a piece of paper to provide cover for accusations of aggressive tax avoidance.

Armed with that signature, those who developed and promoted new schemes enjoyed what is known as 'a reasonable excuse' for selling the scheme, which protected them against action. But even if the boutique advisers turned out to have given bad advice and their clients were required to pay the tax they thought they had avoided, the advisers themselves – those who develop, endorse, fund and promote these complex schemes – got off scot-free.

8

HSBC in Switzerland: About More than Cheese and Chocolate

An exchange at one of our evidence sessions in October 2011 between Permanent Secretary for Tax Dave Hartnett and myself illustrates the essence of the unfairness that pervades the UK tax system.

'How do you justify the difference in treatment of rich people ... and the way your department treats the overpayment of tax credit to single parents?' I asked him.

'We know the people who have been overpaid tax credits,' he replied, 'and can address that, but we do not know the identity of people in Switzerland and we cannot establish who they are ... A pragmatic solution to a long-standing difficulty.'

That approach is the reason why ordinary, law-abiding taxpayers have lost confidence that every individual is treated equally by the tax authorities.

The suspicion that there is one law for the rich and powerful and another for everybody else was starkly demonstrated by yet another set of leaks and another tremendous piece of work by investigative journalists. The leaked documents helped us to shine a light on another scandal that reinforced that loss of confidence. And, of course, our investigation took place fifteen months before the Panama leaks hit the media in April 2016, when the content of 11.5 million documents from the Panama-based law firm, Mossack Fonseca, were revealed to the public.

We had known since 2010 that HMRC had received information from a whistleblower about Swiss bank accounts held by citizens from the UK and elsewhere that could involve tax avoidance – and possible tax evasion. HMRC had put out a press release in 2011 telling the world that they had 'begun criminal and serious fraud investigations' and threatening that if people did not come forward voluntarily, HMRC would 'begin an investigation into their affairs, which could include a criminal investigation or result in penalties, in certain circumstances, of up to 200 per cent . . . This is not an amnesty.'

At our hearings with HMRC officials, we had regularly asked about progress in investigating the information on the Swiss bank accounts. They always assured us that they were making progress and that they were both pursuing the money and, where appropriate, initiating prosecutions.

In February 2015, five years later, the whistleblower, presumably frustrated by the lack of progress by tax authorities, gave the documents to the media. The *Guardian*, working in collaboration with journalists from France and from the Washington-based International Consortium of Investigative Journalists, released the data, and their revelations blasted a hole through HMRC's claim of being both tough on the people who had hidden their money in Switzerland and successful in securing substantial monies for the British taxpayer.

The revelations were astounding. In 1999, HSBC bought a Swiss private bank as part of a wider deal. By 2007, it held over thirty thousand accounts in that bank which between them contained assets worth some £78 billion. Those who kept their money in Switzerland came from all over the world.

In 2008, an employee from the Swiss bank, Hervé Falciani, a computer engineer, leaked documents relating to the accounts and gave them to the French tax authorities. The Swiss authorities pursued Falciani across Europe and eventually found him guilty of industrial espionage, sentencing him to five years in prison in his absence. Both the French and Spanish authorities (he fled to Spain to avoid assassination threats) refused to extradite him. In fact, the French authorities indicted HSBC for money laundering in November 2014.

By 2010, the French authorities had released a disk to HMRC containing details of the accounts held by UK citizens that they had received from the Falciani leaks. There were 6800 different documents and the monies held in Switzerland by UK citizens amounted to £40 billion.

Although, in the following years, HMRC had given us broad assurances that they were pursuing the individuals and the unpaid tax, it was only after the Falciani leaks were made public in 2015 that HMRC became more open about what they were doing.

During our hearing in February 2015, HMRC told us that the documents related to 3600 individuals. They had traced 3200 of them. Two thirds of those people were open in their discussions with HMRC. But officials thought about one third of the cases – around a thousand individuals – raised serious concerns. However, that was then whittled down to 150 individual cases where HMRC was considering criminal proceedings. When we saw the officials in 2015, they had prosecuted only one case and recovered only £135 million in tax. According to information given to me by the investigative journalists, the French and Spanish together were handed fewer documents than we received, but between them recovered three times as much as our tax authorities did: France recovered £200 million and Spain £185 million.

By the time the information was made public, I had become a little desensitised to bad behaviour, however what we saw here was not just aggressive tax avoidance, but what looked like tax evasion. Tax evasion is illegal. There is no grey area, nor any debate about morality to be had; it is a criminal act. And for the first time we had evidence of the active role played by a reputable bank in facilitating avoidance and possible evasion.

Individuals held their money in Switzerland for a reason. Clearly some had a perfectly legitimate explanation, but for many Switzerland offered a good place to hide money. As my colleague Stewart Jackson ironically quipped during the hearing when we were discussing why people banked in Switzerland: 'It is because of the cheese and the chocolate.'

Not only were these bank accounts held in Switzerland, but many were 'hold-mail' accounts. This meant they were much more secret: there was no direct communication between the bank and the beneficial owner of the account, so that nobody could link the individual to the bank or to the money held in the bank. One of our HSBC witnesses tried to justify the existence of such accounts: 'A lot of these people were worried about their wealth being known and kidnapping.' He went on to admit: 'It wasn't considered a red flag at that time, because all the Swiss private banks were doing it.'

However, group chief executive Stuart Gulliver was a little more straightforward. When pressed by Dame Anne McGuire MP as to whether these secret accounts were set up to avoid or evade tax he admitted: 'I would agree that there is a higher probability that hold-mail indicates areas of concern that we, as a bank, should take note of.' He told us that he had instituted a review of these accounts in 2012 – well after the whistleblower had leaked the documents to the tax authorities – and that the number of clients with hold-mail accounts had been reduced from 14,868 to twelve. Would that have happened if the whistleblower had not released data to the authorities?

Another shocking discovery came to light during the hearing. One of our witnesses, who was the former group general manager and CEO of HSBC's Global Private Banking, admitted openly that the bank was involved in aggressive tax-avoidance schemes. He cited lending money to individuals to invest in artificial film production schemes.

That was all bad enough. But the information released by the whistleblower showed us worse. Not only was HSBC helping its clients use known tax-avoidance schemes, the Swiss arm of the bank was also the architect of new tax-avoidance schemes. They proactively advised their Swiss banking clients on how they could avoid a new piece of European legislation, called the European Savings Directive, which had been specifically agreed with the Swiss authorities so that EU nations could extract some tax from people hiding their money in Swiss bank accounts. The directive placed an obligation on banks to collect tax from account holders on the interest income they received from savings held in the bank. The banks had to collect the money from the accounts and pass it directly to the tax authorities in the country where the account holder resided. It was a clever way of securing some tax from people who were determined to hide their money because the tax authorities themselves did not have to identify and pursue the individuals. Banks became legally responsible for extracting the money from their clients.

HSBC helped their clients avoid this new measure. The bank devised an artificial scheme to take the money out of the tax authorities' reach. The tax directive covered individuals, not companies, and so HSBC helped clients set up shell companies located in tax havens. They would then transfer money from the Swiss bank account to the shell company and in that way clients could avoid paying the tax.

Like PricewaterhouseCoopers, HSBC marketed this tax-avoidance scheme widely. The leaked papers shown to me contained notes compiled by HSBC employees on the files of individual bank account holders. So, for example, one set of notes said: 'Met with Maurice, he will open a Panamanian Corporation as a solution of the ESD [European Savings Directive]. He will transfer his assets to the new account. The opening forms have already been signed.' Another set of notes said: 'Client came to visit us as his bi-annual visit. I took advantage of his journey to ask him to sign the appropriate documentation to avoid falling under the ESD directive.' And yet another: 'We also discussed the impending ESD and despite the very modest benefit in saved tax he has decided to form a company through Mossack and to transfer all assets across.'

Marketing tax-avoidance schemes to clients was one thing. But the data from the whistleblower seemed to show that HSBC was also colluding in tax evasion, the criminal end of the tax-avoidance spectrum. The notes revealed deliberate and planned evasion of tax by individual bank customers.

One client appeared to have brought the money he had in Switzerland into the UK by using a credit card issued by HSBC. This enabled him to take funds directly out of his Swiss bank account without the UK tax authorities knowing about the existence of the money. HSBC visited him at his home and the following appeared on the notes of his account with the Swiss bank: 'I nevertheless mentioned to my hosts that the Geneva lawyer, who has signature on all the accounts, except 23258 HE, almost certainly knew of its existence as he saw the details of credit card expenditure on Filmor and would certainly wonder from where it was financed ... This situation initially appeared to cause some disquiet to my hosts, though this later gave way to a more relaxed attitude with the sentiment that Genevan lawyers would be discreet, something that I did nothing to discourage.'

Notes on the file of another client read as follows: 'We had previously met last November, when I had promised to come back to her with a "considered" response to questions that preoccupied her: the fact that her account here – which she had inherited on the death of her husband – was not known to the UK tax authorities.'

On another file the note-taker commented: 'I contacted this person on the phone to say that unless he changed his situation he would be subject to UK tax.'

The Swiss bank account of a prestigious UK restaurant owner also looked suspect. It would appear the Swiss branch of HSBC allowed him to withdraw five million Swiss francs cash in one day, the equivalent of £2.25 million, with no questions asked. From the notes, it would seem that while the bank was nervous at handing over so much money without it being legally accounted for, they were more concerned at the possibility that the client would close the account and take the business elsewhere than that he might be laundering money.

The discovery of all these documents hit the headlines in the *Guardian* and both we and the Treasury Select Committee decided they merited public hearings, with both HSBC and HMRC. The Public Accounts Committee certainly had an interest in the matter, because we had asked questions about the Falciani leaks a number of times and had received regular assurances that HMRC had everything under control.

That now seemed to be far from the whole truth with only one successful prosecution. The explanation offered by officials was very frustrating. We were given every reason why things couldn't be done. We were told that we couldn't be told. We were left with unanswered questions which simply added to our suspicions that the tax system was not fair.

Edward Troup, the tax commissioner, summed up the officials' approach when he proclaimed: 'This was tax evasion. I am not going to go into operational details' – code for 'I am not going to tell you anything.'

When we repeatedly tried to find out why there had been only one prosecution, officials replied that the terms of the agreement with the French tax authorities meant HMRC was restricted as to how they could use the information. HMRC could not share it with the UK prosecuting authorities. Miraculously, after the information was leaked to the public and appeared all over the newspapers, HMRC did go back to the French authorities to seek agreement that they could use the information for wider purposes. Of course, the French authorities agreed (in fact, surprise, surprise, they agreed the day before our hearing), but as I write these words, a staggering eight years after the whistleblower first shared the information, only one person has been charged.

An HMRC statement dated 14 February 2015 said: 'In 150 of these cases we sought to collect evidence for criminal prosecutions . . . we could only prepare three cases for submission to the Crown Prosecution Service . . . having examined the evidence the CPS considered only one case to be strong enough to take forward and that was successfully prosecuted in 2012.'

Lin Homer, who was the permanent secretary in HMRC, also justified her inaction by pleading that litigation was expensive: 'Prosecution is one end of the toolkit and it is the expensive end,' she argued.

The frustration we felt at that response was best expressed by Stephen Phillips MP, when he said: 'The evidence from these files is that you prosecuted one person. Now the message that sends to people who might be inclined to evade tax by having Swiss bank accounts and other things is, "Don't worry about it. If you get caught, there won't be a prosecution; there will be a settlement."'

Questions about Dave Hartnett's role also emerged when we examined the HSBC/Swiss issues. As the then head of tax, he had negotiated a deal with the Swiss banks that the Chancellor, George Osborne, assured Parliament would raise £3.2 billion in tax in one year. Indeed, in his 2012 Autumn Statement the Chancellor proudly proclaimed: 'Because of the Treaty we signed we expect to receive £5 billion over the next six years from the undisclosed Swiss bank accounts of UK residents. It is the largest tax evasions settlement in British history.' In practice they raised only a fraction of that sum, £440 million.

Two matters were relevant to our investigation, which was based on the whistleblower's information revealing tax avoidance and potential tax evasion. First, the Anglo–Swiss agreement had been signed in October 2011, nearly two years after the French had handed over the incriminating data. Dave Hartnett knew about the information on HSBC provided by the ex-employee, Hervé Falciani. However, armed with that knowledge he still saw fit to insert a paragraph in the wider agreement with the Swiss, exonerating financial advisers, including banks, from any action on money laundering.

The paragraph reads: 'Swiss paying agencies and their employees will need to comply with their legal obligations in respect of money laundering. Whilst it is never possible to provide an absolute assurance against a criminal investigation, *it is highly unlikely to be in the public interest of the United*

Kingdom that professional advisers, Swiss paying agents and their employees will be subject to a criminal investigation by HMRC [my italics].' We did not receive a convincing explanation as to why, knowing of HSBC's involvement in tax avoidance and possible evasion, HMRC negotiated an agreement that let them off the hook.

Second and more worrying was our inability to establish and understand Dave Hartnett's relationship with HSBC. He claimed that he had not been involved in the decisions about the HSBC investigations. Yet he had held a meeting with HSBC within days of receiving the leaked data in February 2010. What on earth had they talked about at that meeting, we wondered, especially because he apparently took along one of the top officials tasked with working on the investigations arising from the leaks?

Neither Dave Hartnett nor Lin Homer was prepared to tell us. Hartnett claimed that Homer prohibited him from disclosing the details. When pressed to explain what happened at the meeting with HSBC, he replied: 'I don't think I can, Madam Chair, because Lin Homer has made it very clear she is not prepared to go into detail about that note [of the meeting] and I am therefore restricted in exactly the same way.'

Homer insisted she could not share with us the minute of the meeting between HSBC and Hartnett. When I asked her what was discussed, she replied: 'I will have to tell you that we do not discuss individual—'

MH: 'No, this is not about their tax affairs; this is about
     HSBC's role in actively promoting tax avoidance and
     possibly evasion.'

Lin Homer: 'That's what you are telling me. I'm telling
     you that I will not discuss what happened at meetings
     with individual businesses, because it falls under—'

MH: 'It's not about their own tax affairs, Lin. I am not
asking about HSBC's tax affairs. I am asking about
a bank's role in relation to its clients, which is what
this is all about, so it is not a confidentiality of
taxpayers' interest; it is a much broader public interest
issue and I cannot accept that you cannot talk about
it.'

She then agreed to go away and look at the issue once more but wrote to me again refusing to disclose any information because, she maintained, the issues discussed were operational and contained material that related to HMRC's early approach to investigating potential tax offences. Somehow this might betray taxpayer confidentiality.

The best we got from Mr Hartnett was: 'I did not personally discuss any data from the Falciani leaks.' No doubt literally true, but he was there with a director working on the leaked data and I was reminded of Stewart Jackson's cynical observation that they were hardly going to be talking about Swiss cheese and chocolates. And of course, within six months of leaving HMRC, Dave Hartnett was given approval to accept a job with HSBC, where he was responsible for preventing financial crime and other abuses of the financial system!

We gave HSBC a tough time when they gave evidence on 9 March 2015. The Treasury Select Committee had interviewed Douglas Flint, group chairman of HSBC Holdings Plc, and Stuart Gulliver, group chief executive, a fortnight earlier. We saw Gulliver again, together with Chris Meares, who had been group general manager and CEO of HSBC Global Private Banking at the time the Swiss branch and its clients were allegedly involved in tax avoidance and possible evasion.

We also interviewed Rona Fairhead, who had been appointed to HSBC's Audit Committee in 2004 and served as its chair between 2007 and 2010. She then became chair of HSBC's Risk Committee. She held a number of non-executive positions with HSBC and in 2014 her earnings from those positions totalled some £500,000. She was a non-executive director throughout the period when the private bank was engaged in highly questionable practices. At the same time she is now the chair of the BBC Trust.

Clearly HSBC had decided to blame Chris Meares, who had left the bank. At the Treasury Select Committee, group chairman Douglas Flint had said: 'I believe in personal accountability and I do believe people should be held responsible for what they have direct oversight over when they have failed. Yes.'

They thought Mr Meares was responsible. The best he could come up with in response was: 'We had a clear policy that tax evasion is illegal.' HSBC's policy concurred with Parliament's ruling on the illegality of tax evasion. Some comfort. The audacity to believe that saying that was enough astounded me.

Beyond that Meares was at pains to pass the buck to front-line staff. Although the staff all acted in a similar way, he tried to get us to believe they were acting without his knowledge and without management guidance, knowledge or instructions. That really stretched the imagination.

This exchange between Chris Meares and David Burrowes MP, who had recently joined the Public Accounts Committee, illustrates the way Meares tried to deal with our questions. I quote it at length because it constitutes such a clear demonstration of how the witnesses tried to evade responsibility.

MH: 'Do you accept personal responsibility?'
Chris Meares: 'So I take responsibility for control failings
    that may have happened – you have got to be aware

that I am not aware of most of these events that were reported in the press.'

David Burrowes: 'Mr Flint said they – meaning you and others – "certainly bear fairly direct responsibility for what went on in the private bank during their stewardship". Do you agree?'

Chris Meares: 'I think I have responded to that question.'

David Burrowes: 'So you agree?'

Chris Meares: 'I have responded. I have said—'

David Burrowes: 'This particular question is whether you agree with Mr Flint that you bear fairly direct responsibility for what went on in the private bank during your stewardship.'

Chris Meares: 'I have already said, I think—'

David Burrowes: 'Can you answer my question? Do you agree with that?'

Chris Meares: 'I have said that I take responsibility.'

David Burrowes: 'No, no. I am asking you particularly. Do you bear fairly direct responsibility for what went on in the private bank during your stewardship? Yes or no?'

Chris Meares: 'I think I have answered that question.'

David Burrowes: 'Please say it again. I may have got it wrong.'

Chris Meares: 'I will say it again. I take responsibility for what happened during that period.'

David Burrowes: 'Once again, do you bear fairly direct responsibility for what went on in the private bank during your stewardship? Yes or no.'

Chris Meares: 'I take responsibility for the control failings that happened—'

David Burrowes: 'Yes or no? I need you to say yes or no.'

Chris Meares: 'I do not really see—'

David Burrowes: 'It is my job to ask the question and you can answer. So I am asking the question, do you

accept direct responsibility for what went on in the
private bank during your stewardship?'

Chris Meares: 'I take fairly direct responsibility for what
happened in global private banking during my
stewardship. I do not—'

MH: 'Mr Meares, just say yes or no. I think that would
really help our proceedings. We are stuck here.
Either yes or no.'

Chris Meares: 'I think I used exactly the words you said,
but it has to be taken into context, in that I was
running the global private bank. I do not take fairly
direct responsibility for the individual actions of
people in Switzerland that I was not aware of what
they were up to.'

All of this led me to observe: 'All you are doing is evading.
You are evading the evasion.'

So in the end he claimed it was not his fault. Stuart Gulliver,
on the other hand, had a far better alibi. Although he had
worked for the bank for many years and had been appointed as
a director of the Swiss private bank in 2007, he became group
chief executive of HSBC in 2011, after the Falciani data had
been leaked.

It was his own circumstances and his attitude to his own
taxation more than his actions as an employee of HSBC that
gave us pause for thought when he appeared before the committee. He was quiet, direct in his answers and self-assured in
his performance.

He was born in the UK, grew up in Plymouth, owned
property in the UK, sent his children to school in the UK,
voted in UK elections, had most recently been working in the
UK since 2003, but claimed non-domiciled status. He claimed
that he and his family were permanently resident in Hong

Kong. He used to be paid into a bank account in Switzerland that was linked to a shell company in Panama. He claimed he set up these secret bank arrangements to ensure his privacy; it appears he didn't want his colleagues in the bank to know how much he earned.

In establishing this structure he used the services of what we thought was a somewhat dubious agent, Mossack Fonseca, a name that appeared in the Falciani leaks, and an agent with a history of working for questionable clients. For instance, we discovered before our hearing that Fonseca had provided services to the very wealthy Rami Makhlouf, who was a close associate of Bashar al-Assad, and to Zimbabwean companies owned by individuals who were close to Robert Mugabe and known as his bag carriers. But at the time we interviewed HSBC, the Panama leaks of documents from Mossack Fonseca had not been revealed. However, our research had thrown up the role of Fonseca as an agent of doubtful integrity that had close links with HSBC and that provided legal services to dubious clients. The Panama leaks throw up new questions for HSBC. Why on earth did Stuart Gulliver use this lawyer to set up a secret bank account in Panama and what was the relationship between HSBC and Mossack Fonseca in facilitating tax avoidance and possible tax evasion? Even at the beginning of 2015, things looked murky.

It was the Conservative MP Jesse Norman who best expressed the disapproval many of us felt. In the Treasury Select Committee a fortnight before our hearing with bank representatives, he said: 'All right, so we do not need to personalise this to Mr Gulliver but it is perfectly clear that Mr Gulliver is an example of a certain kind of posture, which my colleague Mr Kane described as being at the outer limits of aggressive tax avoidance. That is to say someone who is able to pursue his life in this country for twelve or thirteen years so far, potentially twenty years or more in total, able to enjoy the benefits of living in this country, able to use a house, kids go to school here, all the benefits of that, and yet be resident in Hong Kong, non-domed in Hong Kong by the end of that time for forty-plus years. So my question is this: how on earth can this have been allowed to happen? Why isn't this a tremendous indictment of the non-dom rules that you have? How is someone like Mr Gulliver able to achieve this status of being essentially offshore to everywhere except the lowest tax domain that they choose to pay tax in?'

In the end, after insisting he paid all the taxes for which he was liable, Gulliver had to admit: 'I would agree with you that it has caused reputational damage to the bank in some quarters.' In his evidence to our committee Gulliver said he was working to clean up the bank. He had taken steps to close down some of the worst abuses. However, in doing so he clearly implied that his predecessors had failed to act.

His immediate predecessor was Lord Stephen Green. He had been working for HSBC for many years; in 1998, he became the board member with responsibility for global banking and markets; he oversaw the acquisition and integration of the Swiss bank; he chaired the Swiss bank holding company from 2006, when he became chairman of HSBC, and he had been group chief executive from 2003. He gave up his job at HSBC when he was given a seat in the House of Lords and appointed as a Minister for Trade and Investment by David Cameron in January 2011.

Green was at the helm of HSBC during much of the time that avoidance and potential evasion took place. And it wasn't just the revelations about the Swiss bank that called his judgement at the helm of HSBC into question. Just after he left HSBC, an American Senate Committee had issued a hugely critical report on the bank, with accusations that it had facilitated money laundering by Mexican drug barons and had conducted business with companies linked to terrorism.

Gulliver openly distanced himself from Lord Stephen Green both when he appeared before the Public Accounts Committee and when he gave evidence to the Treasury Select Committee. His statements were pretty open. Here are some examples of what he said:

'What I would hope the British public could see is that the action steps I have taken leave HSBC in a better place today than it was five years ago.'

'I am saying that Douglas [the new chairman, Douglas Flint] and I, and about two thousand people within HSBC, have been working tirelessly for the last four and a half years to change HSBC and make it fit for purpose.'

'So yes, it is being managed the way you would have imagined it always should have been managed, but it is now.'

He clearly left Lord Green and David Cameron with many questions to answer. When the dossier was first published, I remarked in the press that Stephen Green must either be culpable because he had been asleep at the wheel and didn't know what was going on, or he did know and was therefore involved in very dodgy tax practices. In an interview with *Channel 4 News*, Green denied these accusations.

I have never met the man, but he was clearly an interesting character. Not only had he risen to the top of the bank, but he had also been ordained by the Church of England. Indeed, he had written a book called *Good Value: Reflections on Money, Morality and an Uncertain World*, in which he said, when discussing the role directors hold in companies, that 'it is their job – and one which by its nature will never be complete – to promote and nurture a culture of ethical and purposeful business throughout the organisation'. I wondered how the values expressed in his writing married with the activities taking place in HSBC on his watch.

It was obvious to me that we should call Lord Green to give evidence. However, we were a couple of months from the 2015 General Election and the last thing the Conservatives wanted was a public evidence session with a man tainted by his HSBC connections and whom David Cameron had ennobled and appointed as a Trade Minister. I tried twice to persuade my colleagues that we had to call Stephen Green, but failed. This, in my view, was one of the few occasions when politics over-rode what should have happened in a rational, non-partisan environment.

Perhaps if we had been further from the General Election things might have been different. But it remains a bizarre mystery that Lord Green was ever appointed by David Cameron to his government. His appointment took effect from January 2011. The HSBC files had been offered to HMRC in February 2010 and given to them in April 2010. Lin Homer was absolutely clear that she had informed ministers about the files promptly.

Why in these circumstances was Stephen Green given a ministerial post? Was proper due diligence carried out? Did the Prime Minister know about the allegations against HSBC when Stephen Green was running the bank? Or is the establishment so remote, so self-confident and so arrogant that they consider it acceptable to ignore questionable behaviour by fellow members on the basis that they are all part of the same ruling elite and so 'good chaps' really? Would the misdemeanours of a tax credit cheat have been ignored in the same way?

Stephen Green spent three years enjoying the privileges of being a government minister (although he did not take a salary). When he gave up his ministerial post at the end of 2013, he was appointed trustee and chairman of the Natural History Museum, a post he still holds. The only job from which he resigned in the wake of the scandal at HSBC was as chairman of The CityUK's Advisory Council, a trade body for the financial services industry. It feels as though he got away scot-free.

A similar story can be told about another character who featured in this saga – Rona Fairhead. I had met her when she was appointed in 2014 to chair the BBC Trust, an appointment that entitled her to be paid £110,000 per annum. I was always pleased to see women promoted to top jobs, so my feminist instinct was to support her. However, as I came to uncover her role in HSBC, I had to question her competence.

Fairhead appeared to have enjoyed a successful career in business. She had risen through ICI and Pearsons to become chairman and chief executive of the Financial Times Group. She had held a range of non-executive positions within HSBC since 2004, mostly managing risk and audit. She was earning over £500,000 per annum for all these non-executive positions with HSBC on top of her BBC earnings and earnings from other non-executive positions. I naively thought that holding those positions for that level of remuneration might suggest that she would have been vigorous and vigilant in overseeing what was happening in the bank.

Her evidence to us was astonishing. In her view all the blame could be attributed to the tax evaders, the front-line client-relationship staff and those who managed the Swiss branch. Nobody else was to blame. She said: 'Can I go where I think the responsibility lies? I think first and foremost that the people who are most culpable are those people who evade taxes. I think that is where the illegality happens and they are the most culpable. I also hold accountable the front line, who were breaching the policies of the bank. We had clear policies in place and if they breached those policies I hold them accountable. I also hold accountable the management in-country the most, because they should have created a control environment. As you move up – you are shaking your head, but honestly—'

> MH: 'I just think you are getting paid £10,000 a day but I don't know what you do for it.'

Later in the evidence session I was taken aback when she described the actions of the whistleblower in lifting the lid on what was happening as being those of a thief. 'It was not until the end of 2009 that we realised that *the theft* was much more significant.'

Blaming the front-line staff and calling the whistleblower a thief riled me.

It was unbelievable that the chair of the Audit Committee had not been more alert to the dangers. The existence of the Swiss branch in itself should have been a red flag; the fact that there were so many people with secret hold-mail accounts should have been a red flag; the fact that the Swiss branch was securing disproportionately high profits warranted closer attention; the failure to have proper systems in place (which Stuart Gulliver admitted to in his evidence) must in part have been her responsibility; the culture of the bank that resulted in widespread complicity with tax avoidance and possible evasion in Switzerland, Mexico and elsewhere should have been something she identified; the bonuses for which she was partly responsible should have involved better due diligence on her part; her seemingly passive, reactive and superficial approach to her highly paid role was simply astonishing.

I was not the only person on the committee who reacted in this way. The Conservative Stephen Phillips asked: 'Ms Fairhead, you said – and you were in place at the time – that, with hindsight, there were system failings. In other words, this problem ought to have been identified in Switzerland and was not. Given that there were those system failings and that you were in charge of the systems at the relevant time, or at least were the person receiving their output, how can you stay in place as a non-executive director of this bank? Surely you should go, shouldn't you? Someone has to take responsibility for this.'

She limply replied that she could only deal with the evidence that she was given. She said she was unaware of the secret accounts held by the Swiss bank. She claimed that she relied on others in executive positions to raise matters with her. She had created lots of committees and lots of policies and had lots of presentations, but claimed she knew nothing.

In the end I flipped. I was angry that she tried to shift blame on to front-line staff who were only doing what they had been told to do. I was angry that she considered the whistleblower to be a thief. I was angry that she accepted such a high fee yet was so passive and reactive in overseeing the bank. So I went for her: 'Having watched your performance this afternoon, I have to say this to you: either you knew, and if you knew, you colluded in tax evasion—'

Rona Fairhead: 'I categorically deny that.'
MH: 'Or you didn't know, and in that case, I think you were either incredibly naive or totally incompetent. The record you have shown of your performance here as a guardian of HSBC does not give me the confidence that you should be the guardian of the BBC licence fee payers' money. I really do think that you should consider your position and should think about resigning. If not, I think the government should sack you.'

Those were very strong and hard words that I still believe were right, although I concede it would have been better if

I had kept my temper. But as an establishment figure, Rona Fairhead could count on her friends to close in and protect one of their own. It did not take long.

Her friends criticised me, with Michael Portillo proclaiming on television that she was really a very decent person. The *Spectator* criticised me. Another assault came from a fellow MP, Alan Duncan, who wrote a letter that he released to the press twenty-four hours before it reached me. In it he attacked what he called my 'insulting and offensive performance'. He thought calling for Rona Fairhead's resignation was 'inexcusable' and he alleged that I had indulged in 'a self-aggrandising outburst which was nothing short of vile'.

Fair enough, I thought. I had been very tough on our witnesses, so it was perfectly understandable that those who disagreed should subject me to similar treatment.

But I think there are wider implications to this kind of attack, of which I was on the receiving end time and time again during the five years that I chaired the Public Accounts Committee.

All too often our own attacks were on members of the British establishment. In some cases we were criticising top bankers, people appointed by the Prime Minister and others who moved in those closed establishment circles. In other hearings we challenged top industrialists, civil servants and people who had secured their jobs because of who they knew, where they had been educated and the social circle in which they moved.

Criticism of such people regularly occurs below the radar. Our hearings challenged that tradition and forced those unaccustomed to it to account for themselves in public. Of course that is uncomfortable. But as a society, we are not afraid of naming and shaming benefit claimants who cheat the system; we do not hold back from harassing small businesses to pay every last penny of tax they owe; we are quick to condemn those who overclaim on their tax credits. The members of the establishment should also be subject to open and public account and if they do wrong that fact should have an impact in some tangible way. It is simply unfair in my view for the Chair of Audit at HSBC to feel she is blameless and for her to remain secure in her public appointment at the BBC. The same goes for Lord Green who still enjoyed the patronage of the Prime Minister with his appointment at the Natural History Museum.

I think that some people find my forthrightness particularly difficult because I am, of course, a member of the establishment myself. I am an MP, a Dame, a Privy Councillor; my husband was a High Court judge and I benefited financially for many years from a successful family business established by my father (a business that went into administration recently).

Throughout my long public life I have been subject to attacks. In the early days they came from those who couldn't understand how somebody from a well-heeled background could have lots of money and claim to be on the Left in British politics. Surely it would be more appropriate for someone with my background to spend life painting their toenails on Primrose Hill rather than campaigning for equality.

But when I started to criticise the many individuals, institutions and companies embroiled in the tax-avoidance industry that really was a step too far for the establishment. Inevitably they wanted to undermine my integrity by trying to tar me with the same brush. There were attempts to claim that I myself avoided tax and that the family company that my brother ran was also a tax avoider.

The first attempt by the *Telegraph* was swiftly withdrawn by the paper. The second attempt by *The Times* occurred during the 2015 General Election campaign. It involved allegations that money I inherited from an uncle in America and an aunt in France showed I colluded with tax avoidance. My relatives, who had all fled the Holocaust, had set up structures outside the UK that I would not condone, but when I inherited the money I, of course, brought it into the UK, used much of it to set up a charity and always pay my tax in full.

I expect those whom I criticise to give as good as they get, so the questions asked were perfectly legitimate. On reflection, I should have been open about my relatives' tax affairs, but I had not done anything wrong. Yet the determination of the establishment to try to destabilise and undermine anyone who challenges them is chilling.

There was a bemusing epilogue for me personally. I have always banked with HSBC, because my father-in-law was a Midland Bank manager so we banked with the Midland, which then merged to become HSBC. Nowadays HSBC asks all its clients whether they have any relationship with a politician. When my son was setting up a new start-up business, he went to HSBC, which had also always been his bank. He was not asking for any money or loans, he simply wanted to set up a new account for his new business with them. Of course, he disclosed his relationship with me. After weeks of delay and without giving any explanation, HSBC turned him down.

9

Tax Reliefs: Relieving the System of Common Sense

The more I learned about the UK tax system, the more I came to understand how much tax-avoidance behaviour comes from exploiting the huge number of tax reliefs we have in the UK tax code.

Tax reliefs exist for a wide variety of reasons. Some are there to define who should pay tax; so, for instance, we have personal allowances before we start paying any tax. Others are brought in to achieve certain social or economic objectives, be it more investment in research and development (R&D tax credits) or encouraging us to save more of our income (ISAs).

Some are to deal with one-off anomalies that could arise, such as cabin crews on aeroplanes being exempted from paying air passenger duty.

But many are brought in by Chancellors of all political parties as their personal bounties to enhance their own or their party's reputation. Chancellors have two set-piece occasions in the political calendar when they are centre stage, the Autumn Statement and the Budget. Every Chancellor grasps those opportunities to surprise the electorate and stimulate their own popularity both within their party and the country. All too often they do that by introducing yet another tax relief.

And every tax relief becomes an opportunity for tax avoidance.

The permanent secretary at the Treasury was very open when he came to talk to us about this subject in the summer of 2014. 'Taxation is the most political of activities. It goes back thousands of years,' he said. 'The House of Commons came into existence because of taxation. I do not think it is something that you can reduce to the same sort of clarity in terms of objectives as many other areas of public spending . . . the Coalition has recently reintroduced a relief for marriage. Is that allowance really designed to encourage people to go off and get married, or is it just a value judgement that married couples should have a slightly lower tax burden or be relieved of rather more tax?'

He claimed that the complexity of the tax system, with all the associated dangers, was mainly a matter of politics.

In October 2014, the Public Accounts Committee hosted an international conference on tax to explore some of the issues we had exposed through our inquiries during the previous four years. At that conference, Michael Izza, the chief executive of the Institute of Chartered Accountants in England and Wales, expressed a very widely held frustration, telling us that the size of the tax code (now 17,000 pages long) had increased by a third in the last seven years. 'There isn't a single accountant that understands the code from A to Z, neither is there a single member of HMRC,' he said. His recommendation – 'The only possible solution is to set it on fire.'

The sheer complexity meant that people could not even agree on what a tax relief was and how many we had. HMRC tried to claim that defining tax reliefs was 'a term of art rather than a term of science'. They had a list on their website of

398 tax reliefs, whereas the Office of Tax Simplification, set up by the government to simplify the tax system, identified 1140.

We were interested in looking at those reliefs introduced by government to stimulate a change in the economy or in people's behaviour. This included everything from Gift Aid tax relief, introduced to encourage philanthropic giving to charities, to reliefs enacted to stimulate entrepreneurship and encourage the growth of new businesses. Even here, definitions were disputed. The National Audit Office categorised half of the tax reliefs on the HMRC list as constituting reliefs with specific economic or social objectives. The NAO estimated that the cost of these tax reliefs, which were called 'expenditure' reliefs, was around £100 billion. That is a huge amount of money that is spent by the Chancellor and much of it is not held to proper public account.

HMRC was reluctant even to engage in any debate about tax reliefs, saying this was not about the efficiency and effectiveness of public expenditure, but about political choices. We dismissed that argument. Many of these tax reliefs constituted another way of spending money. We were not going to ignore £100 billion of expenditure and we wanted to know whether this was securing value for money for the taxpayer.

Our determination to investigate tax reliefs came from evidence we had already uncovered. Following a number of earlier hearings, we had completed reports on Gift Aid relief and the Charity Commission. Again, we were helped by the assiduous work of journalist Alexi Mostrous, who drew our attention to the story. In an article in *The Times*, he exposed how Gift Aid had been abused and exploited as a device to avoid tax.

We all think Gift Aid is a good thing. We all tick the box on every form and think that the money goes straight to a good cause. When you tick the box, the charity can apply for Gift

Aid from HMRC and for every £1 you donate, the charity can receive an extra 25p from the tax authorities. So your donation of £1 is worth £1.25 to the charity. Yet even this seemingly most altruistic of reliefs is yet another opportunity for tax avoidance. Encouraged by the story in *The Times*, we looked at a charity called the Cup Trust. This charity was established with just one trustee, a company called Mountstar based in the British Virgin Islands, a tax haven. Mountstar's directors were also directors of NT Advisers (a not very discreet code for No Tax Advisers). The Charity Commission had the job of registering this organisation as a charity and checking its bona fide 'public benefit' status. It duly did so and granted the Cup Trust charitable status. Mountstar donated a great deal of money, £176 million, to the charity, but only distributed £55,000 to a charitable cause; that is, for every £100 the charity received, it used only 3p for charitable purposes. However, with £176 million purportedly donated to the charity, it was able to claim the 25p in the £1 tax relief, amounting to £46 million in Gift Aid tax relief. This was a total scam. Fortunately HMRC never paid out the money; but the Charity Commission opened an investigation in March 2010 and then closed it two years later, concluding that the Cup Trust remained legally structured as a charity.

The story in *The Times* and our inquiry in 2013 created such adverse publicity that the Charity Commission reopened its inquiry and suspended the trustee, but over two years later, it has yet to report the outcome of that renewed inquiry.

The Cup Trust scandal led us to investigate both Gift Aid and the Charity Commission in greater depth. In 2012–13, Gift Aid cost the taxpayer £2 billion a year. Only half of that went to charities: the other half went into the pockets of individuals and companies who benefited from tax relief changes introduced by the Labour government in 2000. Under these changes, not only was the charity able to claim an extra 25p for every £1 donated, but higher rate taxpayers could also claim tax back; on every £1 they gave to charities, they could claim back the difference between the higher rate of tax (40 per cent) and the standard rate of tax (20 per cent). Those changes were intended to give companies and individuals a tax incentive to encourage more philanthropic giving. In the 1999 pre-budget statement, the government explicitly said that the changes were being introduced 'to encourage more individuals and businesses to give more, and to make the taxation system simpler for donors and charities to use'. When the changes were introduced, HMRC undertook to monitor and evaluate them, but they failed to do so. By the time we came to look at the issue, £1 billion a year was going back to rich individuals and big corporations in tax relief, but we identified no increase in charitable giving – £1 billion spent to little effect.

HMRC told us that they investigated three hundred charitable schemes every year where they suspected fraud had taken place. In the year before our inquiry (2012–13), they thought £170 million had been lost to the Exchequer through avoidance, fraud and error. Since 2004, HMRC had identified and challenged eight schemes exploiting Gift Aid that had been marketed by tax advisers and widely used by individuals. But 90 per cent of the cases involved – that is 1800 individuals with £217 million of tax at risk – had yet to be resolved by the time of our inquiry.

Mountstar and NT Advisers, who were involved in setting up the Cup Trust, were well known to HMRC. Yet the Charity Commission had not checked them out with HMRC as part of its due diligence before registering them as a legitimate charity. In part, the Charity Commission claimed that they were inhibited by data protection concerns. However, after we made a fuss, the data protection issues were miraculously addressed and resolved, showing that pleading data protection barriers was not a good justification for the failure of two public bodies to communicate properly and for getting things so horribly wrong.

The Public Accounts Committee had issued innumerable reports criticising the Charity Commission. By 2015, the commission was responsible for monitoring 165,000 registered charities that between them boasted an annual income of £69 billion. Yet committee reports in 1988, 1991, 1998, 2001 and then our report in 2013 all found severe shortcomings in the work of this regulator. Its due diligence in registering new charities was clearly inadequate. I can't think why an application for charitable status from an organisation with one trustee based in a tax haven did not alert those charged with undertaking due diligence. As Fiona Mactaggart MP observed at our hearing: 'Section 4 (2) of the Charities Act states that "it is not to be presumed that a purpose of a particular description is for the public benefit". It is down to you as the Charity Commission to assert and discover whether it is for the public benefit.'

When we questioned the Charity Commission, we found it undertook only twenty compliance visits a year. In the previous four years, it had removed only one trustee from their role and it had frozen the accounts of only two charities. It was the guardian of the public interest for the charitable sector and I found its performance pretty dismal.

As ever, the new chairman promised us a brighter future for the Charity Commission with a new chief executive and less money! The chairman, William Shawcross, was another old Etonian who was known for his biography of the Queen Mother. His daughter had been a member of George Osborne's Council of Economic Advisers since 2008. In my view, he was appointed because of his politics, not his experience.

Observations from a distance suggest things have not got that much better since the Cup Trust scandal, if one thinks of the Charity Commission's failure to spot things going wrong in Kids Company and it not appearing to know about the commercial relationship between Age UK and the energy supplier E.ON. The fact that it has still to complete its inquiry into the Cup Trust is, frankly, pathetic.

It was shocking to discover that a tax relief we all believed was a potential force for good was in fact being abused by unscrupulous people as a tax loophole.

It was not the only example. We identified too many reliefs that had been exploited to avoid tax to chronicle them all. What is astonishing is that with so much money at stake, HMRC appeared so cavalier in both monitoring and evaluating tax reliefs. The National Audit Office identified 196 tax reliefs that could be said to have economic or social objectives. HMRC published data on the cost of just over half of these reliefs, but did not publish – and in 25 per cent of cases did not even collect – data on the remaining nearly half of the identified reliefs. HMRC and government simply did not know how much they were spending on tax reliefs.

On the other hand, there seemed to be little logic as to why HMRC collected information about the cost and use of some tax reliefs, yet ignored others. So they held data on seven tax reliefs where the cost was negligible, under £2.5 million a year, including Community Investment tax relief and the relief for Right to Buy transactions. But HMRC did not monitor others where the cost had increased by over 50 per cent in ten years, with costs sometimes going into billions. Without the information they had little evidence about whether the objective of the tax relief was being achieved and/or whether tax avoidance was taking place.

I have already described the film tax relief in the chapter on 'scams for scumbags'. That tax relief was expected to cost £30 million over three years when it was first introduced. In the end it cost £10 billion over ten years before the government finally closed the loophole in the scheme.

We came across a tax relief called the Share Loss relief, which allowed individuals or companies to claim tax relief on money they lost on shares in smaller companies. In 2005–6, that relief cost us, the taxpayer, £385 million. The next year, 2006–7, the figure spiralled to £1206 million, more than tripling in cost. However, HMRC did not properly monitor the use of the relief and the expenditure until it undertook a one-off exercise in 2013 and even then, the figure only came into the public domain because the National Audit Office published it, not because HMRC revealed it.

HMRC has now established that two substantial and aggressively marketed tax-avoidance schemes were used to exploit this relief. They investigated 80 per cent (by value) of the claims for Share Loss relief made in 2006–7 with nearly £1 billion of tax at stake. HMRC also challenged claims from other years. In total, 60 per cent of all claims made under this tax relief were challenged and nearly £2 billion of tax relief claimed is under investigation. How much of that could have been pre-empted if HMRC had been properly monitoring what was happening and had been quicker off the mark?

Entrepreneur's relief, where people enjoyed a reduction in capital gains tax to 10 per cent for certain disposals to encourage enterprise, represents another scandal. When the relief was first introduced in 2008–9, it cost the taxpayer £475 million, but five years later that figure had mushroomed by 500 per cent so that by 2013–14, it cost the taxpayer a staggering £2.9 billion. There had been some policy adjustments, but HMRC could not explain the huge increase in cost. Just imagine the public outcry if spending on benefits or overseas aid suddenly increased by 500 per cent with no public accountability for what had happened?

Another interesting example was the tax relief invented to encourage more research and development expenditure by companies; a relief supported by most politicians, researchers and businesses. We all believe that investment in research and development is vital for economic growth. But the money spent on the R&D tax credit grew from £100 million in 2001 to over £1 billion ten years later. Yet the actual amount of business expenditure on research and development stayed about the same. No surprise when you see the advertisement of a company calling themselves Innovation Plus, who classed themselves as R&D tax credit experts and promoted themselves by saying: 'We have particular expertise in software R&D tax claims and in particular have dealt with a number of cases where clients have been told by other firms of advisers that there was no claim and where we have subsequently obtained six figure amounts for them . . . We often encounter foreign companies who want to know how they can benefit from the UK R&D tax credits. Sometimes they have Research and Development operations in the UK but often they do not.'

Or the advertisement from a firm called Taylor Cocks, who wrote: 'Any good accountant can make you compliant. What makes us different is that we go further . . . we'll find innovative ways to reduce the amount of tax you pay and increase your bottom line.'

Exploiting the loopholes that invariably existed with tax reliefs was the day-to-day business of the tax industry. We knew about accountants and lawyers, but the banks were also heavily implicated. HMRC's Jim Harra felt obliged to admit to us: 'I think historically you are right: banks have been heavily involved in avoidance. Sometimes they have been designers of it; sometimes they have been facilitators of it through the provision of financing.' We had gained some insight into the role of HSBC's bank in Switzerland during our inquiry into the Falciani leaks, but the papers revealed in the Panama leaks suggest the heavy involvement of HSBC and other banks in international tax avoidance and possible evasion. The complexity of the UK tax code makes for rich pickings for those involved in tax avoidance and evasion.

In Opposition the Conservatives had recognised the problems associated with our complex tax code. They had supported the establishment of the Office for Tax Simplification, saying they wanted to simplify the tax code. However, their record in government did not fit with their rhetoric in Opposition.

The Office for Tax Simplification was given a staff of six, some of whom worked part-time. The new unit set about trying to simplify the tax system by abolishing some tax reliefs. They reviewed 155 reliefs and recommended that 47 should be abolished. The government agreed to 43 of them. However, not much good came from that, because over the same three years, from 2011 to 2014, the government introduced 134 new reliefs. We ended up with an even longer tax code.

The reliefs reviewed by the Office for Tax Simplification included a relief in respect of meals provided for employees who cycled to work on a 'Cycle to Work Day'. Another linked to luncheon vouchers and was worth 15p a day, and had probably been introduced after the war. Yet another was one the government refused to abolish. This relief could be claimed by workers who were required to stay late at work until at least 9 p.m. and then take a taxi home. Between 80 per cent and 90 per cent of the claims for this relief came from the big City firms. One major law firm ordered twenty-five thousand late-night taxis in one year. Shift workers, who worked at night (often cleaning the very offices the City folk work in during the day), were not eligible for this tax relief because they had agreed to the anti-social working hours entailed in their contracts. It would seem that the lobbying by the big law firms stopped the government from abolishing this relief.

The Conservative government believes in tax competition and uses tax reliefs to encourage competition. I think this is an absurdly short-sighted approach, which involves a race to the bottom on tax, with other countries simply overtaking us by offering ever-lower taxes and ever-more generous tax reliefs. The result of trying to compete by cutting taxes is to create even more problems for the Exchequer by damaging our ability to raise essential revenue. It is doubtful that competition on tax will ever create sustainable growth and sustainable jobs.

The Patent Box tax relief I talked about earlier was one example where government used tax reliefs to promote competition. Under the Patent Box relief, corporation tax was reduced to 10 per cent on the profits attributable to qualifying patents licensed in the UK, but also those that could have been licensed in countries in the European Union. The products made under the licence could have been produced in the UK, but could equally be produced and sold outside the UK. The only requirement to qualify for this tax relief was that the profits had to be taxed in the UK so that the relief could be offset against them. A blatant invitation for global companies to shift profits to the UK, where we offered a low-tax regime – just like the tax havens David Cameron condemned in Davos in 2013. All the international bodies challenged this new tax relief, and both the EU and the OECD deemed it a 'harmful tax practice'. No sooner was it introduced than the government was forced to rethink the tax relief under pressure from the international community, in particular Germany.

Using tax reliefs to create harmful tax practices, when we are trying to reach international agreement on a new set of rules so that global corporations do pay tax on the profits they make in the UK, is short-sighted and hypocritical.

But there is a wider issue on which we should reflect. Tax reliefs have become a hidden way to increase spending for a particular purpose. Recently, the government introduced new tax reliefs for orchestras, children's television programme productions, and what is called a high-end television tax relief. No doubt these are all good and worthy causes, but providing these new tax reliefs has a cost. Yet that cost isn't considered and compared alongside other budget demands, because it does not appear as an expenditure item in a departmental budget. There is no proper consideration of relative merits or relative priorities. The only person who might make that call is the Chancellor himself, but that is neither transparent nor objective. If the Chancellor wants to give more money to orchestras or children's television, that should be considered alongside other priorities within the Department of Culture, Media and Sport, and the DCMS budget needs to be judged alongside the expenditure plans of other departments. Using tax reliefs is a way of increasing spending on pet projects through the back door. The Chancellor might argue that funding through tax reliefs leads to better decisions because the private sector decides whether to pursue a particular project and take advantage of the tax relief; the market decides. The alternative is for the government to award grants and many argue that the state is not good at picking winners. But the state distributes research monies through the Research Councils very effectively and grants to arts organisations are distributed by the Arts Council. We are able to establish efficient and effective funding mechanisms in some areas, so there are examples of good practice we can replicate.

Using tax reliefs rather than awarding grants represents poor and irrational decision-making. It adds to the complexity of our tax code and every new relief becomes a new opportunity for the tax industry to dream up yet another scheme to avoid paying tax.

Tax reliefs cannot be controlled by setting a finite budget; once you define eligibility for a relief, everyone who claims that eligibility is entitled to the payment, whatever the cost. The National Audit Office found that one in three of the reliefs that they examined had increased in cost by over 25 per cent in five years. Such uncontrolled expenditure is much more difficult to manage, particularly when you want to cut public spending. It just means that the knife has to cut more deeply elsewhere.

At the very least every new tax relief ought to be introduced with what is known as a 'sunset clause'. This means that after a defined number of years it dies away unless ministers and Parliament deliberately decide to extend its life. HMRC would then have to monitor and evaluate tax reliefs properly so that informed decisions on their efficacy and cost were taken.

The current state of our tax code is madness. We can't keep on and on adding yet more pages and yet more complexities by inventing yet more tax reliefs. I haven't come across anybody who thinks we shouldn't radically simplify the tax code. It just takes a bold Chancellor to show some common sense and get on with the job.

10

Where Next on Tax?

During the five years of the 2010–15 Parliament, the Public Accounts Committee held twenty separate hearings on tax and tax avoidance, and we made over a hundred recommendations to government. The unanimous resolve of all members of the committee to pursue the issue was remarkable. From Austin Mitchell, the long-serving left winger and member of the Campaign Group on the Labour side, to Stewart Jackson, a founding member of Conservative Voice, on the right of the Conservative Party, we were united in our determination to continue exposing what we all thought was wrong and unfair in the tax system.

I can't say that our investigations were greeted with the same enthusiasm by tax professionals. Early on, the *Tax Journal*, one of the trade publications, christened me 'Tax Prat of the Year', writing in February 2013: 'The personal crusade of Margaret Hodge against the tax profession as a whole because it will not fall in line with her idiosyncratic and ill-informed views about tax avoidance risks marginalising the Public Accounts Committee and has already made it a joke to those who understand the subject.'

This was not a personal crusade. The whole committee was dedicated to pursuing tax avoidance. And I am certainly not a tax professional and do not pretend to have the technical know-how. But that is precisely the point. The tax system belongs to us all; it should command the confidence of everybody and should not be the secret preserve of professionals, used by them to manipulate the system in their own interest or in the interests of the most wealthy and powerful in our society. We should all understand how the system works and we should all be assured that it and the way it is administered is fair to everybody. The onus is on the professionals to explain the system to us so that we are reassured that it is fair.

What the Public Accounts Committee did was to ask the questions ordinary people wanted us to ask. We held hearings with people whom the public wanted us to call to account. All we did was to shine a bright light on what was happening. So much of what we uncovered in our hearings was so shocking to most people that we successfully stimulated a high-profile debate and encouraged politicians in government to act.

We did not act alone. Development charities and campaign groups were also actively engaged, culminating in the protest by Occupy outside St Paul's Cathedral. The investigative work of journalists and broadcasters uncovered scandalous stories. The fact that so many families were struggling with their personal finances and were therefore particularly sensitive to how much they paid in tax gave the issue powerful relevance.

Until the financial crisis, aggressive tax avoidance was widely considered to be not just normal, but cool. People were proud if they managed to avoid paying their fair share of tax. That cultural norm is now beginning to change and our ability to highlight and popularise the issue contributed to that shift of attitude.

That came home to me when I visited the OECD in Paris to talk about their work in rewriting the international tax rules, aimed at preventing corporations shifting profits from jurisdictions where the money was earned to low-tax or no-tax jurisdictions.

We had a successful and informative series of meetings. It was fascinating to discover that the OECD had been working on changing the international rules for thirty years. That made sense, because the globalisation of companies is not a recent phenomenon, so rules framed when companies operated nationally had clearly become anachronistic and inappropriate for the contemporary, globalised world. Rules originally designed to prevent companies being taxed twice for the same profits were now being used to avoid any taxation.

The OECD had experienced frustration down the years, because they found it difficult to find any traction when trying to persuade national governments to draft new international agreements. Then the UK and the USA came along with our high-profile hearings, particularly the hearings with Amazon, Starbucks and Google in the UK and Apple in the United States. The mood changed and national leaders, led by David Cameron who was chairing the G8 at the time, suddenly engaged with the issues. The dedicated staff at the OECD were overjoyed that their important work was finally being taken seriously.

So while on the one hand our work had turned me into a villain for some people working in the tax industry, for others, whose life's work was working for change, I had apparently become a symbol for all that they passionately cared about. As we were preparing to leave Paris, Grace Perez-Navarro, Deputy Director at the OECD's Centre for Tax Policy and Administration, asked for us to be photographed together. From being derided by the professionals as a 'Prat' when it came to tax, I was, she told me, now a tax rock star; a bizarre concept but a far cry from being caricatured as a tax prat.

So how does the scoreboard on tax avoidance look, several years after we held our first public hearing on the issue? What else needs to be done? A little progress has been made, but much more could be achieved with some boldness and firmer commitment to the cause.

I have no doubt that the public discourse on tax has changed. A ComRes poll carried out for Christian Aid in 2014 found that 85 per cent of British voters said tax avoidance is morally wrong, even if it is legal. Many people tell me that the conversation in boardrooms has changed, with directors now expressing concern that reputations could be trashed and businesses damaged if the company engages in aggressive tax avoidance. Tax professionals have adopted a more conciliatory tone and are sensitive to accusations that they promote avoidance. Leading politicians feel obliged to make the right noises and to be seen to take action to stamp out aggressive tax avoidance.

David Cameron at the G8 meeting in 2013 said: 'I'm going to push for international agreements to fight the scourge of tax evasion and aggressive tax avoidance so those who want to evade taxes have nowhere to hide.'

Similarly George Osborne wrote in an article in the *Guardian* in February 2013: 'Some large multinationals are able to restructure their business to avoid paying their fair share in tax. Some are exploiting the rules by getting profits out of high-tax countries and into tax havens, allowing them to pay as little as 5 per cent in corporate taxes while smaller businesses are paying up to 30 per cent. This distorts competition, giving larger companies an advantage over smaller domestic companies. People are rightly asking for something to be done.'

It is also true that the present government has taken some

welcome action to toughen up on tax avoidance. We are one of the first countries to legislate to introduce a public register of beneficial ownership in the UK, so that there is greater visibility over where assets are held. Such a register will reveal who ultimately owns or controls assets based in the UK. That helps determine where taxes should be paid.

The government has also introduced a diverted profits tax, which they christened the 'Google tax'. The government claimed the new tax was aimed at both those foreign multinational companies who say they are not trading *in* the UK but trading *into* the UK, and/or those UK global companies that try to create tax advantages by using transactions or entities that lack economic substance. If companies engage in what HMRC considers to be deliberate avoidance structures, they will have to pay tax at a punitively high rate of 25 per cent rather than the 20 per cent corporation tax headline rate that now prevails.

The Google tax may be a small step in the right direction but it is also a good illustration of how the government is facing both ways on tax avoidance. Google has not and is not likely to be asked to pay the Google tax. Google's structures – claiming that sales are made in Ireland and not in the UK, and that most of the value added comes from the intellectual property developed in the USA – will not be caught by a tax Chancellor George Osborne claimed was specifically designed to capture Google's profits in the UK.

The Google tax contains major loopholes. It does not apply to loan arrangements such as the ones uncovered in the Luxembourg leaks scandal. So businesses can still set up shell companies in tax havens and use those companies to make loans to other companies in the same group, most of which are sham loans far in excess of what the multinationals actually borrow. This reduces the taxable profits and thus exports profits from the country in which they were earned. Also, nothing in the Google tax rules appears to prevent Internet-based companies from continuing to argue that they do not sell in the UK, but into the UK.

The limited effect of these measures can be seen in the estimated additional revenue this new tax is expected to bring. The *Financial Times*, in an article in January 2014, estimated that the seven big digital companies alone – Apple, Google, Microsoft, Amazon, eBay, Yahoo and Facebook – made combined sales of about £9.5 billion in the UK in 2012, but paid only £54 million in UK corporation tax. Christian Aid carried out a rough calculation suggesting that if those companies had paid the standard rate of corporation tax on the profits from these sales, the UK Exchequer might well have collected as much as £500 million more in tax from them alone. The government itself predicted that the Google tax would bring in only an additional £350 million a year from not just the seven big digital companies but all large multinational companies by 2017–18.

Much of the reality on the ground is thus somewhat different from the rhetoric in the media. The government is convinced that it can attract new businesses to the UK by competing on tax. It has systematically reduced the headline rate of corporation tax from the 28 per cent it inherited in 2010 to the 17 per cent it plans for 2020. But that has not secured real growth for the UK economy. More global companies may choose to put their headquarters in the UK, but that does not bring many jobs to the UK or much added value.

Starbucks rang me in 2015 to announce what they thought I would regard as welcome news. They were shifting their headquarters to the UK. I cautiously asked how many extra jobs that would bring to Britain. There was an awkward pause in the conversation.

'Well,' I asked, 'will it be a hundred new jobs? Less?'

At the end of the conversation, Starbucks admitted that the change would lead to just eight new jobs being created in the UK. They were establishing a financial structure in the country to take advantage of the generous tax reliefs and low tax levels, but they were not bringing jobs to the UK.

In June 2014, Reuters published an article in which they examined seven American companies that had recently transferred the domicile of their companies to the UK. Between them, they employed seventy-three people at director level; only ten of these directors, 14 per cent of the total, actually lived in the UK. One of the companies, Rowan, which is one of the largest operators of oil drilling rigs in the world, when questioned by Reuters as to what changing their domicile to the UK meant, said: 'We changed our corporate structure and we're legally domiciled in the UK but our headquarters and our management team remain in the US.'

The government's belief in tax competition has led to the creation of what many would regard as tax haven conditions here in the UK. Far from being at the forefront of the battle against global tax avoidance, the present government is now trying to beat the tax haven jurisdictions at their own game.

Stephen Shay, the Harvard professor, wryly observed: 'When I go to tax conferences now, I hear people talk about the UK as a tax haven.'

It is not just the low level of corporation tax. The government has changed existing tax rules to make it easier for global companies to avoid tax in Britain. Most notably, a set of rules introduced by Nigel Lawson in the 1980s to try to tackle the problem that was emerging even then of companies shifting profits out of the UK to tax havens. They are called the Controlled Foreign Companies rules. The rules were intended to enable HMRC to tax multinational companies for profits made here, even if they tried to divert those profits to a tax haven.

It is difficult to be certain because of the frustrating confidentiality of taxpayers' affairs, but according to *Private Eye*, Vodafone had fallen foul of these rules. The allegation is that they transferred their profits to Luxembourg and avoided a tax bill of several billion pounds through this arrangement. Vodafone eventually settled with HMRC in 2010 and paid £1.25 billion in tax. If the allegations in *Private Eye* are true, taxpayers lost around £6 billion from this deal. The company was also given five years to pay the bill and, unlike every small company in Britain that would have been forced to pay all the interest charges, the more powerful Vodafone was let off any interest charges incurred by the delayed and deferred payments. It was this scandal that had convinced David Davis that I should look at the issue of tax collection and tax avoidance.

In the wake of this deal, multinationals campaigned discreetly to weaken the Controlled Foreign Company rules. The Conservative government caved in to the pressure and, under the guise of saying they only wanted to tax companies for the profits they made from economic activity in the UK and were not trying to catch the profits multinationals made in other countries, particularly developing countries, they introduced changes to the rules which limited their scope and introduced new exemptions. These changes were buried in a Finance Bill.

With the new changes, finance subsidiaries of UK-based companies that are established offshore in tax havens are let off paying corporation tax, or are charged effectively at only a quarter of the prevailing rate. This arrangement is so complicated that it is not surprising that few people realised what was happening and few even now understand how it has helped to create tax haven conditions in the UK.

To show what it means in practice, imagine that a UK multinational company borrows money in the UK. They pay interest on that loan and can offset the interest charges against their tax bill. So they secure a tax benefit here in the UK. They then place the money in a financial subsidiary in a tax haven. (So they take advantage of the new exemption, which in effect means that profits will only be taxed at a fraction of the corporation tax rate; essentially a 5 per cent tax on profits.) They then use the money to lend to another of their businesses in another country, for instance Germany. The German subsidiary claims tax relief from the German government on the cost of the loan, so the company gets double tax relief and pays very little corporation tax because of the tax exemption.

There are other examples of deliberate changes to rules that act as tax 'sweeteners' for global companies, for example changes in how Eurobonds are treated and the Patent Box relief discussed earlier. Equally worrying is the UK's failure to tackle the secrecy that continues to pervade tax havens. This is absolutely central to combating global tax avoidance and it matters most for the poorest countries. The leaked documents from the law firm in Panama, Mossack Fonseca, vividly emphasise the key role Britain has in stamping out secrecy in tax havens. According to the *Guardian* investigators, the law firm operating out of Panama acted for 113,000 companies that were incorporated in the British Virgin Islands, a UK Overseas Territory that boasts 950,000 offshore companies registered in its jurisdiction and that thrives as a powerful tax haven. Mossack Fonseca acted for nearly one in eight of the companies registered in the British Virgin Islands.

If we are to eliminate tax avoidance we simply need to know who owns the assets that are registered in tax havens: in the same way as we are about to create a public register of beneficial ownership in the UK, we need similar registers in the tax havens and those registers have to be publicly available. Once there is transparency over ownership, it becomes possible to tax those assets in the jurisdictions where people live or where the companies have made their money. The UK government has a pivotal role in encouraging – or forcing – tax havens to set up publicly accessible beneficial ownership registers. Many of today's tax havens are either Crown dependencies or Overseas Territories, linked through our imperial history to the UK. Traditionally UK governments have been reluctant to intervene in these self-governing jurisdictions. However, they have the powers to intervene and have done so in the past.

For instance in 1991, the UK Conservative government used an Order in Council to abolish capital punishment for murder in the Caribbean Overseas Territories (Anguilla, the British Virgin Islands, the Cayman Islands, Monserrat and the Turks and Caicos Islands). In 2000, the Labour government used an Order in Council to decriminalise homosexual acts in the Caribbean territories, against the latter's will.

So there are precedents that would allow government to act decisively on tax. While some British Overseas Territories have agreed to create registers of beneficial ownership, the government has dropped the requirement that these registers should be public, which is essential if we are to know who owns the companies, trusts or wealth that is held in tax havens. The government has said the information should only be available to tax authorities and enforcement agencies.

This is where the government does not appear to be fulfilling promises David Cameron made during the UK's presidency of the G8 in 2013. He promised that the UK would lead by example and that by acting both in the UK and in the Overseas Territories and Crown dependencies, we would ensure transparency. That was a fundamental part of the legacy to be delivered by the UK during its presidency of the G8 countries. The Overseas Territories may have agreed to compile the registers but they will not be public documents. Jersey has put a central registry of beneficial interests in place and, in 2015, Guernsey, which already collects this type of information, consulted on the introduction of a central register of beneficial ownership.

But the Overseas Territories are shying away from giving up their status as tax havens. Bermuda has said a firm no to compiling a publicly available register and the rest are showing little willingness to co-operate. The government could use its powers through an order in Privy Council to impose transparency but, as I write this, the government has refused to act. If it fails to do so, the ambition to have transparent country-by-country reporting of where assets are held and money is earned will be seriously undermined. In the meantime, nearly all the FTSE 100 companies have subsidiaries in tax havens.

David Cameron's approach to tax avoidance has been full of contradictions. At the same time that he was being lukewarm in his efforts to deal with tax havens, he supported the OECD's work on rewriting the international rules.

Similarly, while supporting the rewriting of the international tax rules, Britain is limiting the effectiveness of the proposed reforms. Our insistence on allowing individual countries to pursue tax breaks for businesses in the interests of so-called competition is but one example of how we are actively denting progress at the OECD level.

Our obsession with stopping Europe intruding further into the UK makes us resist moves to share information on a common reporting standard across Europe. We must have transparent reporting on a country-by-country basis of where assets are owned, where sales are made, where people are employed and where profits are secured and so on. This will always involve tricky issues, particularly in relation to the digital economy, but we need to be more consistent and act with greater urgency in the international arena if we are serious about tackling tax avoidance. And once we have reached agreement internationally, we must ensure that all jurisdictions implement the new rules. Implementation of the new laws is as important as their formulation.

But we do not need to wait for new international rules to achieve some important changes and improvements. We could act with greater vigour in the national arena. I have already suggested simplifying our tax code and getting tough on tax reliefs but we need to secure cross-party consensus so that the changes are sustainable.

HMRC needs a radical transformation. In 2013–14, HMRC provided data to the law firm Pinset Masons in which they claimed that the amount collected for every £1 spent on staffing was £18 for local compliance investigations and £97 for large business service compliance investigations. So cutting the staff at HMRC is short-sighted and counter-productive. The government is obsessed with reducing the Civil Service headcount as part of its drive to deal with the deficit. That might have made sense in a department like the Department for Business, Innovation and Skills, but it makes no sense at all for HMRC. HMRC lost forty thousand staff between 2005 and 2015. That is just under 40 per cent of the total workforce, with further cuts expected over the current spending review period. The government will claim that they put extra investment into the tax compliance function, but if you are losing staff at that rate, it is well nigh impossible to deploy the remaining staff in the very targeted way intended. The pressure will always be on public targets to address, for instance, the continuing and abject failure of HMRC to answer the phone. The latest figures at the start of 2015 showed that HMRC only answered half the calls they received from the public and of those they answered, only 39 per cent within five minutes. The pressure to use staff to improve performance here will undoubtedly impact on their performance in dealing with tax avoidance and evasion.

Government should be more nuanced in its approach. Cutting the deficit can be achieved by increasing income as well as cutting spending. Tackling tax avoidance with enough staff will help to reduce the deficit. Making sure you keep trained and experienced staff is equally important and requires a radical change in how people are rewarded and promoted in the Civil Service. It is a disgrace that so many well-trained and experienced tax inspectors are enticed into the private sector just at the point that they become useful to the state.

HMRC is always playing catch-up. The failure to act speedily simply adds to the problem. So by February 2015, HMRC's backlog of tax-avoidance cases was sixty-five thousand. On the Public Accounts Committee we identified many examples where delay had exacerbated tax avoidance, such as happened with the Liberty tax-avoidance scheme described in the chapter on boutique advisers. This was one of the biggest tax schemes ever created and was first promoted in 2005. Sixteen hundred individuals used it to avoid tax – including celebrities like Gary Barlow, the Arctic Monkeys and Katie Melua. HMRC knew about the scheme in 2005. However, it took until 2009 to close the scheme down and HMRC only got the first cases in front of the tribunal in 2014. They were so slow off the mark that thirty people got away with avoiding tax through this scheme because HMRC failed to issue the appropriate notices in time.

HMRC needs to act promptly and much more assertively to defend the taxpayer's interest. The tax authorities always remain reluctant to challenge tax avoidance in the courts. Their reluctance to litigate means that far too many people get away with tax avoidance. The fact that over two years HMRC won fifty-one of the sixty decisions they took to tribunal simply proves that they are far too cautious in their approach. Interpretation of the law is at the heart of what is acceptable tax planning and what is unacceptable tax avoidance. HMRC should always be on the side of a tough interpretation and should always reflect what Parliament intended.

If that means they lose a few more cases, that would not matter. The mere threat of facing a challenge in the court would act as a strong deterrent to those who exploit loopholes in the law.

That leads me to another area in need of reform. The greatest challenge to restoring confidence in the British tax system stems from the secrecy that surrounds it. Time after time before the Public Accounts Committee, officials hid behind the mantra of the confidentiality of taxpayers' interests and refused to divulge information we sought.

We would never have known about the Goldman Sachs deal if the whistleblower hadn't sent in that brown envelope. The Luxembourg leaks and HSBC's complicity in avoidance and possible evasion were only exposed by whistleblower revelations. The confidentiality of taxpayers' interests is destroying confidence in the integrity of the system. Other countries that we admire, like Sweden, allow public access to tax records. And I agree with David Cameron, who told us that 'sunlight is the best disinfectant'. The government now needs to act on that.

This is not simply about MPs publishing their tax returns. Media focus on that, in the wake of the revelation in the Panama papers that David Cameron's father ran an offshore fund, diverted attention from the bigger picture of corporate tax avoidance. As a first step, select committees should have access to papers on a confidential basis. The House of Commons Intelligence and Security Committee enjoys access to secret information provided by the security services on a confidential basis, to assure Parliament that the security services are behaving appropriately. A similar system could be set up for HMRC, creating a select committee of both Houses of Parliament which meets in confidence and holds HMRC to account. The committee would have the power and authority to examine the details of negotiations between HMRC and large corporations to assure Parliament and the public that companies are paying their tax in full. As we have seen, HMRC is a non-ministerial department; no minister is able to oversee the tax settlements it has agreed. Some way needs to be found whereby there is proper accountability for the way HMRC administers the tax system.

I would argue that transparency is essential to ensuring fairness. If we had greater visibility about how HMRC operated, we would have greater confidence in the fairness of their approach. The confidentiality of taxpayers' interests has become sacrosanct and nobody dares challenge it. But why should the tax affairs of a publicly quoted company be secret? I am not talking about individuals, where I can see an argument for privacy; this is about public companies. Their accounts are publicly quoted; the actual tax they pay is publicly available. Why can't we be privy to the arguments or negotiations that take place between the company and the tax authorities? Would the world fall apart if that was opened up? I think not.

We should tear away the shroud of secrecy. I would love us to experiment with the FTSE top 100 companies, placing the negotiations between them and HMRC in the public domain and seeing whether that results in any disasters. If it does, we could reconsider the issue; if it doesn't, we might consider extending transparency. I have absolutely no doubt that this would do much to ensure confidence that HMRC does treat everybody equally and fairly.

Throughout our deliberations on the Public Accounts Committee we constantly came up against the over-cosy relationship between HMRC and Treasury on the one hand and tax advisers and big business on the other. There is a world of difference between ensuring good working relationships and securing undue influence and preferential treatment. Of course, tax officials and Treasury policy advisers should work with their stakeholders, but too often they appear to act in the interests of one group of stakeholders at the expense of the rest of us. It was David Cameron himself who warned before the 2010 General Election that the 'buying of power and influence' was the next big scandal waiting to happen.

The membership of Government advisory bodies needs to be more diverse and all interests should be represented. Why not have some different academics who do not buy into the tax professionals' agenda, representatives from charities concerned with tax avoidance, and tax campaigners sitting alongside the tax professionals and big business?

Stronger policing of the revolving door that pervades this closed world is also urgently required. It is not acceptable to find those seconded to government to help write new tax rules immediately returning to the private sector to exploit those rules for a purpose that Parliament never intended, using loopholes they themselves helped to create to avoid tax. Allowing senior tax officials to take up posts with the Big Four accountancy firms or with the banks within six months of leaving their posts is completely wrong.

The private sector places strong restrictive clauses on staff to prevent people abusing their knowledge and expertise. The government should introduce similar restrictions for all its staff and it should place restrictions on those who are seconded to work for the government which would apply on their return to their private sector jobs.

Again, I would go further. The tax-avoidance industry is huge and those who work in it make a lot of money as accountants, advisers, bankers or lawyers. Yet they are not held to account when their advice leads to aggressive tax avoidance that is outside the law. It was astonishing to find that the threshold for suggesting schemes to clients was so low. As long as the chance of a scheme being successfully challenged was less than 50 per cent, the industry marketed the schemes. For the most egregious advisers, as long as they secured a legal opinion that gave them cover against action by their clients, they did not seem to care whether the scheme was legal or not.

In my view, the time has come for us to create a new offence that would hold advisers responsible and accountable for the advice they give. They too should be prosecuted by HMRC if the tax authorities come to the view that a scheme they have promoted is unlawful. They too should face penalties for promoting illegitimate tax-avoidance schemes.

Such a law would close down most aggressive tax avoidance overnight. It is the advisers who identify most of the loopholes and dream up most of the schemes. One of our most shocking sessions was the one with the head of tax at PwC. In my view, his unashamed and condescending insistence that he had not lied to the Public Accounts Committee and that PwC did not market avoidance schemes really took some beating. In the face of such attitudes, it is clear that only a law holding them to account for their advice would shift attitudes and deter bad behaviour.

I would also be much tougher on those who, by using artificial structures, deliberately avoid paying their fair share of tax on the profits they make in our jurisdiction. Why should these very same companies earn money from securing public contracts that are funded by the taxpayer? Any company that is shown to aggressively avoid tax should be banned from securing public contracts. When we put that proposition to Lin Homer she pleaded European procurement rules in her defence. She claimed those rules prevented her from excluding bidders on the grounds that they avoided UK tax. Meanwhile HMRC was itself giving business to companies like Accenture which was reported in the press to be paying very little tax on the profits they secured from their work in the UK.

Again, the government did eventually do something about this but the action they have taken is weak. European procurement rules do permit the exclusion of companies from tendering on specific criteria; the European rules allow authorities to apply tax and propriety issues at the early selection stage of a procurement process. Government has chosen to interpret the criteria in a very narrow way; only those companies who evade tax (which is of course illegal), or who fail to tell HMRC that they are using a scheme that could be deemed illegal, can be excluded from tendering for a government contract for a limited period of ten years. But it is avoidance, as well as evasion, that we want to capture so that companies that aggressively avoid tax do not benefit from contracts funded by the taxpayer.

Getting to grips with the reality of tax avoidance in Britain today and exposing it to the public gaze was one of our most important achievements. It is ironic that, while we in Britain happily lecture about probity to so many developing countries, our own practice falls far short of those standards and allows those with the most to contribute the least into the common pot for the common good.

There are people who argue that greed is part of human nature and very difficult to design out. I hold a more optimistic view. Most people sign up willingly to a set of common rules that are designed to benefit us all. They understand the importance of everybody being treated equally and fairly. They understand the moral as well as the legal dimension of tax in society. In the old days, tax was raised to fund warfare; today it supports welfare, defined in the widest sense. Without that support, the stability and cohesion in society, on which we all depend, is threatened.

I know there is still a long way to go to secure the changes in culture, policy, law and practice that I think are necessary for a fair and trusted tax system. I can't let go of this issue. It is so important. That is why I have helped to set up an All Party Group in Parliament on Responsible Taxation. Working with all those who share our ambition, I hope we will keep the public focus on the issue, maintain a beady eye on what our government is actually doing and achieve the changes we believe are needed to secure a just tax system for the UK.

11

Unconscionable Waste

Why value for money matters

Wasting public money is unforgivable. It need not inevitably go with the territory. All politicians – and all public servants – pledge commitment to the principle of value for money but too often fail to translate that commitment into good practice on the ground. Working to secure best value for the taxpayer's pound should be at the heart of all our politics.

The issue matters wherever you sit on the political spectrum. People on the right want to reduce public expenditure and cut taxes, so they need to eke best value from every pound spent. Those on the left want to maintain and grow public expenditure because they see public services as vital to opening the opportunities that transform and equalise life chances. They need to persuade people to part with their hard-won earnings by demonstrating that they can be trusted to spend the money wisely.

This is all even more important in present times. When most people are struggling to make ends meet, the imperative to show that their contribution, made through the taxes they pay, is being well spent, becomes ever more important. How on earth can anyone justify a situation in which families are struggling to find the money to pay their taxes, while politicians preside over waste in the expenditure that that money buys?

The emphasis on good value tends to diminish when times are good. If money is more freely available, the pressure on securing better value becomes less urgent. This may be neither logical nor right, but it reflects reality.

But these are not good times for public spending. Politicians legitimately argue about how quickly we need to reduce the deficit, yet everybody accepts that we should not be spending more on current services than we secure in income through taxation. So in a climate where expenditure is being cut to reduce the structural deficit, it is critical that we get the most we can out of the resources that are there.

If the issue is so important, why is it not more central to our political discourse? I think it is because politics tends to concentrate on ideas for the future rather than implementation in the present. We love to think and talk about new policy initiatives that sit comfortably with our ideology. It is much more interesting to dream up new ways of tackling inequality if you are on the left, or privatising public services if you are on the right, than to worry about the efficiency of day-to-day services.

Furthermore, every minister in every government wants to leave their mark by introducing a new initiative. Once I counted eighteen new initiatives to tackle urban regeneration taken in as many years by successive ministers of both the main political parties. Some were led by government from the top, like the Urban Development Grants and the Urban Regeneration Grants, others were bottom-up approaches like the New Deal for Communities and City Challenge. They ranged from enterprise zones to garden festivals. No initiative was allowed time in which to work. Ministers measure their success by the announcements they make rather than by the work they have done to secure better value. They know their time in office is limited, and they feel their place in history will only be secured by the new programmes they promote.

The same is true at every level of politics. Members of Parliament prefer to dissect new policy proposals rather than current budgets. The departmental select committees of the House of Commons spend their time exploring the challenges for the future. They rarely use the reports on past and present departmental expenditure produced by the National Audit Office for the basis of an inquiry.

Yet I know from my email traffic and from my post bag that there is widespread obsession with waste in public services. People hate it. They want us to uncover it and deal with it. They expect us to ask the tough questions. They want us to do better. This does not mean that most people think that public spending is a bad thing and should on principle be cut. Of course there are those on the right of the political spectrum who do want to reduce the size of the state radically. But anger at public waste is felt by everybody, including those who enthusiastically support more investment in public services.

If it matters to our voters, it should matter to us. A commitment to reconnect politics with people means we should respond to the concerns that people express rather than trying to dictate our own agenda. For all these very sound reasons, striving to cut out waste and secure better value should be central to our work.

Of course some mistakes will always be made. Some innovations, because by their nature they are untested, will result in failures. But a relentless focus on efficiency and effectiveness can still yield huge rewards: better services, stronger outcomes, more for less, and renewed confidence in the value and importance of public spending.

What really startled me as a result of holding regular hearings over five years was the sheer enormity of the problem. The money governments waste runs into billions; and though billions are regularly squandered, we seem unable to learn properly from past mistakes. In every job I held as a minister, I like to think I tried to secure value for money. Most of my fellow ministers would say the same. But somehow, for the short periods during which we were in post, we operated in the silos of our portfolios, and we never saw the wider picture and understood the regular, familiar and repetitive nature of our failures.

Chairing the Public Accounts Committee gave me a new perspective. As we assiduously followed the taxpayer's pound, I was able to look across government at the whole, vast range of its projects and programmes. It became clear that if we could fundamentally improve the effectiveness of our expenditure, it would release huge amounts of money that could be invested on unfunded but essential priorities now considered unaffordable. The room for improvement was immense; the waste a frustrating and unforgivable scandal. In these next two chapters I describe some of the stories that involved simply huge amounts of wasted money. They are not the only stories but they are the ones that stick in the mind.

Ministry of Defence

Our early studies of the Ministry of Defence (MOD) were unbelievably awful. The level of waste, particularly in procurement, was eye-watering. Every year we looked in detail at the MOD's biggest investment projects. These were schemes to build new planes, new ships and submarines, and new equipment for the armed forces on the front line. I recall one memorable hearing, when during around two hours of taking evidence we uncovered some £8 billion of wasted expenditure, where taxpayers' money had been spent with absolutely no benefit for the armed services in terms of new equipment and support. Projects had been abandoned; deliberate delays added unnecessary costs and changing specifications halfway through a contract added further millions. It was as if the MOD tore up £8 billion worth of banknotes and tossed them into the air, as though they were a shower of confetti.

I had never in the past taken an interest in defence equipment; I thought of it as 'toys for the boys'. But seeing the sums involved, I realised that I needed to get my head around these complex, technical projects if I was to pursue the taxpayer's interest properly, so I worked to understand them better and I learned a lot.

One unforgettable story of unconscionable waste concerned the contract to build two aircraft carriers to replace the three existing Invincible class aircraft carriers. The decision in principle to replace the carriers was taken by the Blair government during a Strategic Defence Review in 1998. At the time the estimated cost of the replacement ships was around £2.8 billion. However, moving from a policy decision to policy execution took for ever.

By July 2007, no contract had been signed, the defence budget was wildly overspent, but Gordon Brown was anxious to proceed. He was determined to keep the jobs in the shipbuilding industry in Rosyth. The justification for building two new carriers was dictated more by the government's industrial policy than by its defence priorities. At the time Gordon Brown said: 'This is a major project for the future of the shipbuilding industry, and a major addition to the strategic strength of the Royal Navy.' In 2012, when he thought the Coalition would pull the plug on the contracts, he said: 'I have a duty to speak out for the shipbuilding and dockyard workforce.'

The prevailing culture in the MOD in 2008 was to identify some money in the budget to justify and fund the start of the project and then hope that the Treasury would come to the rescue with more money once the contract had been signed. Some described this approach as a 'culture of optimism'. 'A culture of recklessness and irresponsibility' would be a more apt description.

A contract to build the carriers was signed in 2008 at a projected cost of £3.65 billion – a 30 per cent increase on the original estimate of £2.8 billion. The MOD justified committing to the contract by saying they would find savings from another part of the programme, by reducing or delaying the provision of armoured vehicles for front-line troops.

When Des Browne, Defence Secretary at the time, announced in Parliament that the contract had been signed, he said: 'These will be named HMS Queen Elizabeth and HMS Prince of Wales. They are expected to enter service in 2014 and 2016, respectively . . . The carrier programme will sustain and create some ten thousand jobs across the UK.'

Estimates of how big the black hole in the defence budget was when the contract was signed have varied hugely, ranging between £6 billion and £36 billion. The variation in the estimates simply confirms the failure of all those involved to have a firm grip on the budget.

Within seven months of signing the contract, the MOD failed to identify alternative savings and therefore could not fund the work. They dealt with this big financial hole by pausing the contract and deferring work for two years. They acknowledged that while deferral might give immediate savings, it would also lead to additional costs because the MOD was trapped into expensive specialist overheads and had to keep the facilities, the infrastructure and many of the people in place. When they took the decision to defer, the estimated

additional costs were £900 million. Within months of deciding to defer the contract, the MOD found that the actual costs
of deferral had risen by a further £650 million, to nearly £1.6
billion.

The cost to the taxpayer from signing a contract for political and industrial rather than defence reasons, with no budget
available to fund the work, leading to a decision to defer most
of the work within seven months of embarking on the contract, was an astounding £1.6 billion. The Labour government
under Gordon Brown was to blame for this tumultuous waste.
Nobody was held to account.

Things did not improve under the Coalition; the new government failed to learn the lessons. Shortly after the 2010
General Election, the Coalition government undertook another
Strategic Defence Review to try to bring down the deficit in the
MOD's budget. Again, the politicians took decisions without
a proper understanding of costs. They considered cancelling
the contract for a second aircraft carrier, but on the back of a
threatening letter from the main contractor, BAE Systems, they
claimed that it would cost more to cancel the second carrier
than to build it.

In a letter to the Prime Minister from Ian King, BAE's chief
executive, written in October 2010, the company said: 'If both
carriers are completed the cost will be £5.25bn. If Prince of
Wales is cancelled the direct cost of the programme will be
£4.8bn. However in these circumstances, and under Treasury
rules and the agreements I have outlined, there will be con-
sequential costs, including those relating to rationalisation,
which we estimate would amount to £690m.' He then went
on to say: 'The cancellation of Prince of Wales would mean
that production in all BAE Systems shipyards would cease at
the end of 2012 . . . all three yards would have to close by early
2013 with the loss of more than 5000 jobs in BAE Systems and

many more across the UK in hundreds of companies in the supply chain ... And a potential termination liability under our agreement with MOD would also arise.'

I know from my dealings with BAE when I was a minister at the then Department of Trade and Industry that they can be very aggressive in their demands of government. We do not know how strongly the claim was challenged but it persuaded the government to continue building both aircraft carriers – then immediately to mothball one, leaving it sitting unused in dry dock.

The government also decided to change the specification for the carriers; they chose to fit them with 'cats and traps' – catapults and arrestor gear – which would enable a different variant of the Joint Fight Striker aeroplane to be used on the ships. In the Defence Review the government argued: 'As currently designed the Queen Elizabeth will not be fully interoperable with key allies, since their naval jets could not land on it. Pursuit of closer partnership is a core strategic principle for the Strategic Defence and Security Review because it is clear that the UK will in most circumstances act militarily as part of a wider coalition. We will therefore install catapult and arrestor gear.'

The extra costs arising from the revised specification were estimated at between £500 million and £800 million.

Less than sixteen months later, in May 2012, ministers came back to the House of Commons to say that they had changed their minds – again. The additional costs of the new specification had increased by 150 per cent to over £2 billion. There was a further bill for £2.5 billion to £3 billion to retrospectively refit the first aircraft carrier to take the different planes.

Why had the costs changed? In part because it took the Ministry of Defence eighteen months to understand the technological implications and hence the costs of the proposed modifications. In part because officials in the department had simply failed to account for obvious things like inflation and VAT in their original estimates. The ballooning revised estimates persuaded ministers to change their minds and revert to the old specification. Suddenly the argument about the better capability disappeared.

The extra costs to the taxpayer of this second change of heart were estimated by the National Audit Office to be around £74 million.

The latest estimates suggest the costs for building the aircraft carriers will exceed £6.2 billion. The delay in getting the carriers into service runs into years. The carriers can carry thirty-six aeroplanes, but initially the MOD agreed to buy only eight – although that figure is creeping up, with a recent commitment to deliver twenty-four planes by 2023. At the NATO summit in 2014, the Prime Minister announced that the government had changed its mind again and would bring both aircraft carriers into service: 'This will ensure that we will always have one carrier available 100 per cent of the time,' he said.

The wasted millions were inexcusable. Balancing the books in the short term without regard to long-term value for money was irresponsible. But what is particularly disconcerting is that civil servants let this happen. Gordon Brown's determination to protect jobs in Rosyth and David Cameron's whim in choosing a different plane and a new specification should have been challenged, and the bad decisions could and should have been stopped.

The permanent secretary is the accounting officer for the department's budget and has clear powers and responsibilities. He or she is personally accountable to Parliament for the use of public money. If officials believe that ministers are taking decisions relating to proposed expenditure that do not demonstrate value for money, or fail the tests of regularity and propriety, they are required to write formally to ministers and seek a written ministerial instruction, also known as a 'letter of direction'. The issue then becomes formal and public and so the minister's justification has to be robust.

Letters of direction are rarely issued and they represent the ultimate sanction. One would hope that a mature discussion between politicians and civil servants would mostly result in defensible decisions. However, the decision in the first instance to proceed with the aircraft carriers with no money in the budget and in the second instance to change the specification with no thorough knowledge of the costs involved should have been challenged.

Sir Bill Jeffrey, the permanent secretary when Gordon Brown first insisted on signing the contract, wrote to us and said: 'The aircraft carrier project was clearly a very high priority for the then Government, and Ministers' agreement to undertake an examination of the equipment programme with a view to reducing its cost provided a means by which the programme could be brought into better balance before long.' He said this despite knowing at that time that the budget was already over-spent and despite his judgement, again at that time, that a review the department was about to undertake on the cost of the MOD equipment programme was likely to reveal an even bigger black hole in the department's budget. The permanent secretary at the Ministry of Defence was supported by Sir Nick Macpherson, the permanent secretary at the Treasury, who said he 'had no reason to second guess him' on his decision not to seek a letter of direction. Nobody acted. Nobody accepted responsibility for the waste and the politicians have moved on. Nobody felt they should be held to account.

The flip-flopping by the Coalition government on which planes to buy and whether to change the specification to include cats and traps was deliberately obscured by all involved. The National Audit Office was initially refused access to the papers on which the 2010 decision to change direction had been taken. The Audit Office regularly examines confidential material in considering value for money on behalf of the taxpayer. Obviously they do not divulge to Members of Parliament or others information that is confidential or commercially sensitive. But without the information, the Audit Office could not reach a value judgement conclusion. Refusing access to papers was pretty unprecedented. When the Public Accounts Committee asked Ursula Brennan, who by that time was the new permanent secretary at the Ministry of Defence, to explain the refusal she was uncharacteristically candid:

> Ursula Brennan: 'The view of the government is very clearly that the National Audit Office were given access to all the papers that had the information that related to value for money. What they were not given access to were papers that they do not generally get given access to, which relates to policy.'
> Nick Smith MP: 'Sorry, did you just say that the Prime Minister blocked the NAO asking for the papers that it wanted?'
> Ursula Brennan: 'I am saying that it was confirmed with the Prime Minister whether or not the National Audit Office should have access to the Cabinet papers.'
> Nick Smith: 'So the Prime Minister stopped the NAO having the papers that it wanted?'
> Ursula Brennan: 'Yes.'

We wanted to understand two things. First, it was hard to believe that cancelling the second aircraft carrier could cost more than building it. The National Audit Office had estimated a £200 million saving, which the Prime Minister claimed was wrong. Second, we wanted reassurance that the decision to switch to cats and traps had been taken with proper evidence and information on costings. These questions were valid and went to the heart of value for money. The public through Parliament had the right to know. Hiding behind an assertion that these were policy issues and should therefore remain private was not good enough.

I raised the issue directly with the Prime Minister in the weekly Prime Minister's Questions. The chair of the Treasury Select Committee and I wrote a joint letter to the Prime Minister, urging him in the interests of transparency and accountability to release the papers to the auditors. We also raised the issue through the Liaison Committee, which brings together all the chairs of all the select committees, and regularly interrogates the Prime Minister.

In the end we won that particular battle and the Prime Minister caved in. The chair of the Treasury Select Committee and I received a letter from him, in which he qualified his previous remarks: 'Turning to my comment in Parliament on 19 October 2010 that "we were left in a situation where even cancelling the second carrier would cost more than to build it", it might be helpful for you to have read my next sentence that "I have this in written confirmation from BAE Systems". To be clear I was quoting BAE Systems, not the MOD or NSC [National Security Council] papers.'

The National Audit Office was given access to all the papers. We saw the letter from BAE. I remain sceptical as to whether this claim that it would cost more to cancel than to proceed was ever properly interrogated and challenged. When the National Audit Office saw the papers, we uncovered the lack of reliable and properly costed information that ministers had when taking the decision to switch to cats and traps.

One might forgive the MOD for one mistake – even a huge one like this. But our regular reviews of the defence programme revealed a continuous stream of waste and a deep-seated culture going back for generations that all too often resulted in money being squandered.

The Public Accounts Committee has found it necessary to produce between two and three reports on defence procurement every year since the committee was founded. The words of Harold Wilson in 1960 still resonate today: 'I will merely say that Seaslug [the first surface-to-air missile] was estimated at £1 million to £1.5 million expenditure and, as the Committee reports, the latest estimate of the direct cost of developing the missile and its control and guidance system is £40 million, while the total estimated all-up cost is £70 million, including the ship-borne radar developed by the Admiralty.'

Later in his speech he said: 'The failure of the Seaslug contractor – I quote the Committee's report – "to provide competent leadership and to co-ordinate the work of other firms developing equipment for the project" . . . We have here a system where the financial control on behalf of the taxpayer is exercised, not by trained civil servants with a lifetime experience in these things, but by private contractors whose training is quite different and whose enthusiasm for saving the taxpayers' money may be less than wholehearted.'

Today, austerity and the cuts in public spending may have provided a spur for change, but the underlying problems persist, not just in the procurement programme but elsewhere in the Ministry of Defence.

There is still strong pressure to commit to spending more than they have. The Ministry constantly rescopes projects, adding unnecessary costs; they still under-price projects to secure immediate approval, only to jack up the costs after having been given the go-ahead. Delay is used to ensure the immediate short–term budget is not overspent. Too many schemes are innovative, untested and gold–plated, with specifications for commissioning the most expensive, up–to–date and complicated equipment. The programme is therefore susceptible to unknown overspends because problems inevitably arise. There is no proper link between responsibility and accountability, with those responsible for a particular project being moved on to another job after a couple of years. Too few people have the abilities required to do the job, such as commercial or project management skills. Too many people who are trained in managing major defence projects at the Ministry of Defence then leave for better paid jobs in the private defence sector.

The MOD is itself like a huge unwieldy tanker and any effort to turn it round is inevitably thwarted by the embedded culture. The tussles for power between civil servants and the armed forces; the tussles between the three services themselves, especially for resources; the power of the big players in the defence industry in threatening redundancies and dictating costs; the lack of people with appropriate skills who stick to the job long enough; the constantly changing political imperatives: all of this inhibits the reform required to get better value.

To fund their overspending, the MOD often uses the special arrangement it has with the Treasury to get more money. Under what are called 'urgent operational requirements', the MOD can finance equipment it cannot fund from its own budget by pleading that it is urgently required in the theatre of war. The department regularly reduces a budget overspend by cancelling contracts to provide new and better armoured vehicles needed in places like Afghanistan or Iraq because such contractual commitments are easier and less costly to break than the big contracts for big items. More than once the MOD cancelled contracts for medium–weight tracked and wheeled armoured vehicles that were easier to deploy than heavy tanks over large distances and offered a balance between firepower, protection and mobility. The Ministry of Defence then extracted money from the Treasury to buy vehicles funded as urgent operational requirements: for example, the Mastiff Protected Patrol vehicles were bought under this arrangement. Over one eight-year period, from 2003 to 2011, £2.8 billion was taken directly from the Treasury to make up for the cuts to the armoured vehicles programme in the MOD. All of it taxpayers' money.

We gathered regular evidence of the lack of financial control occurring elsewhere in the Ministry of Defence, on top of the waste in the procurement of defence equipment. At one point we looked at the MOD's real estate. They own and have access to an astounding 1.5 per cent of all the land in the UK. This vast estate is valued at around £20 billion.

The government started to sell assets like polo fields in Edinburgh and Brompton Road Tube station, which bizarrely the MOD owned. However, at the beginning of 2015, Michael Fallon, the Defence Secretary, admitted in a speech that the MOD still owned an incredible fifty-seven separate sites within the M25 and that they still held fifteen golf courses. One such course is occupied by the US Air Force and a few are shared with the general public, with Upavon golf course in the rolling Wiltshire countryside leased to private owners. But most of the golf courses, including a pitch and putt centre and a driving range, are still controlled by the Ministry of Defence.

The MOD has little idea as to whether or not the armed forces need all the land that they own or lease; they have scant information on the relative value of sites, which sites are operationally more important or more intensely used, what the conditions are and how much they cost to run. The only clear fact we established was that in the ten years from 1998, personnel numbers had dropped by 13.4 per cent but the built estate had only reduced by 4.3 per cent. A straightforward way of creating efficiency savings, you would have thought. While that obvious fact was agreed by all concerned, translating good intentions into reality seemed beyond them.

We highlighted the big number disasters, but we also came across many smaller disasters that resulted in unnecessary waste. Such as the writing off of £6 million spent on buying ten thousand high-tech earplugs that had been especially moulded to enable soldiers to hear each other on the battlefield while blocking out the noise of explosions and gunfire. These had apparently been tested by senior officials before payment had been authorised. The listening and hearing levels of those officials must clearly have been unique, because once they were tested by front-line soldiers on the battlefield, the earplugs were found to be ineffective and the money was wasted. Another example was the writing off of £7.2 million spent buying mobile mine detectors that were later deemed unsuitable. Another the failure to secure prompt delivery of spare parts; in the case of the Typhoon aircraft, the Ministry of Defence dealt with the shortage of spare parts by cannibalising other planes in the fleet. That meant losing the use of the cannibalised planes, which of course had to be grounded. On the day of one of our hearings in 2011, three Typhoon planes were grounded for this reason. Nearly £400 million worth of aircraft sitting on the ground that could and should have been being used to train the forty-eight pilots whose job it was to fly Typhoons.

I have described a few of our inquiries. There were many more occasions where we were shocked by the many millions of pounds regularly wasted by the department on procurement. And while all this money was being wasted, the number of serving soldiers was being drastically reduced to meet the budget deficit. It just does not make sense.

One final example (although there are plenty of others) illustrates the way the same mistakes occur time and time again. We examined in detail the management of the Typhoon project. The origins of this went back to Margaret Thatcher's premiership; in 1987, she approved the proposal to develop and build Typhoon fighters. This aircraft remains at the core of the Royal Air Force capability today. The project was a collaboration between four countries: Britain, Spain, Italy and Germany. As with the aircraft carriers, the MOD was over-optimistic about the costs when gaining approval to proceed.

The contract committed the UK to buying aircraft in three phases. We did cut the number purchased over time, decisions dictated by both budget overspends and military requirements. However, in 2004, the budget overspend was particularly challenging, so ministers and the Ministry of Defence decided unilaterally to pull out of the third phase and simply removed £1 billion from the budget in an attempt to balance the books. Yet the UK was contractually committed to buying the third tranche of planes and, of course, was held to this commitment by our partners. A report in the *Financial Times* in May 2009 said: 'Mr Brown has come under intense pressure from Germany, Italy and Spain – the UK's partners – to stop holding up the third production run by making an overdue £1.4 billion payment. The Prime Minister is anxious to avoid antagonising Angela Merkel, German Chancellor and a key ally.'

So the short-term cut in the budget was illusory and in 2009, £2.7 billion had to be added back to pay for the third tranche of Typhoon aircraft; yet again, the books had been balanced in the short term with scant regard to long-term value for money.

The Typhoons were originally conceived as air-to-air fighters, but in 2004 the MOD had decided to retire early the

Jaguar aircraft, which were used for ground attack, probably to make short-term savings to balance the budget in that year. So the department decided to invest £119 million in upgrading the Typhoons that had already been built so that they could replace the Jaguar aircraft for ground attack.

Then, in 2009, the MOD decided to retire the Tornado F3 aircraft early, again to meet a shortfall in the MOD budget. So they changed their minds again on how they would use the Typhoon aircraft and moved them away from ground-attack missions (for which they had just been upgraded at vast expense) back to air defence. When we held our hearing in 2011, the ground-attack capability had not been used.

In recent years, the discipline of austerity has given a new impetus to efforts to improve. But the evidence that would give us all confidence that fundamental reform has taken place is scant. The deficit in the defence budget has been tackled but, in the main, that has been achieved by employing fewer soldiers and buying less equipment rather than improving efficiency. The Nimrod maritime surveillance aircraft has been scrapped after a total of £3.4 billion had already been spent developing and building the first aircraft. Cost overruns have been avoided by a crude strategy of cutting numbers in the equipment pro-gramme, so we have fewer Puma helicopters, fewer big A400M aircraft and fewer Chinooks. The regular army has been cut by twenty thousand to be replaced by an increase in reservists, with little evidence that those reservists can be recruited.

There have been some improvements. The MOD is trying to move away from always aiming for the latest, cutting-edge innovation to buying off-the-shelf products that offer greater certainty. There have been some tougher dealings with the defence industry and efforts are being made to live within budgets. But many of the problems associated with big projects in the MOD remain unchanged.

12

Not Just the MOD

B ut it is not just the MOD that wastes our money. We found other parts of government where taxpayers were ripped off on big projects and nobody was held to account.

One of the worst cases of project failure emerged from an early study we undertook of the FIReControl project for which the Department for Communities and Local Government (DCLG) was responsible. The project was conceived after the 9/11 attacks and was, in part, designed to improve the resilience of the fire and rescue services to respond to major national emergencies. The idea was to replace the forty-six local fire control rooms run by the forty-six separate fire and rescue authorities and create nine regional centres. All the 999 calls would be routed through the nine regional centres and in this way responses could be more quickly and effectively managed. Co-ordinating the work at a regional level seemed both to offer stronger resilience and better value. The nine centres were predicted to cost less than running forty-six centres. And they fitted perfectly with the ambitions of the politicians of the time, particularly John Prescott, who was vigorously promoting regional government. This was a service, he argued, that should obviously be delivered at the regional level.

The project was launched in 2004 and the nine new regional centres in places like Durham, Wakefield, Cambridge, Merton and Taunton were expected to be up and running by the end of 2009. The cost of establishing the new network of centres was put at £120 million and the department estimated savings of £86 million. Seven years later, at the end of 2010, the department decided to abandon its efforts and scrapped the entire project; the taxpayer was left to foot the enormous bill of around £500 million for this failed venture.

What went wrong? What lessons can government learn from unmitigated disasters like this?

The concept itself was flawed, and proper planning to ensure success did not happen. Central government was seeking to impose a national solution on forty-six independent local fire authorities, that would have to pay the ongoing costs of running the new system. The fire authorities had no say in designing the project and very little attempt was made to get them involved in detailed decisions.

Indeed, their hostility to the project was enormous. The Fire Brigades Union's opposition was also vocal. Their general secretary Matt Wrack said: 'Regional controls might be able to deal with the desktop scenarios dreamt up by management consultants, but not with real life. Not only will they not make things better, on these figures they will be much worse when the public need them most. The government is trying to run 999 emergency command and control centres like control rooms. The public don't want to be listening to Vivaldi's *Four Seasons* as the smoke is flowing into the room.'

In May 2007, he was quoted as saying: 'Fire crews have almost no confidence in the government's ability to deliver the new system and think it should be scrapped. The project is being forced down the throat of local fire services by a central government which thinks it knows what's best for local services.'

But it was not just the trades unions that were hostile to the programme, which is what ministers believed. The authorities themselves were not willing partners. In 2006, Cornwall County Fire Brigade, in its evidence to the select committee on local government, expressed concerns about 'the dependence which the project places on untried and untested technology'. This view was echoed in evidence from West Sussex County Council and the West Sussex Fire and Rescue Authority, who wrote in their evidence: 'We have serious concerns about the general uncertainty, lack of transparency and apparent lack of forethought given to the implications of regional control, not least the technological aspects. The financial costs and resource implications for individual fire services in meeting the demands of regional control do not appear to be appreciated by the Office of the Deputy Prime Minister . . . Neither are we confident that the proposed savings of 30 per cent are achievable. Timescales for the project appear to have been determined based upon the financial model, rather than on a detailed assessment of what needs to be done and how thoroughly. Also communication is poor both in terms of information and timeliness.'

Government had no statutory powers to compel the fire authorities to co-operate and so getting them to buy into and own the project was critical to its success. The government failed to think about incentives designed to bring them on board and failed to secure their co-operation.

The concept was predicated on having one common IT system for all forty-six authorities. That required every authority with different operational needs to change its management and IT systems so that they all aligned with one another. The department simply did not appreciate the complexity of achieving this. They thought they could buy an off-the-shelf IT package that could be easily integrated by forty-six very different and very independent organisations. The department did not even award the IT contract until three years after they had launched the project and the building of the nine new regional centres was well underway. Indeed, the first centres were completed just three months after the IT contract was awarded.

The project was given the go-ahead before anybody had produced a proper business case, a project plan or a procurement plan. It was approved by both the Treasury and the DCLG before the required assessment had been completed by the Office of Government Commerce, so bypassing the checks that existed at that time to ensure that money was not wasted. When that assessment was published, it concluded that the project had developed at 'an extraordinarily fast pace' and the National Audit Office interpreted the conclusions as meaning the programme was 'in poor condition overall and at significant risk of failing to deliver'. Yet nobody thought to pause or stop the work.

By the time the overall costs were properly assessed in 2007, they had risen from £120 million to £340 million, a near-threefold increase. A further reassessment in 2009 estimated that the predicted savings had disappeared altogether and that the project would cost £218 million more than it saved. But still nobody thought the whole thing should be paused or halted.

Moreover the contract with the IT providers was poorly conceived, poorly procured and badly managed. EADS, a firm that had no experience of providing IT services for control rooms, was awarded the contract. They simply failed to deliver the IT systems that would enable the regional centres to function and the inter-operability between all the forty-six fire authorities to work. The department failed to put proper controls into the contract so that EADS could be held to account for failure to deliver. When, in 2010, the department first wanted to walk away from the IT contract, they found that the terms of the contract and their own failure to do proper monitoring meant that they would face a substantial compensation bill for termination. So the department changed the monitoring procedures, made EADS accountable for achieving certain milestones and then took a further six months to establish grounds for terminating the contract.

Although the company gave some money back to the government as part of the termination negotiations, the department was left with equipment worth £5.7 million. They had also paid nearly £12 million to EADS for which they got nothing but which they were unable to recoup from the contractor.

The management and leadership of this project were dire. There were five different people in charge (known as senior responsible officers) during the six years the project was allowed to run. Reporting to these senior responsible officers were four different people who acted as the project director during the six years. Half of the project team working on the project were either consultants or interns and 76 per cent of the cost of the central project team went to consultancies, with the firms earning £68.6 million. PA Consulting, a management consultancy group that had originally been founded by three Englishmen at the end of the Second World War, walked away with £42 million from their work on this monumental failure. (PA Consulting had already run into trouble with the Home Office in 2008 when they lost a USB data stick containing confidential information about prisoners.)

The decision to call a halt to FIReControl in 2010 was too little too late. Nearly half a billion pounds had been spent. The nine regional centres had been built. When we held our first hearing in 2011, eight of these buildings were lying empty, with the taxpayer paying £4 million a month for the leases that had been signed, leases that were twenty to twenty-five years long. When we came back to the issue to see what had happened two years later, we found that tenants had only been found for five of the nine centres and even here, the department was still providing a subsidy for the rent and running costs associated with the buildings. To take just one example, the Castle Donington Centre in the East Midlands, which cost £1.8 million a year to run, was still lying empty. These white elephants stand as a stark reminder of the waste.

So poor planning to ensure a viable concept, no buy-in by those providing the service, inadequate understanding of costs at an early enough stage, constant change of the personnel in charge, poorly devised and badly monitored contracts, and an expensive dependence on outside consultants all contributed to the failure. Again, we were left asking if anybody had been held to account. The consultants are still employed by the government. The responsible permanent secretary between 2005 and 2011 was Sir Peter Housden, who moved seamlessly from the Department for Communities and Local Government into the top Civil Service job in Scotland and has never been called to account. We will never know why he failed to call a halt. We do not know why he did not issue a letter of direction to ministers. A very angry John Prescott phoned me and wrote to me after we published our highly critical report. He was at pains to let us know that he had never been warned about the problems. Indeed, in his letter to me, he quoted the minutes he still had of a meeting held in July 2005, which read: 'In summary, everyone present, including the Accounting Officer

[Sir Peter Housden], agreed there was a compelling case to improve the service and level of national resilience by proceeding now with the FIReControl project. While there were risks involved in the project, everyone agreed doing nothing would be a greater risk.'

Of course, when we held our hearing in 2011, the department's new permanent secretary was able to suggest that he would never have allowed these things to happen. He was not in post and responsible at the time. The real frustration for the committee, and the wider public, is that the system invariably fails to link responsibility to accountability. Until that changes, unconscionable waste will persist unchallenged.

Finally, what about the Treasury? Their reluctance to exert control over major projects means that the checks and balances that prevail in most complex organisations, with the finance function having the ability to pull or pause projects involving major expenditure, is missing as far as government spending is concerned. Until that is put right, the likelihood of money being wasted will endure.

Other IT projects

During the course of our work we came across plenty of other examples of IT disasters. In fact, if any official mentioned a new IT project in their evidence to the committee, we would laugh at the idea that this might be introduced on time, within budget and save money. The Public Accounts Committee has produced seventy-five reports on IT procurement over twenty-five years, from 1992 to 2016. All too often, the same reasons for failure were present, yet all too often, the overall system showed no means of learning from past mistakes.

There were three examples that stood out for me. The first was the National Programme for IT in the NHS. This was launched by Tony Blair in 2002. He had been convinced during a meeting with Bill Gates that a massive IT reform programme was a vital part of the answer to improving and sustaining the NHS. This great reform would bring about a national system for booking appointments, a national prescription service and a national health record service.

The Public Accounts Committee looked at the project a number of times before I came on board. Richard Bacon had doggedly pursued all concerned and was determined not to let go of the issue. Credit must go to him for insisting that the saga should be exposed to the public. In 2011, we considered a report on just part of the programme – the delivery of the individual health records system.

The aim for this part of the project was to have all our health records held electronically on one big national system, so that whenever and wherever you showed up at a healthcare setting, the NHS doctors and nurses could have instant access to your notes.

The sums involved in developing this national IT system were mind-boggling. For the entire system, costs rose from an initial £2.3 billion in 2002 to an estimated £11.4 billion nine years later, when we looked at the care records in the summer of 2011. At the time of our hearing, the Department of Health and the NHS had spent some £6.4 billion on the project as a whole. Just imagine what that money could buy in terms of front-line doctors and nurses and much-needed medical equipment.

Within the £6.4 billion, the department had already spent £2.7 billion on the care records system and was looking at £7 billion as the total spend on the records alone. The idea that if you walked into any health setting from Cornwall to Carlisle, health professionals could have immediate access to your health records was seductive. Tony Blair was clearly convinced, so much so that he pushed officials to bring forward the programme so that it could be delivered in time for the 2005 General Election.

So yet again, political imperatives, macho-style concepts and electoral cycles overrode sensible planning, leading to untold waste on a project that officials admitted was beyond the capacity of the department to deliver. As with FIReControl, government sought to impose a national IT system on independently run hospital trusts and GP practices. As with FIReControl, the government decided what it wanted to do in secret and did not consult the NHS professionals as it developed its proposals and the contract specification. Not only did they want to impose national systems on varied local networks and protocols, but they ignored the concerns expressed by healthcare professionals around patient confidentiality. For instance, would an HIV/Aids patient want their records so readily available? Only after the department had committed to the contracts and only after they ran into difficulties, did they start to consult the professionals who would be the users of the system.

At our hearing, BT, one of the contractors, told us: 'It is considered the largest civil IT programme in the world.' Sir David Nicholson, the then chief executive of the NHS, said that it was 'a laudable ambition' but 'inherently risky'.

The department was trying to do something completely new and untested, doing it hastily and without securing the buy-in from the users. Most important, they had not defined the product; they did not know what they were buying – with our money. One of the very basic requirements of any IT contract is that the IT systems should meet the requirements of the user and not the other way around. Here the users were being asked to change how they worked to meet the requirements of the system.

One of the contractors, Computer Sciences Corporation (CSC), tried to tell us that working in this way was par for the course.

Sheri Tureen (President, UK Healthcare, CSC): 'As is not uncommon in programmes of this type, the initial development and deployment goes through an early adaptor process and it is really not until you have got to that point where they have exercised the solution that you have a true understanding of whether or not the usability and capability are there.' In other words, you commit to a contract without knowing what you want. A recipe for disaster.

In the end the Department of Health abandoned the concept, but could not extricate themselves from all the contracts. So they are using money identified for one purpose to introduce different, localised, trust-specific solutions which mean that if you do have a serious accident in Cornwall, doctors will not be able to access your records from Carlisle.

The government signed contracts with four firms. Accenture walked away from the £2 billion contract in 2006 and declared in their accounts a provision of $450 million for expected losses. In 2008, negotiations to 'reset' the contract with Fujitsu ended up with the departure of Fujitsu and long-drawn-out negotiations to terminate the contract that cost the Department of Health many tens of millions.

By the time we conducted our inquiry, there were only two contractors left, BT and CSC. Both had massively driven up the price, delayed the implementation and were, in the main, providing interim IT solutions to health bodies that could no longer afford to wait for a more comprehensive IT system, or had been enticed by the offer of central-government-funded investment in their local IT infrastructure. The contracts were so poorly written that officials told us it would cost more to terminate them than to continue spending – our money.

CSC had committed to introducing a new 'Lorenzo' system for care records around the country. Because of the problems in designing the system, they ended up introducing over 130 interim systems at a cost of £105 million. Originally the contractors committed to delivering all the new records systems by 2010. At the time of our hearing in 2011, only 10 of the 166 health trusts in the North, the Midlands and the East of England had received the most basic Lorenzo software. No mental health trust had got a system and the Pennine Trust, frustrated by the fact that CSC had missed so many deadlines, decided to reject the CSC Lorenzo solution and install its own IT systems.

The story from BT was not much better. For instance, BT renegotiated the contract for London, cutting by half the number of acute trusts covered, cutting out all GP practices and taking the London Ambulance Service out of the contract. Despite this dramatic reduction in the scope and the functionality of the £1 billion contract, the only saving for the taxpayer was some £73 million.

The controls and the data on the contract were so poor that the National Audit Office and the Department of Health could not provide agreed figures on costs. But it seemed bizarre, to say the least, that BT was selling IT systems to community and mental health trusts at an average of £9 million each in the South of England, while at the same time Bradford District Care Trust had bought the same system and the same services from another supplier, CSE Healthcare Systems, for £1.3 million.

Uncovering this incompetence and waste led us to call for the programme to be halted. The government responded by issuing a press release just before the Labour Party Conference in September 2011, announcing that it was axing Labour's profligate and wasteful scheme. In reality, they have remained tied into the contracts with both BT and CSC, contracts that are delivering far less functionality to far fewer sites.

And shortly after the government proclaimed the end of the National IT Programme for the NHS, a new Secretary of State for Health, Jeremy Hunt, announced that the NHS promised to be paperless by 2018. In the 2015 Spending Review and Autumn Statement, the Treasury gave the NHS yet another £1 billion for new technology to support and produce integrated care records by 2020. Richard Bacon described the NHS IT programme as 'one of the worst and most expensive contracting fiascos in the history of the public sector', but the government has set off on the same journey yet again. I have no doubt that they sincerely believe that they will do better this time around. But I simply observe that the ambition has not been moderated and the political and electoral imperatives have dictated the timeframe. It feels like a case of *plus ça change.*

In 2010, the Home Office unveiled plans for a new immigration casework system. This would allow all the interactions with any applicant to be stored in one place; the new system was designed to replace twenty redundant or inadequate systems. This formed the first of two Home Office IT projects that would ultimately be cancelled – at a cost of £1 billion.

Both projects were designed to improve some of the shambles in the immigration system. The Home Office was using a hopelessly old and inadequate immigration casework system. Much of the work was (and still is) paper-based, with all the errors that can bring. For instance, the team tasked with dealing with applications for permanent migration did all their work by hand – paper applications with the information then being transferred to another separate paper file and so on.

But in August 2013, the department cancelled this first project, claiming it simply did not deliver what was expected.

The bill for failure was £347 million. The Home Office has now decided to spend a further £200 million on incremental improvements to their IT capability, abandoning the big bang approach. I have no doubt that that sum will creep up over time.

The other Home Office fiasco was more political. It concerned what was known as the e-Borders IT programme that had been commissioned by the Labour government to identify who was coming into and who was leaving the country. During the political battles in the run-up to the 2010 General Election, the Conservatives campaigned against this, arguing that it was intrusive and wasteful. So they cancelled the programme. Yet £260 million had already been spent, so after lengthy and expensive litigation with the American suppliers, the Home Office agreed to pay £150 million to the suppliers in settlement of the dispute. The legal costs to the department were £35 million.

In total, the Home Office had spent £1 billion on these two projects and gained absolutely nothing.

The failure to have systems in place that allow government to exercise control over immigration has discredited successive administrations. Our inquiry established that the Home Office could not even accurately count the backlog of applications for immigration. They claimed that the backlog was around 29,000. Some of these applications went back to 2007 and nearly 40 per cent had not even had an initial decision on their application against which they might exercise the right to appeal. The Home Office simply did not have the reliable database they needed.

We also uncovered the fact that there was a pool of 175,000 people whose application to stay in the UK had been rejected. Some of them left the UK voluntarily, but new people whose applications had failed were added to the pool and so the total number still in the country but not entitled to stay hardly shifted over time. The problem was that the Home Office did not know who had left voluntarily. In 2012, they employed Capita to undertake a one-off exercise so that they could identify those people who were still in the UK but whose application to stay had been rejected. Capita could not find fifty thousand of these people. They had disappeared without trace.

Even worse, we were told that in 84 per cent of the cases where individuals should have been deported, the Home Office did not even hold the minimum essential information, like the person's address or the postcode where they lived, to enable the process of deportation to take place.

A working IT system would at the very least have allowed officials to concentrate all the management information in one place. It would not have resolved all the dysfunctional practices that appear to be so strongly entrenched, but it would have helped.

Instead ministers chose to have yet another bureaucratic reorganisation. They abolished the UK Border Agency and brought the Immigration Directorate and staff into the Home Office as an integral part of that department. Maybe they thought that by means of yet another major reorganisation, people would believe they were 'doing something'. But what inevitably happens in these circumstances is that the focus of those working in the organisation shifts to thinking about the new headed notepaper and the new organisational charts. It would have been better to concentrate on getting the IT right.

The BBC and one of its major IT projects told a similar story. This project, known as the Digital Media Initiative (DMI), was designed to transform programme-making at the BBC.

The aim was to enable BBC staff to share, manage and use all the video and audio content created by the BBC in the past, to create new content at their desk or at home on a desktop. Director-General Mark Thompson waxed lyrical on the importance of this in the first of two hearings we held in 2011. 'The point about DMI is that it is a fundamental re-engineering of the way the BBC makes television across much, not all but much of its television production activity,' he said. 'DMI was designed to help us take lots of what is tradition-ally disparate and typically high-cost professional activities, bring them to the desktop, and enable what in the jargon we would call an "end to end digital workflow". That means that essentially one person is able to grab content, manipulate it, edit it, finish it and then deliver it to a number of platforms, and then to be able to see not just rushes shot for a particular programme, but also the entire BBC deep archive and be able to manipulate that as well. It allows multiple users to be using the same material, potentially at the same time.' He later went on to tell us: 'DMI ... is critical to projects like Salford and to aspects of our W1 [the BBC's New Broadcasting House in Langham Place, W1] Project. If you like, it sometimes comes across in the report as if this is a "nice to have"; it was an abso-lutely essential "have to have" for the BBC over this period.' Later in the hearing, Thompson said, 'I believe it will end up saving the BBC and licence payers very significant amounts of money.'

He said all of that in 2011, when the BBC was explaining to the Public Accounts Committee why they had sacked Siemens, the original contractor, and decided to bring the project in-house, adding around £40 million to the projected costs, a 50 per cent increase on the original estimate. Two years later, the entire project was abandoned as costs continued to rise. The BBC wrote off £100 million of licence fee payers' money.

It was then we discovered the capabilities that had been created were not fit for purpose. The archive database was described by the then director of operations as 'incredibly chunky. It was designed for something far more ambitious, far bigger, and it was designed to access digital archive as well as the physical stock-and-loan archive. As a consequence of that, it is really difficult to operate. Our estimates are that it can even take up to ten times longer to use the archive database than the legacy system.'

Later he went on to say, in response to a question, that the annual operating costs of the new archive system were £5 million, as compared to the £780,000 spent annually running the forty-year-old system it was designed to replace: 'You are right that it is appalling value for money. We have managed to negotiate that £5 million running cost down to £3 million per annum, but it is still significantly more than the old legacy system.'

Some similarities with other IT failures emerged; some new insights arose. The BBC is an incredibly bureaucratic institution. Ownership of and responsibility for the project was difficult to pin down.

John Linwood, who had been the chief technology officer during a crucial phase and who earned £287,000 a year, strenuously asserted that he was not responsible for the business case justifying the project, only for the delivery of the technology. He blamed the users, the clients, for the failure. In evidence he told us: 'Perhaps Siemens suffered some of the same challenges that we did internally, which is that the business did not and could not define a consistent set of requirements, could not speak with one voice; did not take ownership of the project; and did not engage to the level they should have.'

If he is to be believed, that suggests the familiar lack of clear and consistent leadership and again an absence of buy-in from users. However, his evidence was contested and he had lost his job – although he went on to succeed in an unfair dismissal case against the BBC.

We found it difficult to establish the full story because there were so many people involved and they all had a different story to tell. There was definitely a lack of clearly defined responsibility and accountability and that meant the BBC failed to respond to warning signals that the programme was in trouble. That blurring of accountabilities in the BBC was evident in other inquiries we held on the BBC.

To be fair, when we recalled him after the project had been abandoned, Mark Thompson accepted ultimate responsibility. 'It failed as a project,' he said. 'It failed in a way that also meant the loss of a lot of public money. As the director-general who was at the helm when DMI was created and developed and who, in the end, oversaw much of the governance system that, as we will no doubt discuss, did not perform perfectly in this project, I just want to say sorry. I want to apologise to you and the public for the failure of this project.'

However, two years earlier he had been robust and confident in his defence of the project. When, at that time, I had ventured to suggest to him that 'it looks to me very iffy that this high-risk option [bringing the programme in-house] is performing as well as you think', he replied: 'What is happening at the moment is that DMI is out in the business. There are many programmes that are already being made with DMI, and some have gone to air and are going to air with DMI already working . . . Crucially, is it on track now to fully deliver over the course of this year for BBC North and Salford? Yes, it is. Are there going to be any significant further delays in benefit from the way we are delivering it? No, there won't be.'

When the programme was scrapped it was obvious that his earlier evidence did not reflect the reality. Indeed, we established that only one television series, ironically called *Bang Goes the Theory*, had used the new technology. It wasn't that Mark Thompson had deliberately lied to the committee; but he had been misled or had misinterpreted what he had been told. Or perhaps, although he was ultimately responsible, he simply did not understand the technology that he was responsible for authorising. Those more closely involved had told him that they had 'deployed' new IT developments; he took that as meaning the systems were being 'used', which was not the case.

This case study demonstrated a reluctance by those directly involved to be honest about the state of play; they only wanted to give out good news stories of progress. It also showed the lack of strong and effective governance and control arrangements, so common to all the failed IT projects.

The governance failure became apparent in other ways. The BBC Trust was responsible for oversight of the programme. At our first hearing, Anthony Fry, the BBC trustee who chaired the Trust's finance committee, assured us that they had the capability to oversee properly what was happening. 'I do not think there has been a single meeting of the finance committee where the subject of DMI in its various guises has not been discussed . . . I am going to spend every FCC [finance committee] worrying the heck about this. This is a big contract . . . I think we have now a sufficient flow of information to actually understand what is happening and where the problems may or may not be occurring in the delivery of the contract.'

Two years later he was forced to admit: 'There is no question that a number of mistakes were made by the BBC Trust, which I freely admit to and as the chairman of the finance committee am happy to take responsibility for . . . With the benefit of hindsight we did not have – as the BBC Trust – a sufficient knowledge around technology to be able to question properly, in my view and in my judgement, the statements that were being made ... If you are asking me whether we could have done more, the answer is, by definition, we clearly did not do enough, and as chairman of the finance committee I must take responsibility for that. We should have scratched more; there is no doubt.'

So lots of '*mea culpa*', but Mark Thompson was already comfortably settled in America as CEO of the New York Times Company and Anthony Fry moved seamlessly into the prestigious role of chairman of the Premier League. The BBC has implemented other IT projects successfully. The BBC's iPlayer has transformed our consumption of BBC programmes; the digital switchover programme was well managed. They can do it, but the successes do not excuse the failures.

The same can be said of other parts of government. Crossrail is a fine example of a complex project that is being delivered on time and within a budget even though the money available had to be cut to meet the deficit reduction demands of the Coalition government. Similarly we hosted a brilliant Olympics in London that came in within budget, although the massive contingency in the budget was almost all spent. The Public Accounts Committee came across other well-run programmes, like the rebuilding of the prison estate, which benefited hugely from having the same senior staff with the appropriate experience and knowledge in post throughout the period of change. These staff were also well supported by a management team with the necessary commercial, contract management and estates management skills.

The government has tried to improve performance by creating a new Major Projects Authority (MPA) in the Cabinet Office, tasked with examining the biggest projects across government and intervening if things go off track. It was the MPA that called a halt to the wasteful National Programme for

IT in the NHS. Their work led to the cancellation of the first competition process for the development of carbon capture and storage facilities. But they are under-resourced so cannot look at all major projects at any one time. They too became victims of power struggles with ministers and departments. The Treasury still funds schemes that the Major Projects Authority considers poor value and strong ministers override their judgements, as I will describe when we look at the implementation of Universal Credit. And they were not able to stick to their commitment to publish regularly their assessment of major projects, calling into question the government's commitment to transparency.

We went to some lengths to praise the good. We knew it would be difficult to get media attention when things went well, so we tried to work in other ways. For instance, we introduced PAC awards at the Annual Civil Service Awards ceremony and gave public recognition to both successful projects and departments where we had observed the greatest improvements over the past year.

But the hard truth is that there is too much waste and things go wrong too often. The same mistakes are made with tedious regularity and institutions regularly fail to learn from each other or from the past. As I will argue later, we need a radical rethink about how we can reform the Civil Service so that its highly able staff can be more effective in the modern world. We need to link responsibility to accountability in our structures and conventions, so that those who are responsible for a project become and remain accountable for the outcomes. These reforms may not instantly grab the attention of either the media or politicians; but ordinary folk who foot the bill with their taxes expect and want us to do better. We should not let them down.

13

Ideology Trumps Pragmatism

first came across A4e in 2009 as I drove through the stunning Derbyshire countryside to the Grade II listed castle, Thornbridge Hall. With other Labour Party stalwarts, I was going to David Blunkett's wedding, which was held at the house. As I walked into the castle with its huge rooms, grandiose furniture, chandeliers, indoor swimming pool and bar, I found that I had walked into a place marked by conspicuous affluence and prosperity.

Thornbridge Hall belonged to Emma Harrison, who held 86 per cent of the shares in A4e, a major player in Britain's welfare-to-work world. In 2009, she was a great friend of David Blunkett; they were both Sheffield born and bred, and friendship with a leading Labour politician helped her grow her business.

Two years later, we started to examine the Coalition's welfare-to-work programme – the Work Programme. This was a five-year project set up to support over three million claimants at a cost of between £3 billion and £5 billion. By this time Harrison had moved seamlessly across the political divide from one David – David Blunkett – to become a close ally of another David – David Cameron. She was awarded a CBE and he appointed her as his tsar for troubled families. She was also poised to take over the chairmanship of the Institute of Directors.

Emma Harrison had made good – entirely out of public contracts funded by the taxpayer. She says of herself that she failed academically at school, but developed her entrepreneurial skills from the age of nine when she set up the school tuck shop. She worked her way up in her father's business and always sought the limelight, appearing in *Make Me a Million* and *Secret Millionaire*. She got her first welfare-to-work contract from the Labour government in 1997 and by the end of Labour's time in office, A4e had become the biggest supplier of Labour's Flexible New Deal, a programme that sought to incentivise private companies to succeed in moving unemployed people into jobs by providing most of the money on a payment-by-results basis. Her business continued to grow under the Coalition, so that by the beginning of 2012, A4e was earning around £200 million a year from public contracts.

Emma Harrison lectured other budding entrepreneurs, telling them that to be successful 'we have to find our own way'. She encouraged them to establish a vision, to walk towards it, to inspire and encourage leadership and every day to engage in 'marketing, marketing, marketing, marketing'. Making friends with leading politicians seems to have been key to her own marketing strategy: she grew her business through relentless networking. By the end of the financial year to April 2011, she had made so much money out of taxpayer-funded contracts that on top of her £365,000 share of the £4.7 million paid out in salaries to A4e's top management team, she gave herself an £8.6 million dividend – on which, of course, she paid no National Insurance. This was £8.6 million taken from profits earned off the back of trying to secure often destitute, unemployed people a job.

Her motto was 'doing well by doing good' and she boasted that when people first contacted A4e they were told: 'We'd love to meet you. The kettle's always on.'

However, there was a gaping gulf between the rhetoric and the reality. The Work Programme exists to help people who have been out of work for a while find a job. When I was Employment Minister in the Department for Work and Pensions (DWP) in 2006, we had embarked on some innovative schemes that for the first time tried to encourage those locked into long-term disability benefits back into work. We saw work as the best route out of poverty. We experimented with awarding some contracts to private firms because we thought they could be more flexible and therefore more effective in this difficult area. Away from the limelight of twenty-four/seven media attention, they could innovate freely to find what worked best. It might, for instance, make sense to buy a new interview suit for someone who had been out of the labour market for years, a payment the red-top press would lambast if those directly employed in Jobcentre Plus made it. A private company was more likely to be able to spend money unnoticed on such items.

However, the very first National Audit Office report considered by the Public Accounts Committee in 2010 – just after I had been elected chair – was on this programme and showed that our experiment had failed. The government-run Jobcentre Plus outperformed all the private contractors in all ways. A4e had been one of the contractors involved and had only succeeded in finding work for 15 per cent of applicants, failing to meet its target of 36 per cent. And this was despite the fact that the job was made easier because many of the people entering the programme volunteered to take part rather than being compelled to and were therefore highly motivated to find work.

Under the Coalition government, the Department for Work and Pensions and ministers completely ignored the implications of evidence from this experiment by Labour. They also chose to ignore the poor performance of A4e on the previous programme when allocating contracts to companies in the spring of 2011 for the new Work Programme:

> Richard Bacon: 'Are you seriously saying that you
>   could not take into account the fact that A4e had
>   dreadful performance in the immediate predecessor
>   programme or one of the immediate predecessor
>   programmes?'
> Robert Devereux (permanent secretary of DWP): 'How
>   could I do it fairly under procurement rules?'
> Richard Bacon: 'I'm not asking you to ask me a question.
>   I'm asking you a question to which I'd like a yes or
>   no and I think the answer is—'
> Robert Devereux: 'Is no.'

Both Iain Duncan Smith (as Secretary of State for Work and Pensions) and Chris Grayling (as Employment Minister) were driven by an ideological conviction that the private sector would be more efficient and cheaper than Jobcentre Plus. They had immediately determined to hand over the welfare-to-work advice and support to private companies. They simply charged ahead, driven by hubris and belief rather than evidence. A4e was a major beneficiary of this expanded privatisation programme, becoming the second-largest private provider of the Work Programme.

That is when A4e and Emma Harrison hit my radar again. The company had secured the contract that covered my own constituency and, in preparation for our hearing on the whole Work Programme, for which A4e was coming to give evidence – alongside officials from the Department for Work and Pensions – I visited the company in Barking and Dagenham. A4e had subcontracted the work to a local voluntary organisation, Lifeline, with which I had worked closely down the years. Lifeline had grown out of a local church, under the dedicated, hardworking and ambitious leadership of Avril McIntyre. It had been providing advice and support for unemployed people for years, with contracts from Jobcentre Plus, local colleges and the Skills Agency. When the Work Programme was introduced, the only way it could remain active in this policy area was by becoming a subcontractor to A4e. But the way in which they were forced to work made the job impossible.

Lifeline received an initial payment of £350 from A4e for each client that was referred to them, described as 'the attachment fee'. A4e received a £400 attachment fee from government, but top-sliced £50 each time as a management fee. During my visit to their premises in Barking and Dagenham, I asked A4e's Matthew Jackson what they gave Lifeline for the £50 they top-sliced. He said A4e set up introductions with national employers such as Tesco. But Lifeline already had strong relationships with the local Tesco – they had been placing their unemployed clients there for years. So the £50 of taxpayers' money taken from Lifeline and its clients was a complete rip-off.

In the meantime, the funding was so tight that Lifeline was only able to provide one employment adviser for every 120 clients. On a thirty-six-hour week – and without taking into account training, holidays and sickness – that meant less than twenty minutes for each client, to see them, write up notes about them, send them and their potential employers letters and talk to them and their potential employers on the phone. Matthew Jackson's explanation: 'Much of the training and interaction we provide doesn't have to be on a one-to-one basis; clients can be dealt with in groups.' These were people who had been out of work for six months or more and who were finding it hard to secure a job. It was clear that they were not able to access the appropriate support they needed to help them back to work.

What I saw in my own constituency incensed me: a large private company taking taxpayers' money for minimal effort and yet putting in jeopardy the viability of a good local charity and showing scant concern for the service received by the charity's unemployed clients.

I came straight back from the visit to A4e in Barking and Dagenham to Westminster and asked my assistant to scour the Internet to see what she could find out about A4e. That's how we tracked down the £8.6 million dividend Emma Harrison had paid herself. She was clearly doing very nicely out of the Work Programme and other government contracts: no money for friendly cups of tea for the clients, but large dividends funding plenty of champagne in Thornbridge Hall for the major shareholder.

A week later, on 8 February 2012 at our committee hearing on the Work Programme, I asked the A4e representative a question about the dividend, so placing the issue in the public domain. Revealing that dividend evidently touched a raw nerve with the media and the public. Emma Harrison and A4e were catapulted into the headlines with people crawling all over her company and her lifestyle. From the *Mail* to the *Guardian* and from Channel 4 to the BBC, she found herself in the limelight – for the wrong reasons. One fact, the figure of £8.6 million, uncovered through a quick Internet search, unleashed a torrent of additional information and massive media coverage.

The number of whistleblowers who contacted me was overwhelming: they were people who had worked for A4e and

A4e clients who claimed evidence of malpractice, wrongdoing and poor service. I received an A4e internal audit report full of evidence that A4e staff across the country had been fraudulently filling in forms and timesheets; claiming for placing clients when the work lasted only a couple of days; not providing training that they were claiming to provide; and cutting corners. Whistleblowers also contacted me about other Work Programme companies, in particular Working Links, raising similar concerns of poor practice and potential fraud. Working Links had been established in 2000 as a management buyout from Jobcentre Plus, and had evolved into a major private provider of welfare-to-work services.

Working with my staff, we carefully selected four witnesses from the list of whistleblowers, people who had concerns about both A4e and Working Links. They told strong and credible stories that needed to be heard publicly, with the protection that giving evidence in Parliament affords. The evidence was damning of the entire Work Programme and would have exposed its considerable weaknesses.

That was too much for one of the new Conservative MPs on the committee, who was driven by political ambition. It seemed to me that he was unique on the committee in seeing his role as simply defending his party political interest, not the national interest.

Matthew Hancock told me that he saw his time on the Public Accounts Committee as a training ground for the ministerial office that he succeeded in gaining in 2013. Not yet forty, he was made a member of the Cabinet in 2015, rising on the coat tails of his former boss George Osborne, for whom he had worked before he became a Member of Parliament. Matt Hancock was not universally popular with his Conservative colleagues on the Public Accounts Committee, but because of his close links with the Conservative Party leadership, he was feared and one could always sense the atmosphere when he entered the room.

A public hearing with whistleblowers, which would have seriously damaged the credibility of one of the government's flagship programmes, was not what Hancock or ministers wanted. It was clear to me from widespread, informal discussions that Chris Grayling was particularly active and aggressive in trying to influence the backbenchers on the committee, a practice completely at odds with parliamentary rules.

Parliamentary convention demands that there is no interference by the executive in the workings of select committees; they are and must be seen to be independent of the executive so that the executive is held to proper account by Parliament. This is, of course, impossible to police – but, in my view, the last thing Chris Grayling wanted was a public hearing based on evidence from whistleblowers.

We were all expecting a dramatic hearing. The whistleblowers had demonstrated great bravery in agreeing to give their evidence in public. But the hearing never happened. I was taken unawares by the Conservative members. Matthew Hancock, supported by other Conservatives, used our briefing meeting before the public session to argue that the witnesses should be heard in private. Their weak excuses were that whistleblowers made unreliable witnesses and MPs had not had time to assess the written evidence submitted by the witnesses. With their inbuilt majority, the Conservative members successfully ambushed the committee, got their way and made sure that the public never heard the evidence. As one of the whistleblowers later said: 'It has taken a lot for us to come and speak in public about what we see as fraud. We have been silenced.'

So we heard the evidence in private. Austin Mitchell later remarked in public: 'You have just sat through a long closed session which produced some fairly damning indictments of the structures and the practices in A4e and Working Links and gave several indications of possible fraud.' It was left to the department to investigate those allegations.

The day after our aborted hearing, the papers were full of stories that the committee had been 'gagged following the intervention of Tory MPs'. The press had been sitting outside the room in the committee corridor, waiting for the hearing, so it was pretty straightforward for them to surmise what had happened. No doubt their suspicions were later confirmed by MPs from all sides.

Matthew Hancock was clearly livid that the scheming had been exposed, so again he worked on his party colleagues to present me with an angry letter as we convened for another meeting the following day. In that letter he claimed: 'Yesterday's private session heard many serious claims without any supporting evidence ... Today's press coverage is very concerning, as it shows a clear attempt to politicise the committee' by suggesting 'the witnesses were "gagged".' The letter demanded all sorts of public statements from me denying the gagging of witnesses, but once the story was in the public domain, such statements would have been pointless, and, in my view, untrue.

This was one of the very rare occasions in my time on the Public Accounts Committee when partisan interest ran counter to the public interest. Fortunately Matthew Hancock's rapid promotion to ministerial office meant there were few other occasions when crude party politics interfered with the work of the committee.

The Department for Work and Pensions claimed to have investigated the whistleblower allegations and found them to be untrue. But the accusations were so many in number and so consistent in the stories they told that it is hard to believe that they all proved unfounded. It was left to the media to publicise the stories. Channel 4 got hold of a leaked report which showed that of the 93,000 individuals referred to A4e in the first twelve months of the programme, only 3400 (3.6 per cent) found sustained work, despite A4e collecting £46 million in attachment fees – that crudely translates to £13,500 of public money for each person who found a sustainable job.

The *Daily Mail* and the *Mail on Sunday* undertook extensive investigative work around the country. They tracked down Amy Rae, who had worked in A4e's Edinburgh office and who told the journalists that she had never been given any money to train her clients and so had no option but to send them home. 'There was nothing we could do with these young people. It was heart-breaking because these were unemployed eighteen- to twenty-four-year-olds, full of hope, desperate to get training so they could get a job. They believed we could help them.' When inspectors from the Department for Work and Pensions arrived: 'I had to stage-manage a completely bogus training session, complete with a fake chart. It was awful. It was all lies, a façade. We just pretended.' She also alleged that A4e claimed taxpayers' money for finding people jobs that lasted just a few days: 'People would be found a job on a construction site that only lasted a day and that was enough to claim the money. It was easy because there was just a tick-box on the form to say that the job was "expected to last at least 13 weeks", but often labourers were being put out of work again after twenty-four hours.' Similar allegations against A4e were made by staff in Bradford, Woolwich and Newcastle.

Finally in March 2015, ten A4e employees who worked in Slough were convicted of fraudulent activity. Six of these former employees were jailed and the other four got suspended prison sentences for what Judge Angela Morris called 'deceitful and unscrupulous practices'. They had claimed 558 successful job outcomes for claimants, but nearly a third of the claims were fake, with employer details, timesheets and job-seeker signatures falsified to inflate the numbers. They even offered bribes to penniless claimants to get them to complete bogus forms.

But these employees were not operating in isolation. A4e had created what I felt was a bullying culture where all that mattered was achieving the numbers and the payments. Employees told us that they worked in a highly pressurised environment where they were expected to hit impossible targets. At the trial of the Slough staff, Steven Pidcock, representing fifty-two-year-old Julie Grimes, said: 'She was immersed in a culture of dishonesty that she didn't have the moral fibre to resist. It doesn't start from the roots – this sort of thing starts from the top of the tree.' A far cry from 'doing well by doing good'.

After she was exposed, Emma Harrison was forced to resign as the Prime Minister's champion for troubled families and she had to give up her ambition to become the chair of the Institute of Directors. She also resigned as chair of A4e (although she kept her shares) and was replaced by Sir Robin Young. I had known Robin Young as a civil servant since the 1980s. I first came across him as the person in charge of implementing the much-hated poll tax. He failed to stand up to ministers on that issue and so ingratiated his way up the Civil Service ladder, finally becoming permanent secretary at the Department of Trade and Industry.

Appointing somebody who had been a senior civil servant and a member of the club to chair A4e at that particular moment was a clever move to help secure the continuation of government contracts. Indeed, within a fortnight of Emma Harrison stepping down as chair of the company, A4e was awarded a £30 million contract by the Skills Funding Agency to provide education in prisons. The company is now active in the newly privatised probation service market.

In 2015, A4e was sold to Staffline Group for £34.5 million. With her 85 per cent share holding, Emma Harrison is likely to have walked away with millions. Staffline immediately realised that the A4e brand was too contaminated and changed the name to PeoplePlus. PeoplePlus still has nine of the forty contracts on the Work Programme.

A4e may have provided the most dramatic moments as we scrutinised the government's Work Programme, but the way the company worked was symptomatic of the intrinsic problems that the programme faced. The government awarded forty contracts to eighteen large contractors under the Work Programme banner. The company that was awarded most work was Deloitte-Ingeus. This was a joint venture between the welfare-to-work provider Ingeus and the big accountancy firm Deloitte. Deloitte made non-cash donations to the Conservative Party to the value of £450,000. Chris Grayling, who was the minister responsible for awarding the Work Programme contracts, had himself received £27,978 as a 'donation in kind' from Deloitte in 2009.

The government was also guilty of wasting £63 million of taxpayers' money terminating existing contracts associated with delivering the Flexible New Deal programme, which they had inherited from the Labour government. In some instances the contractors who were compensated for the termination of their Flexible New Deal contracts were the same companies that were awarded new contracts under the Work Programme. A4e, for example, got paid compensation for the closure of the Flexible New Deal and was then awarded a new Work Programme contract in the same geographical area.

The government had high expectations of the Work Programme. Previous efforts to provide advice and support to the unemployed had resulted in about one in four clients (25 per cent) securing work. Ministers claimed that the success rate of this new programme would be 36 per cent – the target that A4e would fail to reach – yet private providers were confident they could exceed this, predicting a 38 per cent success rate.

The first participants joined the programme in June 2011. It had taken years to set up previous programmes; this one was introduced in twelve months. The business case was only constructed after the key decisions to proceed had been taken; there was no piloting and no consideration given to alternative ways of achieving the same objectives. The IT programme, which was essential to check private contractors' claims that they had placed people in work against the benefit records, was only put in place a year after the programme had started.

Rushing into action without proper planning, intelligent use of evidence and appropriate infrastructure in place inevitably leads to wasted expenditure. The official responsible for setting up the Work Programme, Alan Cave, left before full implementation of the policy. He joined one of the Department for Work and Pensions' main contractors, Serco.

It was the ideological conviction of the two key ministers Chris Grayling and Iain Duncan Smith that forced the pace. They believed that payment by results and private companies running the programme was the way to go, and would save money and result in better outcomes. Their determination to be proved right created a dangerous culture in the department, in which uncomfortable truths were kept hidden and only good news was permitted.

Both the National Audit Office and the Social Market Foundation reported that the government's predictions for the programme were over-optimistic. Ian Mulhearn of the Social Market Foundation, a recognised authority on welfare-to-work policy, wrote in January 2012: 'The Department said it expected providers to get some 40 per cent of the main client group into work, the NAO say past experience (in a better economic environment) suggests that they'll only achieve 26 per cent. This backs up a similar analysis we undertook back in August 2011 estimating the performance would be 27.8 per cent. At the time Chris Grayling tried to brush off our figures on the *Today* programme and he's doing the same with the NAO.'

Indeed, Chris Grayling said of the NAO report: 'I'm really disappointed that the NAO is producing a report which is partially based on guesswork, when it's private companies and not taxpayers who are carrying the risks.'

So determined were ministers to be proved right that they refused to allow anybody to see the early figures that would have allowed people to judge for themselves. Any guesswork was the direct result of the department's determination to keep the data secret. Private contractors were sworn to secrecy, as this exchange at our first hearing on the Work Programme shows. When asked if they were reaching the 40 per cent target in terms of putting people into work, Geraldine Blake (chief executive, Community Links) replied: 'No. I don't think that I am actually allowed to tell you what our performance is. Is that right?'

> Baroness Stedman-Scott (chief executive, Tomorrow's
> People): 'Under the terms of our contracts—'
> MH: 'ERSA [the Employment Related Services
> Association] published something and it is the trade
> association.'
> Baroness Stedman-Scott: 'In that case, I respectfully
> ask you to speak to ERSA. In the confines of the
> contract that we have signed, we are unable to give
> you detailed information.'

Richard Bacon: 'You are contractually prohibited from
    stating what your performance is?'
Baroness Stedman–Scott: 'That is correct, sir.'

Even charities that worked as subcontractors had to sign a
contract saying they would 'not do anything which may attract
adverse publicity' and 'shall not make any press announcements or publicise the contract in any way'.

Shrouding the programme in secrecy did not stop ministers
making upbeat claims for it. Chris Grayling had form on the
misuse of statistics, having in 2010 tried to exaggerate violent
crime statistics which in the view of Sir Michael Scholar, the
head of the UK's Statistics Authority, was 'likely to damage
public trust in official statistics'.

So when ERSA, the trade body representing the private
providers, issued its own figures, claiming that one in five
people who had been on the programme for six months had
found work, Chris Grayling said on BBC Radio 4's *PM* show:
'The Work Programme is doing a good job and is on track. It
is helping long-term unemployed people into work.'

ERSA's figures were wrong. Indeed, Chris Grayling so
riled Sir Michael Scholar by using ERSA's figures that Sir
Michael wrote to the minister saying: 'We would regard it
as unacceptable if attention were distracted from the official
statistics release by proximate release of more detailed data
or of selective early disclosure of data designed to deliver a
political message.'

When the official statistics were finally published before
Christmas in 2012, they painted a different picture. In the first
fourteen months, only 3.6 per cent of claimants on the programme moved off benefit and into sustained employment, less
than a third of the 11.9 per cent the DWP expected to achieve
in the first year, with not one of the eighteen private providers

meeting their contractual commitments. The department was forced to admit that if there had been no programme at all and no expenditure incurred, it would have expected 9.2 per cent of the claimants to find a job and move off benefits by their own efforts. So hundreds of millions of pounds was being wasted to little or no effect.

The government simply refused to confront the reality. When the national statistics were published, their press release was astonishing. 'Tens of thousands of long-term unemployed are getting off benefits and into jobs through the government's Work Programme,' they proclaimed. The new Minister for Employment, Mark Hoban, trumpeted that the 'Work Programme is succeeding in getting people off benefits and into work'.

The truth was that 31,000 of the 877,880 people referred to the Work Programme had found work and that represented 3.6 per cent. To this day it is unclear as to whether ministers and civil servants were deliberately misleading the public or whether they simply believed their own rhetoric.

Substantial evidence was available. For example, the Department for Work and Pensions carried out their own evaluation of the first phase of the Work Programme, which was eventually published when the official statistics were revealed. This report made two strong points, arguing first that there was not enough money to provide proper individualised support to claimants and second that this led to private providers 'creaming' off those who needed least help and 'parking' those who needed most help, without giving them any support.

'Providers' resource constraints are impacting on the level of service,' the report went on. 'Available evidence to date suggests that providers are engaging in creaming and parking, despite the differential payment regime. Those assessed as hardest-to-help are in many cases left with infrequent routine contact with advisers and often with little or no likelihood of referral to specialist and possibly costly support.'

Ministers and senior civil servants simply denied that this was happening. The voluntary sector, which had traditionally played an important role in providing welfare-to-work support in local communities, had been promised a substantial amount of work under the new programme. Cabinet Office Minister Francis Maude said that 35–40 per cent of the value of the contracts would go to voluntary organisations. Both the National Council for Voluntary Organisations and the Association of Chief Executives for Voluntary Organisations submitted clear evidence that the voluntary sector was not getting referrals and that many had had to shut down their welfare-to-work units. In Barking and Dagenham, Lifeline withdrew from the contract with A4e.

Stories abounded about how poor and inappropriate the service was. For example, claimants were made to do so-called work experience, for which they received no money, but if they refused to comply they were threatened with losing their benefits. This ploy was exploited by companies which, in effect, enjoyed free labour from the work experience.

One plucky claimant, Cait Reilly, a twenty-four-year-old geology graduate, hit the press when she challenged the department in the courts – and won. She wanted to work as a curator and had sensibly and luckily secured voluntary work in a local museum to strengthen her CV. But her Work Programme provider insisted that she took up a work experience post in Poundland stacking shelves and told her she would lose her benefits if she turned down the offer. Similarly an HGV driver from Nottingham, Jamie Wilson, was expected to work thirty hours a week for nothing for six months stripping furniture; all he wanted was another driving job. Both claimants won their cases. When Chris Grayling was challenged on the *Today* programme about these inappropriate placements, he just denied that they were happening: 'There is no circumstance in which we would mandate any individual to take part in work activity for a big company. That doesn't happen.' It did, and the government then tried to introduce retrospective legislation to overturn the court's judgements. That retrospective legislation was found to be flawed by the High Court in the summer of 2014.

Over five years, from the start of the programme in June 2011, the department only terminated the contract of one contractor, the Newcastle College Group, which was delivering the Work Programme in North Yorkshire. At one point the department estimated that flawed contracts meant that they had paid £11 million in bonuses to companies 'for performance they may not have actually achieved'. And, of course, the department dismissed the accusations made by the whistleblowers and took no action against the companies about whom concerns had been expressed to members of the Public Accounts Committee.

The most recent national statistics show that between June 2011 and June 2015, just 26.9 per cent of claimants referred to the Work Programme had been in work for three or six months. In fact, 70 per cent of claimants for whom the providers secured payment from the government have returned to jobcentres and gone back on to benefits.

The success rate for the Work Programme is similar to that of previous programmes, like the Flexible New Deal, which were terminated at great cost to taxpayers. Its performance remains far below the ambitions and expectations set by ministers in 2010. Billions of pounds have been spent on the Work Programme. Those who face the most difficult barriers to getting a job, such as the thousands with long-term mental health conditions, have had scant help. One of my constituents, a man in his fifties with a mental health condition, has been on benefits for years. 'I would love to work,' he says. 'I always run out of money at the end of the month. I am not a benefit scrounger. With my condition I just can't get a job.' The Work Programme has failed him and it has certainly not passed the test of providing value for money to the taxpayer.

14

Pig-Headedness and the Public Purse

B ut the Department for Work and Pensions is the scene of other disasters. All too often pig-headedness has cost the taxpayer dear.

The attempt to introduce Universal Credit represents the highest-profile story of waste in that department. It was a flagship programme for Iain Duncan Smith. As with the Work Programme, ministers appeared unable to accept any responsibility for the problems, simply blaming officials when things went wrong. Civil servants dealt with the unrealistic ambitions of ministers by creating a fortress culture from which only 'feel-good' stories were released, while difficulties were hidden. The public and Parliament were denied access to the facts, with the department running to the courts to resist freedom of information requests.

And of course the whole project was riddled with the usual characteristics that lead to failure: lack of proper planning; a failure to see the project as a massive transformation project rather than simply a new IT venture; a failure to address the complexities involved; lack of consistent and good leadership; unrealistic timetables; and so on.

Iain Duncan Smith approached the introduction of Universal Credit with missionary zeal. It may be that George Osborne got it right when, according to the journalist Matthew D'Ancona, he said: 'You see Iain give presentations and realise he's just not clever enough.'

The basic concept of a Universal Credit is not politically controversial. At present government runs six separate working-age benefits, from Jobseeker's Allowance to working tax credit, child tax credit, income support, housing benefit and disability benefits. The system is complicated and cumbersome for both the customers, who may have to claim several benefits, and the government, which has to administer several separate benefits. In 2012–13, there were thirteen million claims for these benefits and the government spent £67 billion. It may seem completely logical to merge the six benefits into one single working-age benefit, and that is what Universal Credit attempts to do. With one benefit it should become much easier to make sure that the benefit system works to provide good incentives to encourage people into work.

As Employment Minister I had considered this option but decided not to attempt the merger because it was hugely complicated, enormously risky and unpredictably expensive. All of the six benefits have different rules and use different systems; integrating such complex systems is a mammoth task that would impact on millions of people and cost billions of pounds.

Alistair Darling also toyed with the idea, as he told a struggling Iain Duncan Smith, who had been brought to the House of Commons to explain himself after a highly critical National Audit Office report was published in the autumn of 2013. Darling asked Duncan Smith: 'Like many Secretaries of State for Work and Pensions, I looked at something like universal credit some twelve years ago and I was advised then that it was technically very difficult, if not impossible, to implement it at anything like an acceptable cost and that whatever cost I was quoted, it was likely that it would end up costing an awful lot more. I have listened to the right honourable gentleman this morning claiming that this project is on track and on budget, which I find extraordinary when the NAO says that it is anything but that. I have also listened to him blaming all those around him for letting him down, so will he tell us what advice he received when he gave this the go-ahead in 2010?'

In response, the stubborn minister, deaf to all criticism, told the ex-Chancellor: 'I intend to deliver it on budget and on time.'

The department published a white paper on Universal Credit within six months of the 2010 General Election and embarked on the design and build in January 2011. At that time they planned to introduce Universal Credit in just two years, by 2013. It is extraordinary that the permanent Civil Service failed to insist on a realistic timetable and appeared to fail to understand the complexity of the transformation. The avuncular Sir Leigh Lewis was permanent secretary in the department in 2010, but he was about to retire and probably only stayed in post to help with the transition to a new government after the 2010 General Election. He was always anxious to please his ministers and was probably obsequious rather than straight in his dealings with politicians. Because of the secrecy that surrounds discussions on new policies, we will never know whether Leigh Lewis simply failed to warn Iain Duncan Smith that Universal Credit could not be delivered in the timescale and in the way envisaged or whether the obstinate Duncan Smith ignored the advice and naively believed that when he commanded something to happen, it would.

There were regular rumblings around Westminster that

the Universal Credit project was a potential car crash. Civil servants would raise their eyebrows and ministers would give you a knowing look. It has now emerged that there were many internal reviews, all of which gave clear warnings that things were going wrong. The recently established Major Projects Authority, created to provide independent assurance of all major government projects, and the internal audit within the Department for Work and Pensions reported in March 2011, November 2011, April 2012, September 2012, January 2013, February 2013 and April 2013. The IT suppliers and contractors reviewed progress in July 2012, January 2013 and February 2013. PricewaterhouseCoopers reviewed the financial controls in April 2013. In February 2013, after pressure from the Cabinet Office and the Treasury, the department had to 'reset' the project: that is, halt it and start again.

But it was only when the National Audit Office published its report and we held our hearing in September 2013 that the lid started to be lifted on what was really happening. The Audit Office and our inquiry revealed a litany of failure. By April 2013, £425 million had been spent, with £303 million going to four IT suppliers that had been contracted to design and build the Universal Credit systems. The National Audit Office said in its report: 'Throughout the programme, the department has lacked a detailed view of how Universal Credit is meant to work. The department was warned repeatedly about the lack of a detailed "blueprint", "architecture" or "target operating model" for Universal Credit.'

Basically the Department for Work and Pensions approached the project as if it were an IT assignment rather than a business transformation venture. The new systems costing £303 million were not fit for purpose. So when the department started trialling Universal Credit in April 2013, the system could only deal with the most straightforward and simple claim from a single person, someone who had no family and no disability, and who was only entitled to Jobseeker's Allowance. The system could not tackle the benefit claim of a family, a lone parent, a disabled claimant; it could not cope with any change in the claimant's circumstances, although the new system, once it was up and running, would have to deal with an estimated 1.6 million changes reported each month. It was not capable of tracking whether claimants were meeting all the conditionality obligations to ensure continued eligibility for benefit (claimants had to demonstrate that they were trying to get work); the system was not secure and could not protect claimants' personal details, being susceptible to fraud and cyber attacks.

The governance arrangements were hopelessly inadequate. The permanent secretary, Robert Devereux, who had come into the job at the beginning of 2011, admitted that he only saw the project leader every two to three weeks, and Iain Duncan Smith claimed to have been unaware of any problems until he received the IT suppliers' report in the summer of 2013. By the time we saw the civil servants, there had been five different people in charge. One of the officials had to withdraw on the grounds of ill health and another, Philip Langsdale, tragically died three months into the job. The lack of continuity in leadership clearly did not help.

The PricewaterhouseCoopers report on financial controls (given to me on the night before our hearing) revealed a shocking failure to control expenditure, with the Department for Work and Pensions, in effect, issuing blank cheques to contractors. Accenture and IBM received 65 per cent of the £303 million spent on IT contractors. They were paid on a 'time and materials' basis, submitting one-line invoices, with the department having no information on which to measure performance. The department simply could not

link payments to results as most of the management information required to do this was owned and controlled by
the suppliers. Ministerial approval was not consistently
sought, and PricewaterhouseCoopers found that in a sample
of twenty-five contracts over £25,000 that they examined,
ministerial approval had only been obtained in eleven cases.
PricewaterhouseCoopers also revealed that personal assistants
authorised purchase orders, although they had no authority to
do so. In one case a PA completed a purchase order for £8.7
million and in another case a PA completed two purchase
orders – one for £1.1 million and another for £22.6 million –
when the delegated financial approval limit for her boss, the
programme director, was £10 million. PwC also reported
that the department had spent over £30 million on licences
it did not need.

We tried to establish how much of the £303 million would
have to be written off. Getting to the truth proved impossible.
The department admitted writing off £34 million. But they
continued, and continue, to use the other systems that are not
fit for purpose while trying to develop new digital systems. By
using these inadequate systems, they can claim they have not
written off the investment. In my view, that is not the whole
truth; if the department ever achieves a working digital system
for all claimants, they will scrap most of the £303 million
already spent on systems that did not deliver what was needed.

We were able to uncover many of the problems – but almost
certainly not all of them – in three ways. Clearly the National
Audit Office report provided us with solid evidence. We also
received a brown envelope containing a memo written to
Iain Duncan Smith by the consultant who had been brought
in from the Cabinet Office to rescue the project. The author
of the memo was Dr Norma Wood, a formidable individual,
clever and straight talking, who had extensive experience in

running big projects and transformation programmes in the private sector.

It was she who had persuaded the government in February 2013 to stop and start again if they wanted to implement Universal Credit successfully. It was on the basis of her advice that the programme was euphemistically 'reset'. The memo was far clearer about how much money had been wasted paying suppliers for IT than the DWP officials had been in the evidence they gave to the committee. Some of the language is technical but Dr Wood argued that 'the Pathfinder technology platform will not support Universal Credit in the future'. (The pathfinders involved testing the new systems and new technology in a limited number of locations across the country. She was basically saying that the £303 million-worth of new technology used in the trials would not work nationally.) Dr Wood went on: 'Pathfinder had no agreed and aligned High-level Business, Application, Data, Security and Infrastructure Technical architectures and no traceability to strategic objectives and policy intent. Pathfinder has been substantially de-scoped and compromised so that it is not fit for purpose.'

She went on to assess what she called 'nugatory spend' – worthless waste of money – and concluded: 'But the order of magnitude of the nugatory spend is substantial and is possibly in the region of £60–£100 million in addition to the £101 million identified at the time of the Major Projects Review Group [one of the review groups].'

That leaked memo revealed, at best, a lack of transparency by the Department for Work and Pensions or, at worst, deliberate attempts by all concerned to mislead the public and Parliament on the true costs and real waste associated with the mismanagement of this project. The memo had been sent in May 2012, well before the publication of the National Audit

Office report and only a few weeks after Iain Duncan Smith had answered a parliamentary question on Universal Credit, claiming: 'The implementation of Universal Credit is proceeding exactly in accordance with plans.'

Dr Wood gave evidence to our inquiry in September and was refreshingly honest.

Norma Wood: 'The pathfinder was actually designed before we did the reset. One of the reasons why we had to do the reset was that there were a number of issues. For example, the pathfinder could not handle changes of circumstance. It was very narrow in scope. It was only for single people who were unemployed, so there were no couples or any of the other arrangements. It did not cover changes of circumstance, which had to be handled manually. When we designed the steady-state, we designed it for 10 million people – about 7.5 million households – and there are 1.6 million changes per month, so it was important that that was included ... The second thing was that it did not include ... conditionality – what we call the to-do list, to try to keep it straightforward. This is where the claimant agrees to make a commitment to do certain things in response to benefits, so it is absolutely at the heart of the policy intent ... There were also security issues with the pathfinder. It hadn't included elements that were really important. When I say security, I mean three things: fraud and error, cyber-security and identity ... I guess the other thing to add – then I will pause – is that the programme was not conceived as a business transformation programme. It was very IT-driven, and this is a major change in business operations.'

Later Richard Bacon asked her: 'Have you described the pathfinder as having been so substantially de-scoped and compromised that it is not fit for purpose?'

Norma Wood replied: 'I think at the time we did the review, that was our conclusion ... Unless it can handle the functionality that we have just described – the 1.6 million changes, putting work upfront and centre, and handling couples – I fail to see how it can be scalable.'

Norma Wood had been brought into the Civil Service on a temporary basis. She was one of the most honest, clear and capable people we interviewed. She could and should have been offered a permanent job overseeing major government projects. But, as I shall discuss in the chapter on Civil Service reform, the permanent civil servants are not good at accepting outsiders. Protecting their own takes precedence over securing the best people to do the job and openness is not regarded as the best policy by many civil servants.

Ministers were determined not to take the blame for the shambles. Speaking on the *Today* programme on the morning of the publication of the critical National Audit Office report, Iain Duncan Smith said: 'I fully accept, because I could've written this report myself that the problem was that those charged with actually putting together the detail of the IT – I'm not a technologist and nor are you, we rely on people telling us, that that is correct – did not make the correct decisions.' Later, on the same day, in Parliament he said: 'The reality is that today's NAO report shows there were problems in the running of this programme. I intervened when I discovered that and changed it, but I never expected to have to do that. When I arrived I expected the professionals to be able to do this properly.'

The determination to blame officials went further, as I soon discovered. Ministers wanted to use the National Audit Office document and our Public Accounts Committee report to sack Work and Pensions' permanent secretary, Robert Devereux.

Iain Duncan Smith and people close to him privately approached the Conservative members of the committee to ask them to make sure we placed the blame fairly and squarely on the permanent secretary's shoulders. If our report was strongly critical of Devereux, this would give ministers the ammunition to fire him.

I received several phone calls too, one from a minister supporting the campaign to sack Robert Devereux and one from the Cabinet Secretary trying to make sure I stayed out of that particular battle and did not use the report to undermine his staff. Devereux also asked to see me, but I thought that would be completely inappropriate.

Devereux is a difficult character, extremely bright but irritatingly cocky. He used his performances at the Public Accounts Committee to avoid answering questions directly and fully, and to demonstrate how clever he was at deviating from the matter and using statistics to obscure the truth. He was not my favourite witness. I also thought he had shown incompetence in his stewardship of the Universal Credit programme. He was the accounting officer; he had failed to monitor progress properly and thus identify the early warning signs; he did not know that he was only being given 'good news' by his staff and that the reality was hidden from him; he was ultimately responsible for the lax authorisation of expenditure to contractors. But that did not mean that he alone should take the blame.

During the hearing Devereux was careful to tell us that the Secretary of State knew as much as he did, at the same time as he did [my italics here and below]:

'The message on that review in July, which was the critical thing *for me and the Secretary of State*.'

'Were there things that became apparent, particularly *to me and the Secretary of State*.'

'We were envisaging, and we consciously knew – *the Secretary of State knew this*.'

'It was that which caused *me and the Secretary of State* to decide . . .'

Ministers were also to blame, he was telling us. They had set an impossible task within a ridiculous timetable. They really thought that if they showed strong and determined political will about a policy it would magically happen.

But it was wrong for ministers to try to influence a parliamentary committee and it was wrong for them to try to use us to dismiss a civil servant. It was an important moment for the committee to demonstrate our independence and integrity, and it is a real tribute to my Conservative colleagues that they resisted the strong pressure to do the minister's dirty work for him. We all felt everybody was responsible for the mess and that is what we concluded in our report.

If ministers really believed that the permanent secretary was not up to the job, they should have had the guts to sack him directly. Instead, Robert Devereux has recently been awarded a knighthood. The fact that he is still in post, working with a new minister, tells us a lot about the relative power of ministers and civil servants, an issue to which I shall return – and demonstrates yet again the difficulty of holding people properly to account for mis-spending our money.

The Public Accounts Committee returned regularly to look at Universal Credit. We were determined to try to hold the Department for Work and Pensions to account for this £2.4 billion project. When we held our final session just before the 2015 General Election, the department had spent £700 million and yet fewer than 18,000 claimants – 0.3 per cent of the eligible population – were receiving Universal Credit. Remember, the scheme was originally supposed to be fully implemented by 2013. Yet another new person had taken charge of the project, Neil Couling, who was appointed at the end of 2014.

Ministers continued to deny the ongoing difficulties. Mark Harper, who had become Minister of State for Disabled People by then, said that he had spoken to front-line staff at the hundred service centres rolling out Universal Credit and received 'nothing but positive feedback'.

Iain Duncan Smith continued to be somewhat economical with the truth. He was asked a question in the House of Commons in November 2014 by the Conservative Nigel Mills MP, who said: 'I welcome the progress announced in the Secretary of State's statement. Will he confirm that the Treasury has now signed off *the whole business case* and laid to rest the fear that it was not going to do so?'

To which the minister replied: 'That is exactly what was being asked before the summer break and the answer is that *the Treasury has done that.*'

When, a couple of weeks later, officials gave evidence to us on Universal Credit, Sharon White, then the second permanent secretary at the Treasury, explained that the Treasury had not signed off on the project: 'It took until September 2014 to agree the strategic outline business case . . . I don't think we have agreed with the department a date for the final business case.'

When I asked her: 'Just to be absolutely clear, all you have signed off is the strategic business case?' she replied: 'That's right . . . I do not want to put a date on it because it is not something we have agreed with the department or with ministers.'

The Department for Work and Pensions has now adopted a twin-track approach and is running two systems. In their final hearing with us, they admitted that if the digital system does eventually work – if they finally succeed – they will still have to write off most of the £344 million early investment in IT. Another commentator, Rory Cellan-Jones, the BBC's technology correspondent, believes that a further £100 million will be spent to keep the old system going, bringing the bill to around £450 million. Finally the National Audit Office, in a little-read footnote to their report at the end of 2014, says: 'The Department . . . plans to complete moving areas on to new digital systems by December 2017. We estimate that the total inefficiency in the Department's planned use of live service to this date will be around £150 million in staff costs . . . This does not include the costs of [the old] IT systems' maintenance.' So the estimates of wasted expenditure are currently around £600 million.

The project remains years away from being delivered, and further delays, with the costs that brings, are inevitable. The Office for Budget Responsibility showed their scepticism in their latest forecast report when they wrote: 'In our view there remains considerable uncertainty around the delivery of such a complex and wide-ranging change. On the basis of the evidence we have reviewed, we judge that . . . the second part of the roll out is more uncertain . . . and we have assumed for this forecast that it will be delayed by a further six months beyond the new plans.'

The last words on this saga belong to two eminent and experienced men; sadly they only spoke publicly after they had left government. One was Baron Bob Kerslake, a senior civil servant who had been a very successful local authority chief executive in Sheffield, but who, like other outsiders, could not survive within the Civil Service and was retired as head of the Home Civil Service in 2015 by being given a peerage. He was a very honest, unassuming and effective administrator. He reportedly told the Institute for Government that Universal Credit was 'undeliverable' in the timetable originally set out by the DWP but that 'this was not recognised at the time by the department, because of a prevailing culture of deference within the Civil Service'.

The other comments were made by Lord John Browne, the ex-chief executive of BP, who had first come into government under Tony Blair. I had worked with him on the tuition fees policy when I was Minister for Higher Education and had always found him to be incredibly bright, quick and able to provide excellent and helpful analysis and insights into any issue. He had been the lead non-executive Civil Service director for the Coalition government. When he resigned at the end of 2014, he gave an interview to the *Financial Times* in which he referred to Universal Credit as 'one example of a major project going awry ... You have to do much more analysis and planning in order to set both a financial and a time target. That takes a lot of skill and it takes a lot of work. And with political announcements, sometimes these political announcements are made with insufficient analysis behind them. As was the case with Universal Credit.' Pig-headedness triumphed and money from the public purse was squandered.

15

Other People's Money

On 10 November 2012, George Entwistle agreed to resign as director-general of the BBC. He had been in the job for just fifty-four days, but had worked for the BBC for over twenty years. He left because he had been unable to provide effective leadership when the BBC was rocked by a major crisis arising from its failure to deal properly with Jimmy Savile's decades of sexual abuse of young children.

Yet Entwistle walked away with a severance payment of £450,000, double his contractual entitlement, plus the legal costs incurred in agreeing this pay-off. He was awarded a further £107,000 to pay the legal and other costs related to his appearance as a witness at the Pollard Inquiry into the Jimmy Savile affair. He was granted £6000 to cover PR costs spent protecting him from journalists door-stepping him during this crisis and he was granted a further twelve months of medical insurance. All funded by licence fee payers.

George Entwistle went for everything he could get. He was leaving because of his failure and he knew that everything he took was paid for by the public through the licence fee. Instead of pursuing unbridled self-interest, he should have shown greater dignity and reflected on the impact his actions would have on the reputation of the BBC. He could have accepted less or he could have returned some of the money when public fury at the pay-offs was unleashed.

But his was not an isolated case. As the Public Accounts Committee started to ask questions about George Entwistle's severance package, we uncovered a longstanding culture and an expectation at the top of the BBC that senior executives had an unquestionable right to walk away with hundreds of thousands of pounds of licence fee payers' money when they quit.

Examining only three years to December 2012, we found that 150 senior managers had received severance payments, the total cost of which was £25 million; 22 had been paid more in lieu of their notice than they were contractually entitled to. This money, spent on getting rid of staff, could have funded Radio 4 for four months or Radio 1 for eight months.

These revelations shocked us all. They were the clearest example of how irresponsible people in the public sector can be with other people's money – our money.

Unless and until everybody in the public sector takes decisions about spending other people's money in the same way as they take decisions about spending their own money, waste will be rife. The story of the BBC pay-offs is a dramatic illustration of the 'other people's money' culture, but it is far from unique. We came across similar stories in the National Health Service, in which managers accepted huge pay-offs and then immediately took another lucrative job in another part of the NHS. We found examples among private companies delivering public services with the taxpayer's pound, where excessive profits, bonuses and dividends were paid out. And, of course, we are all familiar with the scandal of bankers' huge bonuses after the banks were bailed out by the taxpayer.

It was a tragedy that a British institution that is so loved and valued, that is rich in talent and widely acclaimed as the world's leading public service broadcaster, should inflict such damage on itself. Yet it did and I think it happened largely because the top executives lost sight of their responsibility to act as guardians of the public purse. In the present director-general Tony Hall's words, 'We lost the plot.'

During Entwistle's short-lived tenure as D–G, the BBC was plunged into one of the greatest crises it has ever faced. It had emerged that *Newsnight* had dropped investigations into allegations of sexual abuse of children by Jimmy Savile, investigations that later rocked the nation when they were broadcast on ITV. Entwistle responded by asking the editor of *Newsnight* to 'step aside' while inquiries were conducted into why the BBC investigations were abandoned.

A bruised *Newsnight* team, keen to restore their damaged reputation, then decided to show a film they were offered by the Bureau of Investigative Journalism and the reporter Angus Stickler, which alleged that a senior Conservative of the Thatcher era (later revealed to be Lord McAlpine) had sexually abused children in a care home in Wales. No sooner was the programme shown than the alleged victim, on whose evidence the report was based, said that the person he had previously identified as Lord McAlpine was not the man who had abused him. He said: 'I'd like to offer my sincere and humble apologies to Lord McAlpine. That certainly is not the man that abused me.'

All hell broke loose. It emerged that the later discredited journalist had not shown the victim a picture of Lord McAlpine; he had not corroborated the story by finding other victims; he had not put the allegations to Lord McAlpine.

George Entwistle failed to get a grip of the crisis. He gave a disastrous interview to John Humphrys on the *Today* programme, when he admitted that he 'found out about the programme after it went out' because he 'was out', and that a tweet trailing that *Newsnight* was going to reveal that a top Conservative from the Thatcher era had sexually abused children in a care home 'was not brought to [his] attention'. He also admitted that he hadn't known the alleged victim would retract his evidence until after the victim made the statement, although the story revealing the retraction had already appeared on the front page of the *Guardian* that morning. Entwistle claimed he was busy preparing a speech and hadn't read the *Guardian*: 'when something is referred to me and brought to my attention I engage with it,' he pleaded in justification.

He had to go, but did he deserve such a generous pay-off?

Both the Public Accounts Committee and the Culture, Media and Sport Committee took evidence on George Entwistle's pay-off. After the evidence session in November 2012, our committee agreed to look more widely at pay-offs in the BBC. While this investigation was taking place, we learned that the BBC had failed to give us a full account of Entwistle's financial settlement. He had been given yet more – a further £25,000 for twenty days' work between the date his resignation was announced and his actual day of departure. He hadn't worked during those twenty days, because both Tim Davie, who immediately became acting director-general, and Tony Hall, who was appointed within twelve days, did not need him. Yet he still walked away with another £25,000.

Stewart Jackson MP reflected the views of the committee when he said in our second session with the BBC in the following July: 'Entwistle was paid more or less the equivalent of what one of my constituents earns as an average annual salary. What did he actually do in those twenty days?'

Lord Patten, the chair of the BBC Trust who had negotiated the severance package, replied, 'Very little.'

An exasperated Jackson came back with: 'So you paid the outgoing director-general £25,000 of public money to sit on his backside and do nothing for twenty days, and you are quite happy that that is a satisfactory and appropriate use of licence payers' funds?'

This 'oversight' by the BBC turned out to be par for the course. During the ensuing months we uncovered more evidence of a cavalier attitude to licence fee payers' money. We tried to establish who was responsible for negotiating the deals and who was accountable for signing them off. People blamed each other, changed their story, suddenly found documents they had previously said didn't exist and remembered conversations they originally claimed had never taken place.

The BBC's governance structure is complex and has proved unfit for purpose. Put in place by Labour after the tragic death of Dr David Kelly, it will now be changed yet again, in part because of the Jimmy Savile cover-up and in part because our hearings revealed its weaknesses. The BBC has a paid executive led by a director-general with non-executives who sit on the executive board and chair the remuneration committee. The BBC Trust is a separate body that is there to provide strategic oversight and represent the licence fee payers' interest. The blurring of the roles of the executives, the non-executives and the Trust enabled everybody to try to pass the buck.

We held three hearings on the BBC pay-offs. In the first, we concentrated on the Entwistle pay-off. In the second hearing in July 2013, we looked at all the senior management severance and redundancy deals.

After the second hearing I got so fed up with the inconsistent and conflicting stories that I decided the only way to establish the truth was to hold a third hearing and call all the key people to give evidence together. So on 9 September 2013, they all sat together in front of the committee, seven senior figures: Mark Thompson, the former director-general; Marcus Agius, former chairman of the BBC executive board remuneration committee; Lord Patten, chairman of the BBC Trust; Anthony Fry, BBC trustee; Sir Michael Lyons, former BBC Trust chairman; Lucy Adams, the director of human resources; and Nicholas Kroll, the administrative director charged with supporting the BBC Trust.

'We are not a court of law,' I said at the start of the session. 'But we are trying this afternoon to get at the truth, and only you, as witnesses, can help us to do that. It is extraordinary that the committee has felt the need to ask seven key players in the world's leading public service broadcaster to come together to attempt to establish on behalf of the public and the licence fee payer who knew what at what time and who is responsible, and therefore answerable for decisions taken by the BBC.' It was to be an unedifying spectacle, but it had become necessary given the contradictory evidence we had received to that point.

The hearing was based on information provided by the National Audit Office. In the three years to December 2012, 228 senior managers left the BBC, of whom 150 received a severance package. These packages averaged £164,200. The National Audit Office examined a sample of sixty cases in detail and found that in fourteen of them the managers were paid more than their contractual entitlement.

A number stood out. Sharon Baylay, the former director of marketing, ecommunications and audience, was made redundant after only seventeen months at the BBC and walked away with nearly £400,000, including a year's pay in lieu of notice and £1763 to pay for BUPA health cover. Caroline Thomson, who had been led to believe that she would be promoted to the director-general post, was then made redundant and left with a cheque for £680,400, including £14,000 to pay for the legal fees incurred by her in negotiating the package. John Smith left his post as chief executive of BBC Worldwide on 31 December 2012, at the age of fifty-five, and immediately started drawing a pension of £212,000 a year. He had negotiated a £2 million pension top-up and £1.6 million in severance pay five weeks before he signed a contract with Burberry to join them as their chief operating officer. (After the publicity generated by our inquiry, he paid back £200,000 to the BBC.) Pat Loughrey received £866,000, including £300,000 pay in lieu of twelve months' notice, even though he had already worked his notice and been paid for it. Before he left the BBC, he secured a £200,000 a year job as warden of Goldsmiths College, University of London. Roly Keating, the director of archive content at the BBC, became the chief executive of the British Library. Having got the offer of a new job, he negotiated a severance pay package worth £376,000. In the light of the adverse publicity, he returned the money to the BBC.

In many of the cases extra money was paid out for private health insurance, legal fees and in the form of long-service awards. In one case, a senior manager received £49,000 for training and information technology equipment. In another case, an agreement was reached to buy at least £60,000 of consultancy services from the departing manager over two years, at a daily rate of £1000.

The individual case that sparked most attention was that of Mark Byford, the former deputy director-general. The BBC, supported by the BBC Trust, wanted to reduce senior manager numbers by 20 per cent and cut the associated salary bill by 25 per cent. In that context, the decision to scrap the deputy post and pay the redundancy package was taken in October 2010, but Mark Byford did not leave the BBC until June 2011. He

left with just under £1 million. He received a redundancy payment equivalent to a year's salary and another year's salary 'in
lieu of notice', although the decision to make him redundant
had been taken nine months before he left. He also received
£73,000 for leave accumulated before 2004. There was no
contractual obligation to pay the money 'in lieu of notice'.
That was fabricated to reward the man with half a million
pounds over and above an already very generous redundancy
package. As I remarked at the time: 'An ordinary worker on
average earnings would have to work for forty years to earn
the £1 million that Mr Byford got in redundancy pay.'

The size of Byford's settlement astonished us, but Mark
Thompson seemed agnostic. When I repeatedly asked why
he didn't think that £500,000, which was a fortune to most
people, was not enough to secure the redundancy of somebody
whom he felt the organisation no longer needed, he responded
by telling the committee: 'We were in the middle of a series of
gigantic projects to include Salford and the new Broadcasting
House, and also the preparation of the broadcasting of the
royal wedding and the Olympic Games ... We wanted Mark
Byford, through this difficult transition, fully focused on the
enormous task that we had. We did not want him worrying
about his future or taking calls from head-hunters; we wanted
him fully focused.' It seemed grotesque that an extra half a
million pounds of public money should be given to a man to
keep him 'fully focused'. Mark Thompson and Mark Byford
had known each other for thirty years and were friends outside the workplace. That camaraderie at the top of the BBC
may well have influenced the approach taken to pay-offs for
senior staff.

Yet as soon as it became clear that the public were shocked
by the size of the pay-offs, everybody involved started scut-
tling for cover. At our July 2013 hearing, Lord Chris Patten,

an experienced and seasoned politician whom I had known for years and who had become chair after the pay-offs had been agreed, said: 'It was a question of shock and dismay for us to discover how many [pay-offs] had been beyond contractual and had therefore been even higher than they needed to be.'

When I then asked him: 'Where they exceed contractual obligations, should the Trust have known?' he came back with: 'Yes, and if you call a previous director-general of the BBC in due course, I will be as interested as you in why we didn't know.'

He was, of course, referring to Mark Thompson.

The claim that the Trust did not know that the pay-offs went well beyond contractual commitments was confirmed by the other trustee who gave evidence with Chris Patten. Anthony Fry claimed: 'We were assured they were within contractual terms. We were told that they had been signed off in the proper fashion.'

Mark Thompson was clearly furious that the Trust was feigning ignorance and placing the blame on him. He sent me a twenty-five-page memorandum with accompanying documentary evidence. In his submission he said: 'The redundancy settlements with Mark Byford and Sharon Baylay were made with the full prior knowledge and extensive involvement of the BBC Trust ... The BBC Trust did understand these cases in detail before any decisions were taken, and the claim that they were kept in the dark about these cases and the wider policy and practice is untrue.'

Further on in the memorandum, he wrote: 'Although it was not part of the formal process, I had also consulted the Chairman of the BBC Trust on the severance packages because of the seniority of the managers involved and the likely sensitivity.'

And yet later: 'In practice, the Chairman and Trustees wanted to be consulted in advance about the significant changes to the remuneration, numbers, or employment policy and practice in relation to the whole senior management population. Given the saliency of senior pay at the Corporation, I believed this to be a reasonable request.'

Who was telling the truth? It was extraordinary to find these establishment figures squabbling, like children, over differing versions of the facts. As committee member Chris Heaton-Harris wryly remarked: 'It is the most bizarre game of "Whac-A-Mole" I have ever seen in my life. You hit one fact down and out pops another bunch of questions.'

Argue they did. Anthony Fry was fulsome in expressing regret and concern. In July he told us: 'I was in the vanguard of people within the Trust, and more importantly the executive board, arguing that the size of the contractual obligations, including pay, was simply totally out of kilter with what the public and licence fee payers expected. It is fair to say that there were a series of particularly unpleasant discussions that took place ... Frankly, not to put too fine a point on it, I thought they were completely out to lunch in regards to what they thought was acceptable pay in a public body ... Did I expect to find out that in addition to what were already huge payments, payments above contractual obligations were paid on this sort of scale? No, I did not.' And a little later in the evidence session: 'There were a number of occasions when – not to put too fine a point on it – people like me were asked in not particularly pleasant terms to get back in our box, because these were not matters that were appropriate for us to be dealing with under the royal charter.'

When Mark Thompson gave evidence in September, he contradicted Anthony Fry in an equally robust way: 'I just want to say that I cannot recall ever using the words "back in the box" or anything like that; or ever speaking angrily, disrespectfully or arrogantly to Anthony or any other trustee . . . The Trust was very clear that it wanted to see action and we complied with that. The idea that there was some resistance to that is simply not borne out by the facts.'

> Anthony Fry: 'I don't accept that . . . From the time that I joined the Trust and the remuneration committee, I felt that on a whole lot of areas such as perks, the level of pay and the level and appropriateness of bonuses . . . the records will show that there were months and months of arguments between the Trust and the executive which I, as an incoming trustee, found in many cases extremely challenging.'

We may have found it difficult to establish the facts; we did, however, uncover an utterly dysfunctional set of relationships. Similar tensions emerged with the evidence given by Lucy Adams. She had been the director of human resources at the BBC on a salary of £320,000 a year. She appeared before us parading designer glasses and eye-catching jewellery. She gave evidence both in July and in September.

Her first appearance was marked by her attempts to distance herself from the decisions, particularly the one to give Mark Byford £1 million.

'There was very much a prevailing culture that payment in lieu of notice was an acceptable way of managing severance arrangements,' she said. And later: 'I don't think, as the NAO pointed out, that it was acceptable for him to get such a large payment in lieu of notice.' Also: 'He had an expectation – I appreciate that is not the same as a contractual term – of a payment in lieu of notice of twelve months because of the custom and practice with other executives. Mark Thompson was very keen.'

It was difficult to believe that on such a major HR issue, she, as HR director, had nothing to do with it. As Stewart Jackson said to her: 'In what other organisation in the public or private sector does the director of human resources sanction double redundancies for senior officials as "custom and practice"?'

Later in the evidence session Stewart referred to the £49,000 paid to one senior manager for IT equipment and the £60,000 promised to another for guaranteed consultancy work. He said: 'If this was any other organisation, that would be called corporate fraud and cronyism, and you presided over it.'

Adams's evidence about a letter that went to the Trust before the deal with Mark Byford was sealed was extraordinary. The letter set out the restructuring proposals and spelled out the cost of making Mark Byford and Sharon Baylay redundant in the way proposed. Clearly we thought the head of human resources would have helped to draft such a note, although it was sent in Mark Thompson's name. But in July, Adams denied all knowledge. 'I am not aware of the letter that went to the Trust. I did not actually write that letter,' she declared.

I just did not believe her: 'Ms Adams, are you telling us that you never saw the memo dated 7 October 2010? You never saw it?'

Lucy Adams: 'I don't believe so, but what I did do is
provide—'
MH: 'You don't believe so? Either you did or you didn't.'
Lucy Adams: 'I don't believe so. I can't say with absolute
certainty.'
MH: 'I can't believe, knowing how organisations work,
that it didn't go around as a draft and wasn't shared
with you, as director of HR. I find that incredibly
difficult to believe. I don't believe it.'

Sure enough, at the beginning of September, I received an apologetic letter from Lucy Adams in which she wrote: 'Since the hearing, I am now clear which document was being referred to and I can confirm that I was involved in drafting that memo.' In fact, she was shown on the document to have authored it. It had always seemed implausible that she would not be involved in drafting the note to the Trust and it was hard to believe that she did not know which document we were referring to, as she must have reviewed this key piece of paper to prepare for her committee appearance.

By the time Lucy Adams came before us in September, a week after she had written to apologise, we had also seen a copy of the letter she had sent to Mark Byford setting out the terms *she* had clearly negotiated with him. We also had copies of various emails she had sent that provided clear evidence of her central role in negotiating Byford's package. For example, she wrote to some of her colleagues in September 2010: 'I then met with MB [Mark Byford] and talked him through his contractual entitlement as per [the] schedule. He expressed surprise that it was two years but believed me as I said [. . .] I had been through the file.'

She also wrote: 'There then proceeded to be a series of detailed phone calls with MB, MT [Mark Thompson] and between MT and the Chairman – reviewing MB's potential exit package. All of these discussions were based on the assumption of two years' redundancy.'

She was not the innocent bystander she would have had the committee believe. She was a central player in the deals. At the September hearing Mark Thompson said as much: 'The actual negotiations with Mark Byford were led by Lucy Adams, the director of the HR division of the BBC, and not by me.' Later Thompson was asked by Stewart Jackson to respond to her allegation that he had stopped her reforming the system.

Stewart Jackson: 'In her evidence on 10 July, Lucy Adams
        specifically made reference to the redundancy
        payment cap that she sought to bring in as policy,
        which she identified you as blocking? If you were
        interested in value for money, as you said, why did
        you take that action?'
Mark Thompson: 'I didn't. I don't know what you are
        referring to.'

We clearly had to allow Lucy Adams to give her side of the
story, but I was sceptical that she would be anything other than
economical with the truth. When challenged on why she had
told us she had nothing to do with the note sent to the Trust
about the redundancies, she said: 'I was shown the document
after that meeting and, of course, I recognised it as a document
with which I had been involved, so I immediately clarified the
situation.' Her interpretation of 'immediately' was bizarre, as
after the 10 July appearance, it took her until 2 September to
put the record straight.

I was angry and snapped: 'Just to be clear on that, because
I am not having any more lies this afternoon ...'

'You can't accuse her of lying,' Adrian Jenner, my loyal
clerk who worked tirelessly to keep me in check, whispered
in my ear. The hearing was being televised live and all the
BBC staff at the Westminster studios at Millbank were apparently glued to their screens. As my clerk was telling me off,
a loud cheer went up at Millbank when they heard what I
had said.

Towards the end of the hearing, another exchange on a
further issue took place between Lucy Adams and Stephen
Barclay MP, who had carried out detailed research on the issue
and had been handed information by a whistleblower.

Stephen Barclay: 'Was it your sense – we have discussed
culture – that these payments beyond contractual
terms were, in essence, sweeteners to BBC staff? Was
that how you saw it?'

As Adams obfuscated, Barclay came back with: 'My question was very specific: did you suggest to HR colleagues – this is a cultural point – that these sort of payments should be viewed by them as sweeteners?'

Lucy Adams: 'As sweeteners? I think that that is a strange
term . . .'
MH: 'Did you use the word "sweetener"?'
Lucy Adams: 'I cannot honestly recall using that word.
HR professionals all over the world recognise that
occasionally you have to pay above the contractual
entitlement.'
Stephen Barclay: 'But in an email you did exactly that.
You said: "Can I get a sense of the scale of the
sweetener?" It seems that that is another document
that you are forgetful of writing . . .'

Later, the Comptroller and Auditor General intervened to address Lucy Adams in front of the committee: 'On a point of order. I have just been shown an email forwarded to Mr Barclay by a whistleblower that appears to have arisen from your using the word "sweetener". I want to let you go away from here. I appreciate that you want to see it and you do need to see it, but may I just ask you to reserve your position and we will look into it later on.'

Lucy Adams left the BBC in April 2014. She did not receive any severance pay and she did work her notice period.

The other witnesses at our September 2013 hearing also

clashed over who knew what and when. Marcus Agius was a non-executive director and chaired the executive board remuneration committee that signed off the high-profile deals. He had also been chairman of Barclays Bank, resigning in 2012 following the scandal over the fixing of the Libor rate. He was quite open in explaining that he had approved the pay-offs: 'After sustained challenge and debate we were finally persuaded that, in the circumstances, it was the right decision on value-for-money grounds.' But he insisted that the BBC Trust was also aware of what was being done. The three trustees, Chris Patten, Anthony Fry and Sir Michael Lyons, argued that the fault lay with the non-executive directors on the executive board. Chris Patten said plainly: 'Well, the non-executive directors should be publicly accountable to licence fee payers and to us. So if you are asking who was responsible for making these payments, the responsibility is for the senior members of the executive and for the executive remuneration board.'

Similarly Sir Michael Lyons, who chaired the BBC Trust when the pay-offs were agreed, claimed: 'I have no memory of detailed discussions which might have justified the claim that the package that was approved by the executive board remuneration committee was done so with the knowledge and approval of the Trust chairman.'

Marcus Agius contradicted this. He said that he was aware of shuttle diplomacy and that 'the subject of the redundancies and the amount of money that was involved was a matter of interest to the Trust'.

Both Sir Michael Lyons and the senior official responsible for ensuring the Trust worked effectively, a man called Nicholas Kroll, who earned £238,000 a year for serving the Trust, appeared to be horribly forgetful. Kroll conveniently forgot that he had received two key documents – and had amended one of them. One was the infamous October memorandum that Lucy Adams initially said she had not written. The second was a paper describing what the BBC mysteriously christened 'Project Silver'. This was a note provided from Mark Thompson's office to Nicholas Kroll in the chairman's office. It set out the options for dealing with the redundancy of Mark Byford and was sent to the chairman before negotiations with Byford took place. This document set out three options and laid out the cost of each. There was a further trail of emails between the BBC Trust and the BBC management.

Yet Nicholas Kroll said in evidence that the reason he never briefed the new chair Chris Patten on the issue was that 'we were not aware of the details of Mark Byford's arrangement – neither in writing nor from any oral contact; and that is the fact of the matter.' Kroll had claimed to the National Audit Office that the 'Project Silver' document and the October memorandum did not exist. It was only after our insistence that Mark Thompson should fly over from America to give evidence that the existence of these documents miraculously came to light. The National Audit Office was so angry that they had been misled on the Trust's involvement, Amyas Morse wrote to Nicholas Kroll in the following terms:

> Thank you for your letter of 16th July regarding the discovery of a further paper relating to Mark Byford's departure. I must say we are concerned with this development. As you will be aware during clearance of our report we made a specific request to see copies of any communication between Mark Thompson and the BBC Trust relating to the severance awarded Mark Byford and Sharon Baylay. We made a parallel request to the BBC. We were initially informed that the Trust did not

have any documents on file and that it did not have any
recollection of being privy to the details of Mark Byford's
severance package and had not received a detailed
summary of the proposed terms. Two weeks later, the
Trust informed us that the Director General's Office had
found a note from Mark Thompson to Sir Michael Lyons
(distributed to trustees) that did set out the cost of Mark
Byford's severance package, although not in detail.

In view of the discovery of another note [Project
Silver] I should be grateful if you could provide the
following:. . .

All this awful evidence told us that these highly paid individuals and respected members of the establishment were either
guilty of gross inefficiency, collective amnesia or deliberate
obfuscation. Tony Hall, the new director-general, had the
grace to admit: 'We got this wrong. We were overpaying.
The fault lies with us, the executive of the BBC.' But Mark
Thompson insisted that the big pay-offs were justified. 'The
price you would have paid in 2009 or 2010 to try to do it
would have been a delay that would have ended up costing
more,' he claimed.

We found grotesque squandering of public money by a
public corporation that in a private company might have been
regarded as a breach of the directors' fiduciary duty to their
shareholders. Had it not been for the high-profile pay-off that
George Entwistle received when he left the BBC, the scandalous BBC custom and practice of awarding enormous pay-offs
to senior staff might not have been uncovered.

The BBC is not alone in its cavalier disregard for safeguard-
ing public money. Similar stories abound across the public
sector. The accountability structures in the public sector are
not yet strong enough to prevent abuse. Regulatory bodies

do not provide sufficient oversight and protection for the tax-payer – or licence fee payer. It may well be time to consider placing a similar duty on public sector leaders that private sector directors have imposed on them through the Companies Act, a duty to act in the best interest of their shareholders (tax-payers) in good faith and honestly at all times. A duty of this kind does already exist for local government. It should become the norm across the whole of the public sector.

A final observation. Before 2010, the Public Accounts Committee had not examined BBC expenditure in detail; that job had been left to the BBC Executive and the BBC Trust. We were determined to follow the public pound wherever it was spent and, with the agreement of the Trust, the Comptroller and Auditor General now regularly undertakes value-for-money studies of the BBC. Our inquiries broke new ground. We demonstrated the importance of open, public scrutiny and I like to think that those inquiries helped to provide a catalyst for change in the complacent culture at the top of the BBC.

16

Four Wicked and Tricky Dilemmas

Throughout the five years of the Public Accounts Committee's work, a number of themes consistently emerged that mitigated against securing best value for the taxpayer's pound. These were and remain tricky issues that do not lend themselves to the relatively straightforward answers that have been identified elsewhere. But they are important, because they lead to waste and sadly are too often ignored and swept under the carpet because they are considered too difficult to tackle.

Four, in particular, are worth discussing: the tension between localism and efficiency, the reluctance to consider the long-term implications of decisions taken today for the taxpayers of tomorrow, the failure to think outside silos and the unintended consequences that that failure brings, and the refusal to prioritise early intervention and early action that could prevent greater costs being incurred later.

Localism and efficiency

There is a systemic tension between the widely accepted devolution agenda and the continuing commitment to cut public expenditure. For instance, devolving decisions makes it more difficult to standardise and rationalise product choices. We regularly encountered examples of expenditure on very basic items where one hospital, one school or one police force bought goods much more cheaply than another. Furthermore, because purchasing and decision-making are increasingly fragmented, government does not take advantage of its bulk purchasing power to drive down costs for the taxpayer and gain more for the citizen. The Coalition government did introduce some welcome initiatives to exploit bulk purchasing on ICT by central government through the Cabinet Office, but the reach was limited and even that initiative met with strong resistance.

Two striking examples of localism trumping efficiency and leading to unnecessary waste stand out. We have forty-three independent police forces led by elected police commissioners. Eighty per cent of their income comes directly from government, but although the Home Office allocates and is responsible for the money, it is reluctant to use its authority to prescribe better ways of buying the things that the police need. One can understand the reluctance to intervene, particularly in the context of the relatively new reform that created the elected police commissioner role. However, the implications of standing aside hover on the absurd, particularly when money is tight.

Police forces spend 13 per cent of their income, £1.7 billion, buying goods. The price they pay for standard items varies hugely: standard-issue handcuffs cost from £14 to £43; standard-issue boots cost from £25 to £114; and high-visibility jackets can be as little as £20 or as much as £100 per jacket. Such differences are indefensible when at the same time financial constraints are forcing cuts in neighbourhood policing throughout the country.

In contrast, the prison service has taken the 'revolutionary' step of standardising uniforms in all prisons. That simple decision saved £2.6 million on an £8 million budget. Apparently, police forces are not able to agree to do the same because they jealously and nonsensically protect their right to decide how many pockets their force's uniform should have and where those pockets should be. And just imagine how much cheaper it would be if there were just one standard white shirt worn by anyone who worked in the police service, the prison service, the fire service and the ambulance service. However, achieving this common-sense practice is probably more difficult than climbing Everest.

We uncovered similar absurdities when in 2011 we looked at procurement in the NHS. We focused our inquiry narrowly on hospital trusts in England and looked specifically at medical supplies. Between them these trusts spent £4.6 billion, not including ICT expenditure or spending on drugs. This represented 10 per cent of their total expenditure and a quarter of everything they spent outside paying for people.

Again, NHS trusts are independent bodies, and as more gain foundation trust status that autonomy spreads to more institutions. But NHS funding is under unsustainable pressure, with growing demand and declining resources in real terms. So securing best value on the purchase of medical supplies should be a priority. However, when we undertook our study we found that the ability to achieve better value just wasn't there. The National Audit Office conducted a survey of sixty-one trusts and their purchases. Eighty per cent of the orders were for less than £50. Between them, the trusts bought 1751 different types of cannula and 652 different types of surgical gloves. One hospital in the sample bought 177 different types of gloves, while another managed with just thirteen variations. Even when it came to A4 paper, the trusts managed to buy twenty-one different varieties.

Not everybody recognised the absurdity of the position, as is illustrated by this exchange with the then chief executive of the NHS at our hearing in March 2011.

> Dame Anne McGuire MP: 'Would it have been clinicians that would have decided in one hospital that they needed 177 varieties of surgical glove?'
>
> David Nicholson (chief executive, NHS): 'The choice of surgical gloves is a very significant issue for surgeons, and you can perfectly see how, in organisations with individual surgeons and their own particular responsibilities, the pressure to increase the number of—'
>
> MH: 'I cannot buy this argument. It is like housewives and their washing-up gloves.'
>
> David Nicholson: 'No. When you stick a knife in somebody and you are in that intimate relationship with an individual on a table, or whatever, you want everything to be right for yourself. Now, what we know is that if you get clinicians together and you work with them together, they will make sensible decisions about that.'

Dame Anne McGuire replied laconically: 'So that is what happened in the hospital where they managed to survive, with that very delicate relationship between the doctor and patient, with just thirteen different varieties of surgical gloves?'

There are not many people who would empathise with the approach of the NHS chief executive. Later in the same hearing, he tried another tack. Ian Swales MP observed: 'You are going into this with wishes and hopes, but you do not have the power to go out and make it happen.'

David Nicholson: 'I think it is more than wishes and hopes.
   I would argue that the alternative, which is often
   described as the Ukrainian tractor factory bit – the
   idea that we could do all of this from Whitehall – is
   nonsense . . .'

This led Richard Bacon MP to remark: 'May I ask Mr Rolfe
[Director of Procurement, East of England NHS Collaborative
Procurement Hub] a question, because when one thinks of
Ukrainian tractor factories, one does not think of Marks and
Spencer. You [Mr Rolfe used to work for Marks and Spencer]
are generally known as a business that finds out what its cus-
tomers want and is good at supplying it.'

To which Mr Rolfe replied: 'You need transparency in the
system. You were asking earlier about the pressure on the individual trust and, more so, on the non-executive director, so
if you have the transparency, you can understand that a good
question for a trust board would be: "What are your top ten
non-pay spends and how do these prices compare with the best
quartile in your region?"'

Mr Rolfe's job title in the NHS illustrated part of the problem. The NHS had recognised that it should get better at bulk
buying and standardisation. So it had established a plethora of
organisations (all of which cost money) to encourage collaboration. There were regional collaborative procurement hubs,
trusts that had established their own informal collaborative
arrangements, trusts that worked with commercial support
units; there was a national procurement council for the NHS
and a national supply organisation that had been outsourced to
DHL. Too many organisations with variable performances. So
one survey of over four thousand individual products bought
through the national supply organisation found that over half
the items were more expensive when purchased nationally.

On the other hand we came across another example where seventeen trusts had collaborated on buying patient warming blankets and achieved a 62 per cent discount rate off the catalogue price.

This inconsistent performance impacted on the confidence the independent trusts had, and have, in the national or collaborative arrangements. A similar picture emerged with the national supply organisation for the police, where only 2 per cent of the items bought by police forces were purchased through the national hub, well below the Home Office's target of 80 per cent being bought through the national supply body by 2015.

Both government departments believed that the financial pressures created by the austerity programme would alter behaviour. It is a depressing reflection on the cultural approach to value for money that it only becomes important when money is tight. But, more importantly, I doubt that we would find that much had changed if we were to return to the issue in eighteen months' time. The root cause of the problem lies with the tension between devolving power and achieving efficiency, and resolving that tension appears beyond the grasp of decision-makers. Surely at a time of austerity, it must be right that we seek better value even at the expense of some localism.

Bill for tomorrow's taxpayers created by decisions taken today

The pressure of politics always drives people towards short-term decisions. The desire for government to act today leads them to ignore the inter-generational inequity that can result from decisions that only look at the immediate effect, not the long-term implications. Everybody instinctively knows that. Yet there is too little information that is publicly available to really hold governments to account for burdening future generations with heavy bills arising from the action – or inaction – that occurs today.

The government has started to produce an annual document – the Whole of Government Accounts – that sets out all the assets and liabilities facing the state over time. At first glance, this seems like a turgid set of tables, but hidden within those tables are some startling facts. They begin to reveal the extent of the problems our grandchildren will face because of decisions taken today. Take one instance, the current system of student finance that, in my view, is completely unsustainable over time. The government knows that some graduates will never pay back their student loans. Initially it assessed that 30 per cent would fail to do so, later raising that to 34 per cent. However, in a study published in 2013, the Institute of Public Policy Research considered that the loan-deficit rate was likely to be closer to 40 per cent of the total debt due.

That study was completed before the government allowed fees to increase further and before the government decided to phase out grants for low-income students. These decisions are likely to lead to yet more people defaulting on their loans. Future governments will have to pick up the tab for the defaults. Estimates for that growing debt are unbelievably big. In its 2015 Fiscal Sustainability Report, the Office for Budget Responsibility estimated that student debt would rise to £600 billion by 2035. That is an astonishing 8 per cent of GDP. An Institute for Fiscal Studies report published in 2014 estimated that 73 per cent of students are likely to have some or all of their debt written off. The only action that the government has taken is to hide the more honest, higher cost, by making over-optimistic assumptions about the repayment rate. The burden on future generations is frightening.

Another shocking figure lies in the amount of money that

has been set aside to meet medical negligence claims and the steep rise in that figure over recent years. In 2010–11, the government assessed that the NHS might need to spend £17.5 billion settling medical negligence claims; by 2013–14, that had gone up to £26.6 billion – that represented over a quarter of the entire NHS budget in that year, a truly scandalous burden on future budgets. The government's rather simplistic response has been to make it more difficult for patients to pursue negligence claims by tightening up on legal aid and by making it more difficult for lawyers to 'ambulance chase'. But this is a sticking plaster answer to a growing problem. People do pursue their rights more assertively today than they did a decade ago and that trend is probably here to stay, however tightly the law on ambulance chasing is drawn. A more sophisticated understanding of the problem, combined with constantly striving for better care standards in the NHS, represents a more honest and transparent approach to this huge financial burden on future generations.

The Private Finance Initiative (PFI), used to fund a vast range of programmes, represents a terrible burden on future generations too. PFI was first exploited by the Thatcher and Major governments in the 1990s and has been used by all governments since that time. Originally PFI offered government two short-term advantages. First, they could account for PFI expenditure off balance sheet, so the spending did not count against public expenditure totals. That advantage has gone and the government has been required to bring PFI expenditure back on to balance sheets. The second short-term advantage was that the costs associated with the projects could be deferred into the future – spend now, pay later. By raising private finance, governments put off paying for capital investment and other programmes today and saddle future generations with the bills.

The Public Accounts Committee regularly examined PFI

contracts. There are well over 700 of them in place, and at present PFI looks like a better deal for the private sector than for the taxpayer. Lending government money through PFI is a very safe investment for any private investor, as the repayment instalments are a first call on the budget of any public body that has signed a PFI agreement. So paying the annual PFI cost of the hospital takes automatic precedence over paying for nurses, paying the annual repayment charge for the school takes precedence over paying for teachers and meeting the annual bill for a new piece of defence kit takes precedence over paying for soldiers.

Over time the government has become a little smarter in how it uses private finance. In the early days, the private finance companies enjoyed unbelievably huge profits from PFI projects as they refinanced the original loans, securing cheaper money and so increasing their profit margins, in part because of the absolute certainty of getting the money back from the taxpayer. Recent PFI contracts more frequently contain clauses that ensure that any excessive profits secured are shared between the private investor and the taxpayer.

But these contracts still leave questions about whether PFI provides value for money, and they certainly leave future generations with a massive burden. The most recent assessment values the assets obtained through PFI at just under £39 billion, but the cost of paying for these assets over thirty years is estimated as being £150 billion, of which £42.2 billion will be spent on interest charges.

In the early years of the Labour government, I, like others, believed that PFI was the only way in which the hospitals and schools that we then needed could be speedily built. My years on the Public Accounts Committee convinced me I was wrong. The debts PFI bequeaths to future generations are simply too high.

Supporters of PFI argue that by bringing in private developers, the costs and risks associated with constructing new
buildings are transferred to the private sector. However, once
the building is constructed, there is no risk to the investor
and the fact that we could only identify one occasion when
a private developer lost money on a PFI project suggests that
very little risk is ever actually transferred to the private sector.
Government can always borrow money more cheaply than
the private sector so it would cost less for government to fund
projects directly. Better value for money would come from
funding more hospitals and schools on the balance sheet out of
current spending rather than paying for the costs of borrowing the money over time. That would mean either a smaller
building programme or higher taxes to pay for the investment,
but that would be more honest – and cheaper. It would also
relieve future generations of paying for projects over which
they had no influence and where repaying the debt pre-empts
all other expenditure.

Furthermore, assets that are acquired through the Private
Finance Initiative lock you into that service for thirty years.
So the government built big district hospitals when the NHS
treated most people in hospitals. Ten years on, that policy has
changed and the NHS wants to treat more patients in their
own homes in the community. Yet the NHS is locked into
paying for the large hospitals for some thirty years and the
cost of this takes the money that they would prefer to spend
on community nurses and doctors.

My last example of the failure to consider future generations comes from the cost of decommissioning the hazardous
and toxic waste created by the nuclear industry. Sellafield was
first created to produce materials for nuclear weapons, nuclear
power and the reprocessing of nuclear waste at the end of the
Second World War. Over time, with no facilities created to

dispose of the nuclear waste, it was stored in buildings and ponds on the Sellafield site, with nobody taking responsibility for decommissioning the dangerous materials. Past generations simply ignored the problems they were bequeathing to future generations. We visited the site during our inquiry. It comprises 1400 buildings, of which 240 contain enough nuclear waste to fill twenty-seven Olympic-sized swimming pools. It was extraordinary and chilling to see these massive ageing ponds and silo-like buildings, all of which contained dangerous materials that had been deposited without even being properly documented, so that those responsible for decommissioning today did not accurately know what they were having to handle.

The challenges the people working there face are enormous, the dangers substantial and the expertise around the world for dealing with nuclear waste is limited. But the cost to present and future taxpayers is spiralling out of control. Every year, the estimated cost goes up and the date for dealing with the waste moves further into the future. In 2010–11, the estimate was £60.9 billion; the following year, it had gone up to £64.3 billion and by the end of 2013–14, it stood at £77.5 billion.

The failure by successive governments to create appropriate disposal facilities from the 1950s onwards was utterly irresponsible. But the inability to control programmes and costs today is also inexcusable. Just because the task is unique and dangerous is no excuse for poor project management and spiralling costs.

Completing a project on time and within budget never happens at Sellafield. Stories of endless overruns and massive overspends abound. In the eighteen months between our two hearings on Sellafield, one project, known as the pile fuel cladding silo project, slipped by six years. Another, the Magnox swarf storage silo retrieval project, nearly doubled in cost to

£729 million in eighteen months. A third decommissioning project concerned a facility known as Evaporator D. This project was first launched in 2006. It was given design approval in April 2009, with an estimated cost of £397 million, and was scheduled for completion by 2014. The design was found to be flawed and the supervision of the project was poor. By May 2012, the costs had nearly doubled to £641 million and the completion date slipped by eighteen months to February 2016. An inspection by the Office for Nuclear Regulation in March 2015 revealed that the project would not be completed before the end of 2016 and that there were still considerable challenges to overcome, suggesting yet more costs and further delay.

Those responsible for managing the decommissioning programme exploit the very natural concerns we all have for safety, security and care of the environment. It seems to me that they are careless with public money, believing that nobody will turn them down when they ask for more because of the great dangers involved in dealing with nuclear waste. So while the Americans put a cap of $750,000 a year on the salaries that can be earned from working in this area, the top earner at Sellafield took home £1.2 million in 2012; £11 million was spent on senior executive staff. A consortium of private companies brought in to improve efficiency on the site failed and, after pressure from our committee, the contract was terminated. 'I am not yet satisfied with performance at Sellafield,' John Clarke, the chief executive of the Nuclear Decommissioning Authority, told us.

'So why have they got £54 million in fees,' I asked him.

'Because a number of things have been done in accordance with the contract,' he replied.

For me, Sellafield represented the most powerful indictment of inaction by past generations impacting on present and future generations. Building nuclear power facilities without providing for the disposal of nuclear waste is simply disgrace-ful. The bill that neglect has handed down to present and future taxpayers is extraordinarily large and to this day still seems out of control. Of course, it could well be that future generations will be saying much the same things about our failure to regulate the banks properly in the 1990s.

Thinking in silos and the unintended consequences

Time and again both the taxpayer and the citizen pick up the consequences of the government's inability to work across departments. This silo mentality is deeply entrenched in the public sector culture. Public bodies look after their own organisation's self-interest and do not think about how actions taken by one department or service will impact on another part of the public sector. Trying to get those in charge of one part of the public sector to collaborate with other parts is absurdly challenging. Yet from both the taxpayer's point of view and the service user's point of view, we would secure better services and better value from closer collaboration and from decision-makers considering the impact of action in one part of government on another part of the public sector.

There are endless examples of instances when reductions in the spending of one department lead to growth in another department's spending. The failure to build enough decent social housing for rent has led to a ballooning in the housing benefit bill for the Department for Work and Pensions as fam-ilies end up finding a home at a higher rent in the privately rented sector. The housing benefit bill in 2005–6 was just under £14 billion; nine years later it had grown to over £24 billion. This was despite attempts to contain housing benefit spending by toughening up the eligibility rules and introduc-ing new hurdles, like the bedroom tax. Cutting investment in social housing without considering the impact on the Department for Work and Pensions' benefit spending reflected a blinkered, departmental approach to a government-wide issue. Ironically, the political consensus in the 1970s to build more council housing meant that families were able to access decent housing at a price they could afford. Taxpayers' money went into subsidising bricks and mortar and very little was spent subsidising families through housing benefit. Today very little public money is spent on house building and nearly all the public subsidy goes into supporting families and landlords through housing benefit.

Similarly local authorities have reduced their youth programmes without any consideration being given to the impact this will have on youth offending, thus simply shifting expenditure from local government to the criminal justice system.

The services most affected by this blinkered approach are the community-based adult social care services. Traditionally such services have been funded by local authorities, with some support given to families through the benefit system and a relatively small amount of money spent by the NHS on adult social care.

Over the last few years, local authorities have borne the brunt of public expenditure cuts, yet out of every £10 spent on services by local government, £4 goes on adult social care. Inevitably, as their funding has reduced, local councils have had no option but to cut those services. Age UK published a report in the spring of 2014 in which they calculated that to maintain present levels of service, expenditure on adult social care would need to increase by £5.4 billion by 2020 to cope with the demands of an ageing population. In fact, we identified a 12 per cent real-terms cut in local authority spending on elderly people in just two years to March 2013, cuts that are set to continue as councils lose more central government money.

So there are fewer services for the elderly in the community, just when demand for these services is increasing because more people are getting older and living longer.

Inevitably that has led to hospitals being unable to discharge patients because there are no services available for them in the community. Elderly patients, who could be discharged, end up blocking beds and making it ever more difficult for hospitals to respond to other growing demands on the NHS. This is a classic instance of unintended consequences, with a decision taken on local authority spending impacting negatively on the NHS.

Local authority cuts to care services for the elderly also impact on the benefits bill. As council-run social services for the old disappear, more people are giving up work to care for their elderly relatives in the community. The value of informal care is around £100 billion a year. Of course, families should take responsibility for their ageing relatives, but if people have to give up work to care, they start to claim benefits and they stop paying taxes on their earnings. One in five of those caring for relatives is known not to be working as a direct consequence of their caring responsibilities.

All of these unintended consequences could be minimised if government worked in a more integrated and collaborative way. There is no benefit to be gained for the public finances if a cut in one area leads to more money being spent elsewhere. In most cases such decisions simply lead to poorer quality services and extra expenditure over time.

Early action

Spending money early could save future public expenditure and create better outcomes. Instinctively we all believe that to be true. Preventing people from drinking or smoking will save the NHS billions on treating everything from lung cancer to liver failure. Investing in children in their early years through programmes like Sure Start will raise educational attainment levels, help children develop their potential and prevent young people from falling into difficulties as they grow up.

But it is hard to persuade decision-makers to switch from spending on acute services – when things have gone wrong – to spending on new preventative interventions, particularly when they are having to respond to financial cuts in their budgets. Early action often requires a bit of a leap of faith. There is understandable scepticism that the savings promised will ever be realised and there is not enough clear evidence demonstrating that early intervention will lead to future savings.

I remember a conversation with GPs in my constituency who were complaining about the extra time they had to spend with patients who were taking part in a government initiative to give up smoking. The initiative required the patients to return to their GPs at regular intervals so that the doctors could check on progress and prescribe more of the pills that dulled the desire to smoke. The GPs found the regular appointments time-consuming and moaned to me about it. I responded by saying that they must surely benefit from the fact that if people gave up smoking they would be less likely to visit the surgery with emphysema or other ailments. To which one GP retorted: 'This won't help us at all. They may not get emphysema, but they will then come back with Alzheimer's!'

Despite the scepticism of the Dagenham GP, the evidence we collected emphasised the importance of trying to shift expenditure to early intervention. One in four offenders in prison had spent time in local authority care as a child; government statistics tell us that 88 per cent of young men and 74 per cent of young women in youth offending institutions had been excluded from school. Intervening early to prevent children coming into care or focusing on reducing school exclusions would not only save taxpayers' money but would help to secure better outcomes for young people.

The most remarkable example of poor outcomes and wasted money arising from a failure to intervene early came from a study we undertook of diabetes. In this case, the NHS funds both GPs and acute trusts and so has the remedy in its own hands. The incidence of diabetes is alarming and growing. There are four million people in Britain today who have a form of diabetes and Diabetes UK estimates that by 2025, five million people will have the disease. The NHS spends a tenth of its budget, around £10 billion a year, treating patients with a diabetic condition; 80 per cent of that expenditure is used to deal with complications arising from diabetes that could have been avoided if earlier action had been taken and simple checks had been carried out. Every year 75,000 people die from complications arising from their diabetes, and 24,000 of those deaths could be avoided if early checks took place.

These statistics are stark. There are nine basic checks that reveal early signs of complications. When complications arise, they can lead to kidney disease, blindness, amputations and early death. Studies have established that fewer than one in five people with diabetes has the recommended levels for cholesterol, blood glucose and blood pressure, and too many people with diabetes are simply not receiving regular checks. That failure can result in patients developing complications. In part patients need help and education to manage their condition and to visit their GP regularly for tests, but GPs also need to prioritise these checks in their daily work. This is an ideal example of where a switch to early action would result in savings and better outcomes.

Such 'wicked' tricky dilemmas described in this chapter help to show how difficult it can sometimes be to tackle waste and get better services for less money. Too often, complexity drives people to put these problems to one side, yet only through discussion and innovation can we hope – at the very least – to make things better for us all.

17

Private Profit and Public Good

Private companies deliver over half of the goods and services funded by the taxpayer's pound, with a small amount provided by charitable organisations. Every year nearly £200 billion of taxpayers' money is spent providing public goods and services through the private and voluntary sector.

It is a new world, which has grown exponentially. In the last decade we have witnessed a 500 per cent growth in the largest companies operating in this market and in 2014, the Confederation of British Industry (CBI) estimated that public sector contracts with private companies accounted for 7.2 per cent of GDP and involved the jobs of 5.4 million people. We are not just talking about the privatised railways, energy or communications companies, or the outsourcing of back-office functions or routine services like rubbish collection. All welfare-to-work advice and support is now provided by private companies (as chronicled in the chapter on A4e). Most of the probation services have been privatised. Free schools and academies are run by private companies and a growing number of health services are delivered by the private sector.

New companies have emerged that rely largely or wholly on

taxpayers' money for their income. Among them, a small group are evolving into privately owned monopolies operating in the public sector. They are reliant on the state for their business, and we are increasingly reliant on them for the outsourcing services they provide. They have become too big to fail.

For instance, a third of Capita's revenue in the UK in 2012–13 came from the public sector – they earned £1.1 billion from public sector contracts. Two-thirds of Serco's revenue in the UK in 2012–13 came from the public sector – they earned £1.8 billion from such contracts. Just over a third of G4S's revenue in the UK in 2012–13 came from the public sector – they earned £0.7 billion from these contracts. Around a third of Atos's revenue in the UK in 2012–13 came from the public sector – they earned £1.4 billion from public sector contracts. Compare this to the entire budget of the Department for Culture, Media and Sport, which in 2012–13 was £1.6 billion, but declined to £1.4 billion by 2014–15.

UK-based Capita claims to be the largest business-process outsourcing company in Britain; it has been responsible for administering, among other services, the Criminal Records Bureau (now called the Disclosure and Barring Service scheme) and the TV licence fee. Serco is another British company whose turnover is mostly earned in the UK. After the scandals in which the company was involved were exposed, its share price dropped from 647p in 2013 to 218.7p in November 2014. G4S is also headquartered in the UK, although it was originally founded in Copenhagen in 1901. It claims to be the world's largest security company, operating in 125 countries. Atos is a French-based IT company that was founded in 1997 and has grown rapidly since then, in part through acquisition – for example by buying KPMG Consulting in 2002, Siemens IT Solutions and Services in 2011 and Xerox's IT Outsourcing business in the USA in 2015.

The privatisation of public services paid for through our taxes is set to grow further. Tony Blair strongly believed that competition was a way to improve public services and the Conservative government believes that the private sector is more economic and efficient at delivering public services than the state. There are further arguments used to favour the involvement of the private sector. Contracting enables the public sector to use specialist expertise that exists in the private sector for public benefit. Used carefully, this should offer economies of scale. The private sector enjoys greater freedom to innovate in the public interest and a clear division between the commissioner and the provider can help to focus public sector officials on the citizen's interest rather than the producer's interest.

My own view is not driven by ideology. It is what works best that should matter most; what delivers best value for money and the most effective service; what is in the public interest. Privatisation is not a panacea for all the problems we face and it should not become an excuse for failing to confront the public sector management challenges we have seen in the stories in this book.

But this new world demands huge changes in the way central government, local government and the health service work; and in how the public sector contracts with the private sector, how they monitor performance and how they hold private providers to account. That huge change – vital if we are to secure efficient and effective public services – has yet to happen.

The Public Accounts Committee did change the way we worked. Until 2010, the committee had never called a private company to give evidence in public about its performance. The committee had traditionally held a government department's permanent secretary responsible for the contracts the department let and managed. We changed that. We thought that calling the companies themselves to account for how they spent our money was as important as hauling senior civil servants before us. We wanted those directly responsible for running services to be directly accountable for their performance. By doing that, we were able to learn and reveal a lot.

Private companies can and do deliver efficiently at times. One thinks of the Civil Service and teachers' pension schemes delivered by Capita, the National Savings and Investment scheme administered by Atos, or the Boris Bikes that are run by Serco. But inevitably, given our remit, we lighted on enough scandals and dreadful waste to establish that there are systemic problems that must be addressed for the new world to work in the public interest.

So while there are many successful public services run by private companies, setting out some of the most spectacular disasters is the best way to identify the potential systemic solutions required to tackle waste and abuse.

Ministry of Justice

High on the list came the contracts the Ministry of Justice had with both Serco and G4S to provide electronic tagging for individuals who were not serving their sentence in prison, but who were monitored in the community and often had to meet curfew conditions. The contract had been signed in 2004 by the then Labour government. In 2008, a routine inspection by civil servants raised questions about the billing for these tagging services but, in the words of Chris Grayling MP, when as Justice Secretary he made a statement to the House of Commons in July 2013: 'Nothing substantive was done at that time to address the issues.'

The warning signs in 2008 were ignored and it wasn't until

2013 that alarm bells really started to ring for civil servants. Whistleblowers approached both the department and the National Audit Office to voice concerns about G4S's practices. At the same time, officials were working on the competition to renew the contract and uncovered what they coyly described as 'data anomalies'. The Ministry of Justice asked PricewaterhouseCoopers to undertake a forensic audit of the contract and that uncovered a huge scandal.

Both G4S and Serco had been billing and charging the taxpayer for people who were not tagged: prisoners who were back in prison and had had their tags removed; ex-prisoners who had left the country; people who had never been tagged but had returned to the courts; individuals who had for many months and, in some cases, years not been actively monitored; and finally, yes, for a small number of ex-prisoners who had actually died.

It was scandalous that G4S and Serco had overcharged the taxpayer millions of pounds for tagging, but it was equally shocking that the Ministry of Justice did not do anything about the overcharging for eight years. They had not monitored the contract properly from the start and they had failed to respond to the warning signs identified by junior officials in 2008.

Shane Croucher, a reporter on the *International Business Times,* secured an interview with two whistleblowers, both of whom had worked for G4S in the south-west of England. The whistleblowers claimed, for example, that G4S sent 'new tagging orders for every offence, even if the person had already been tagged, so the firm could charge the Ministry of Justice twice', and that 'G4S would continue to visit homes of offenders it unofficially knew were in prison or had been released from their tagging orders, but would still charge taxpayers until it received official confirmation from the courts'. Both the whistleblowers, Sarah Bamford and Paul Wakeman, were ex-military people. Wakeman was sacked by G4S on somewhat spurious grounds and is now a bus driver, and Bamford left the company for health reasons.

Ann Beasley, the director of finance at the Ministry of Justice at the time of our public hearing in September 2014, admitted: 'There was overbilling throughout the entire length of the contract.' Later she told us: 'Some changes were made to the contract in about 2009 that were designed to save money – they related to tagging people who were on bail – and that changed the nature of the overbilling. Nevertheless there was overbilling in each of the years.'

Nick Smith MP then asked her: 'Did the overbilling reduce after 2009 or did it go up?'

Ann Beasley: 'It increased.'
Nick Smith: 'So we had a new system that was intended to
      bring costs down, but overbilling actually went up?'
Ann Beasley: 'Yes.'

Both companies paid nearly £180 million back to the government, of which £140 million was for overbilling on the electronic-tagging contract; but they also had to return monies wrongly claimed on other contracts. In Serco's case, this related to a prisoner-escorting and custodial services contract (which was referred to the City of London police), and at G4S, to billing issues on two court facilities management contracts where they had overcharged.

When we saw the two companies they appeared contrite. The crisis of confidence in their integrity caused by the revelations certainly hit Serco's share price hard and led to new appointments at the top of the company. We saw Rupert Soames, a respected establishment figure, who had been appointed CEO of Serco in September 2014. A grandson of Winston Churchill and brother of the Conservative MP Sir Nicholas Soames, he was awarded an OBE in the 2010 Honours and his son, Jack Soames, has served as a Page of Honour. He was fulsome in his apology: 'This has been an absolute earthquake and a disaster for Serco. We pride ourselves on public service which is a huge part of our business. What happened was totally unacceptable and unethical; frankly, we are deeply ashamed of it.'

But the tagging contract was not an isolated case. There were other Ministry of Justice contracts and we had investigated an NHS contract that Serco had secured, the details of which I shall recount shortly. However, Rupert Soames would not accept that Serco had a cultural problem. I put to him: 'You would accept, Mr Soames, that a cultural issue in the company allows that to happen. It is dead easy to blame the little guys down at the front, but it is a cultural issue. They did it for some reason, not just for the fun of it – they felt they could get further or that they would get paid more. There was something in it for them in your culture.'

Implausibly, he denied that this was the case.

G4S were less fulsome in their apology, but more open about the cultural challenges. Regional President UK & Ireland Peter Neden simply admitted: 'We made judgements on a complex contract that were inappropriate.'

When I asked him what he meant by that statement he responded: 'The contract was open to interpretation. We made judgements on the way in which to interpret that and those judgements were inappropriate. We made the wrong judgements and that led to us overbilling.'

Jean Pierre Taillon, who was the managing director of UK government services for G4S, described the scandal as 'a great opportunity for us ... It is not just a change in the central government services leadership. It is also a change in chairman, a change of group chief executive, and a change of leader for the UK and Ireland business.' Despite these strongly heralded changes, in January 2016, *Panorama* revealed bullying and abuse of young people in one of the secure training centres run by G4S.

In response to questioning by us on whether the culture and practices encouraged cheating, Peter Neden said: 'I would agree that managers in the business would have had an incentive scheme that encouraged revenue and profit growth' – suggesting why, perhaps, the cheating took place.

Ministers had announced a government-wide review of both G4S and Serco in July 2013. Serco agreed to allow a forensic audit to take place but G4S did not. They carried out their own audit, conducted by Linklaters, which said that they had 'not identified any evidence of dishonesty or criminal conduct by any employee of G4S'. G4S was referred to the Serious Fraud Office and they have yet to report. The government reported their findings on their audit within days of Christmas 2013.

During the review sixty government contracts with the two companies were tested. Thirty-four of the contracts had billing issues that involved not only overbilling, but in some cases revealed underbilling and a lack of documentary evidence to prove that the companies had actually provided the services for which they had billed government. The review led the NAO to declare: 'It is likely that there is further overbilling in other contracts across government.'

Mark Sedwill, the permanent secretary at the Home Office, tried to tell us that the department had not uncovered any financial irregularity or mismanagement in the four Serco and G4S contracts they examined, but as the Comptroller and Auditor General pointed out: 'They did qualify that by saying they did not have the full information.'

The Department for Work and Pensions undertook a sample review conducted by PricewaterhouseCoopers. We were told by Bill Crothers, the chief procurement officer at the Cabinet Office, that: 'They discovered that payments were being made that they would prefer not to have been made ... What they found was errors and the value of those errors was recovered. What wasn't recovered was the value of an extrapolation of those errors, so the errors were based on a small sample and you should extrapolate it further.'

> MH: 'So they took the small sample, but they didn't take
>   the implications of that?'
> Bill Crothers: 'That is what PwC found.'

We certainly saw a lax attitude across government to the effective monitoring of contracts. Crothers tried to explain that to us when he reflected on his experience in the Home Office: 'We did the procurement and, once we signed the contracts, I was amazed because they [the civil servants responsible for the procurement] all wanted to go. The culture in the services was that the glamour was in the procurement, and contract management was just handed off to "the business". They all wanted to do the next procurement.' The taxpayer is paying a heavy price for that culture.

The frustration the committee felt on behalf of the taxpayer was shared by some civil servants. Stephen Kelly had joined the Civil Service from the private sector and was quickly promoted to head the Efficiency and Reform Group in the Cabinet Office, but he only survived three and a half years and then went back to head up a private sector firm. He was known as the 'human Ken doll' by my office and others knew him to be the 'best friend' of Francis Maude, the Minister for the Cabinet Office – one of the few ministers really hated by the

Civil Service, perhaps because he was so strongly committed to reform. Stephen showed boundless energy, optimism and enthusiasm for improving efficiency, but as he told a journalist on *Computer World* after he left: 'There are some days I've left here and banged my head against the wall.'

In giving evidence on government procurement from the private sector, he was always candid. 'We could give you stories about £68 for a power cable for a PC and then you go to Amazon and it is £10. It was crazy – you cried for the taxpayer.'

Later in the same hearing, he said: 'We were buying boxes of paper at extraordinary prices. For example, we were buying it at between £9 and £73 and you guys [the Public Accounts Committee] called us out. We are now buying it at between £9 and £12 through aggregation and centralisation, and 75 per cent of all government paper is bought at the lowest cost, so we are starting to have an impact but it is a mammoth task.'

When we discussed Serco and G4S, Stephen Kelly said: 'The man in the street I think would say that we should stop dealing with them. In our private sector experience, you would probably take quite draconian action.'

I agree with that sentiment. If you find you have employed a lousy builder or had your hair cut by a hopeless hairdresser, you take your business elsewhere. Not so with government. All too often poor performance was completely ignored.

We established that, even while the government was undertaking the wide review of both Serco and G4S, they were still giving the companies new work by extending existing contracts or by allowing them to rebid for contracts they already had. Once the government review was completed, both companies won new contracts for new work, with the deals, in some cases, being struck so fast it was clear that negotiations had continued throughout the review. These companies have become just too big and too important to fail.

Astoundingly, they are still being paid to provide the equipment for electronic tagging.

In July 2014, Chris Grayling, then Justice Secretary, announced that there had been a new competition for the electronic-tagging contract that involved much-improved equipment. The contract had been awarded to four companies, one of which was Capita – they expect to earn £228 million over the six years of the contract. New satellite tracking tags were to be provided through a separate contract awarded to a small company in Redditch, called Steatite. Chris Grayling told Parliament that 'we will begin using them by the end of the year'.

That was in 2014, and the new tags have yet to be delivered and are unlikely to be available before the middle of 2016. So G4S and Serco are still being paid for their equipment. The Centre for Crime and Justice Studies claimed that by March 2015, G4S had been paid £8.7 million, while Serco had received £4.5 million, all this after the overbilling had been uncovered.

Astonishingly, given this dreadful history, the Ministry of Justice appears, yet again, to have bungled this new procurement. According to the *Guardian*'s Alan Travis, writing in June 2015, the companies that originally bid to provide the up-to-date tagging equipment withdrew from the competition for a number of reasons. Buddi, one of the bidders, said that their 'technical staff estimate that of the approximately 200 data requirements [that were only specified halfway through the tendering process], half were new.' The Ministry of Justice kept changing their minds as to what they wanted and that made bidding impossible. It also emerged that the ministry was expecting the companies to hand over their intellectual property rights to the new equipment, which they obviously were not prepared to do. So all the companies dropped out and Steatite was awarded the contract without competition. They subcontracted to a Taiwanese company and no sooner had the equipment arrived than it had to be withdrawn 'amid a dispute over intellectual property rights and other issues', according to Travis.

You could not make it up if you tried. The strongest criticism of this latest turn of events comes from Reform, the right-wing think tank, which has long promoted both electronic tagging and privatisation. Gavin Lockhart-Mirams of Reform said that the tendering process had been 'mismanaged disastrously'. In a report they published on electronic tagging, Reform said: 'Rather than using competition to drive innovation and performance, the department has given four providers a near monopoly over the provision of electronic monitoring across England and Wales. Given the pace of technological change this shows a profound lack of future-proofing.'

And they recommended that the government should 'scrap the current procurement and quickly move to put in place a more appropriate model that assures standards and competition and accounts for local demand'.

In the meantime, Serco, G4S and Capita are no doubt laughing all the way to the bank.

Sadly this appears to be par for the course in the Ministry of Justice. In 2012, I was approached by a number of MPs who had received complaints about the new interpretation services provided to the courts. Judges had been enraged by the service and the papers were full of stories about cases being adjourned because interpreters were not available. The National Audit Office undertook some work and produced yet another shocking report, which formed the basis of our Public Accounts Committee hearing.

When the Coalition government had first demanded expenditure cuts in 2010, the Ministry of Justice wanted to save money on the costs of interpretation in the courts. Civil servants thought that the pay deal they had with court interpreters was too generous; for instance, interpreters automatically received a three-hour minimum payment even if most assignments were for less than three hours.

Faced with what was obviously a tricky management issue, the department should have had the courage to renegotiate the contract with the interpreters. They didn't. They thought the easy answer was to privatise the service and save £18 million. They chose to procure a contract from a private provider for the wrong reason when they should have had the capability and strength to manage a reduction in costs themselves.

The procurement turned out to be shambolic. In August 2011, the Ministry of Justice signed a framework agreement with a small, regional company called Applied Language Solutions (ALS) for £42 million. Yet the ministry had commissioned a credit-rating report on ALS that clearly stated that the maximum value the company could safely manage was £1 million. Despite having that report, the Ministry of Justice signed a contract for £42 million with ALS. We asked the officials who appeared before us why they had ignored the credit-rating advice:

> Nick Smith MP: 'At the time did either of you look at the report?'
>
> Martin Jones (MOJ): 'I have certainly read the report.'
>
> Nick Smith: 'At that time?'
>
> Martin Jones: 'I didn't read the report at that time.'
>
> Nick Smith: 'Ann Beasley, did you read that report at that time?'
>
> Ann Beasley (MOJ): 'No, but staff working for me did.'

MH: 'Mr Handcock, did you?'

Peter Handcock (MOJ): 'No, I didn't.'

Martin Jones: 'The crucial question for me, as the
          senior responsible owner [the person in charge of
          the project], was that there had been a diligent
          procurement process by procurement professionals
          which had recommended that this was the company
          that was most suitable for this contract.'

Later Ann Beasley admitted that: 'It says that the company
appears to be of sufficient financial stability to undertake
contracts to a value of a million pounds ... That is a generic
contract, so it would include contracts where you were actually paying them on credit and that is what the £1 million is
in relation to.'

Later, in desperation, she said: 'I am in charge, overall, of a
spend on procurement of something like £3.5 billion a year.
I do not read the credit checks.'

Her justification for giving a company a contract well beyond
its capacity was bizarre: the civil servants clearly thought that
simply commissioning a credit check was enough – it ticked the
box – reading, understanding and acting on what it said went
beyond their job description; process was all that mattered.

Before the contract went live, Capita had acquired ALS.
This appeared to be how Capita often operated, growing
their market share of government business through acquisition. They had not tendered for the original contract but
were happy to take over the company and its contracts. Andy
Parker, the chief operating officer at Capita, told us: 'A financial intermediary brought me an opportunity in, I think,
the beginning of September, with a company called Applied
Language Solutions ... We regularly buy companies. We have
done probably 150 acquisitions. A number are brought to us by

financial intermediaries ... It seemed like an attractive marketplace and looked like the sort of business that was of interest to us as a support services organisation and for the efficiencies that we thought that we could bring.'

Capita admitted that they had never run interpretation services and they expected the existing team at ALS to deliver. They also told us that they only informed the Ministry of Justice a week before completing the takeover that they were going to acquire the company. This lack of influence and control by the client seems extraordinary; the department had no say in the takeover and by growing their government business, Capita had secured increasing dependence on them by government.

Capita bought the company in December 2011 and the contract went live in January 2012. The service proved completely chaotic. The Ministry of Justice had told the private provider that they needed to have 1200 interpreters available to work but it emerged that Capita/ALS had only 280 interpreters assessed, marked and security-checked, and therefore available to work under the terms of the contract. The lack of interpreters was the result of differing interpretations of the contract by the department and Capita/ALS. Capita told the ministry that they had registered 2600 people who were willing to work for them; the department required them to have been assessed and CRB (Criminal Records Bureau)-checked before they were registered; only 280 people met that test. The difference in interpretation resulted in chaos; it shows how clarity of specification is vital in a good contract.

The stories we heard were bizarre. Indeed, some may have been fabricated, but the fact they could be deemed credible showed how dreadful the situation was. It was rumoured that the owner of a cat registered the pet as a feline language specialist as a joke, and was then asked by ALS to bring the pet in for a language test. Another case read as follows: 'After reading about Jajo the rabbit I decided to register with ALS. I had no intention of working with them. I only wanted to see how far I could go and how incompetent ALS is. So I registered with a fake name (the name of a fictional character), a fake address (a well-known official residence of a head of state), a mobile number with only ten digits and an obviously fake Skype name. No qualifications, no experience, no security vetting. Two days after I registered I got my first job offer, a forty-five minute job at a court in central London. Soon after that I received an email inviting me to take the assessment test. I did not reply but I carried on receiving job offers. In total, up to now, I have received twelve job offers.'

I don't know whether the story was true, but we did establish that court staff made five thousand complaints about Capita/ALS during the first six months of the contract. Judges were infuriated at the disruption caused. Judge David Ticehurst was reported in the *Bristol Evening Post* in August 2012 as saying: 'Since ALS took over the contract, the courts have been plagued by a failure of interpreters to turn up, and not be as good at English as they should be. Family cases have had to be adjourned, as have criminal cases.' Judge Francis Sheridan at Amersham Court in October that year said in open court: 'The failure to provide an interpreter on this occasion is down to ALS. They should not retain a contract which is too difficult for them.'

Among the cases reported in the press was one in the *Independent* in July 2012 that claimed a murder trial had been brought to a halt when the court interpreter confessed that he was simply an unqualified stand-in for his wife, who was busy. Another local paper reported in November 2013 that two Bradford brothel keepers could not be sentenced because there was no Polish interpreter, and a third paper reported that a burglary case at Snaresbrook Crown Court had to be retried when it emerged that the Romanian interpreter had muddled the words 'bitten' and 'beaten'.

During our hearing with the department, officials claimed that 'there is an awful lot of anecdotal noise in the system' and that 'it is a fact that in the first two months of the operation of this contract, only four cases were adjourned as a result of the failure of an interpreter'. It was left to the National Audit Office director to point out that this was being a little economical with the truth and that the number of ineffective cases doubled in the first three months of the contract: 'Paragraph 3.6,' the Audit Office official said at our hearing, 'shows that in the first quarter of 2012, 182 trials in the magistrates' courts were recorded as ineffective, which means completely stopped.' The ministry was forced to retort: 'It doubled, but the numbers are relatively small.' And, of course, they were unable to tell us accurately how much taxpayers' money had been lost through the debacle.

The reality was that the mismanagement of the procurement meant that cases were delayed, people were kept in prison for longer than was necessary, and justice was denied. During our evidence session it emerged that MOJ officials may have known that Capita/ALS did not have a sufficient number of interpreters on their books; the department may have known that many languages were not covered that should have been under the terms of the contract; they may have known that Capita/ALS had not carried out proper assessments and checks; and they may have known that the company had not implemented the contractual obligation to carry out in-work assessments of the capability of the interpreters.

All of these important matters were specified, but were not delivered by the company. It was only after our hearing that 219 interpreters were removed from the Capita register because they did not have the documentation to prove that they had both the appropriate qualifications and the necessary security clearance.

One would have thought, and hoped, that the department had inserted strong penalty clauses into the contract, which might have acted as an incentive to encourage a better performance. But the department fined Capita only £2200 for the first six months of the contract; in fact, the company faced no fine for the first four months and the £2200 was levied for the last two months of that period. The department justified its leniency by explaining that Capita had invested over £3 million extra to improve the service. That was a welcome investment, but one of the key justifications for transferring services to the private sector is that the associated risks are also transferred. In this case the government picked up the extra costs to the system from the mistakes and did not benefit from the fines they could have levied on Capita. The service was privatised for the wrong reasons; the government failed to carry out proper due diligence; they failed to monitor a badly drafted contract properly; and they refused to exercise the penalty provisions effectively. All of this created loss for the taxpayer and denied justice to individuals.

In keeping with new protocols that we had introduced, the Public Accounts Committee returned to examine the interpreters' contract in 2014 to check on what had happened to our recommendations. We found improvements; the number of interpreters available to work had significantly increased and the Ministry of Justice was carrying out a range of audit checks to make sure that Capita delivered to the contract. In an eighteen-month period up to November 2013, the department clawed back over £46,319 in payments for failure to perform. So things have definitely got better and that must be good news.

Department for Work and Pensions

A powerful example of poor contracting came from the introduction of Personal Independence Payments (PIPs) in 2012.
This was a new benefit, which replaced the Disability Living
Allowance but had the same purpose. It was a non–means-
tested benefit for disabled claimants, to help with the extra
costs they incurred (directly because of their disability) in
living independently. The government expected 3.6 million
individuals to claim PIP by 2018. As this benefit affects disabled people, who may be very vulnerable and in urgent need of
support, it was important to get it and the new contract right.
The government had tightened up the eligibility rules and
wanted to save £3 billion annually from 2018–19 on spending
in this area, as compared with that spent on Disability Living
Allowance.

In July 2012, Atos was awarded two contracts, worth nearly
£400 million, to deliver assessments for individuals who put
in a claim for PIP, assessments that would determine people's
eligibility for the benefit. With contracts covering Scotland,
the North of England and the South of England, Atos was
responsible for 77 per cent of all claims. The other contractor,
Capita, covered Wales and Central England.

Atos had been a big contractor for the Department for Work
and Pensions for a long time. They were providing all the fit-
for-work assessments for the main disability benefit, known
as the Employment Support Allowance (ESA). But they were
in trouble with the ESA's very similar contract. The National
Audit Office criticised their performance in 2012, admonishing
the department for its failure to penalise Atos for underper-
formance and for not setting 'sufficiently challenging' targets.
The company's assessments for ESA were so poor that six
hundred thousand appeals were launched against them and in

nearly 40 per cent of the appeals against the original decisions were overturned. By the autumn of 2013, the backlog of people waiting for an ESA assessment had risen to over three quarters of a million claims and – surprise, surprise – a week after our public hearing on the new PIP contract in March 2014, the government announced the early termination of Atos's contract for the Employment Support Allowance. Atos had failed to deliver ESA assessments on time and to the appropriate standard.

Awarding a contract to a company that was already experiencing difficulties on another similar contract was just foolish. The government usually pleads European regulations for their inability to exclude a company based on its past performance, but in its specification government can make it clear that past performance will be a criterion in assessments of new bids for new contracts. In terms of value for money, they clearly should. Again, one is left wondering whether Atos was just too important to the Department for Work and Pensions to be allowed to fail.

Inevitably perhaps, the company's performance on the PIP contract was abysmal, as we discovered at our hearing. Both the department, in its procurement, and the company, in its delivery, were failing disabled people. Only 16 per cent of the decisions on claims that should have been made had, in fact, been made by October 2013. All committee members came to the hearing armed with examples of constituents who had been let down and were still waiting for an assessment; they, as well as the taxpayer, were the victims of Atos's failure.

The failures were particularly worrying where people were terminally ill and the company was supposed to complete assessments within ten days. The average time taken to reach a decision for a terminally ill claimant was twenty-eight days, 180 per cent longer than agreed. In my own constituency, several people contacted with me with terrible stories. One of my constituents had been diagnosed with ovarian cancer in June 2013; she was undergoing chemotherapy treatment twice a month, and she had also been diagnosed with a debilitating brain condition. She was advised by the Macmillan cancer charity to apply for PIP in August. She heard nothing, so rang my office and finally got an appointment for an assessment in March 2014 – a week after I raised her case at our evidence session. Similarly, another constituent had bowel cancer, which was diagnosed in April 2012 and which had spread. She applied for PIP in September 2013, heard nothing, contacted my office and was finally given an appointment in April 2014, a full seven months after making her first application.

During our oral evidence session in March, Vicky Pearlman of Citizens Advice told us: 'Because of the length of the delays, people are waiting nine months or more to get through the process. Most people are new claims and they are without any kind of support for their disability needs during that period.'

Lesley Hawes, chief executive of a disability charity in Barking and Dagenham, told the committee: 'We are finding in our area that we are getting more people needing food parcels or relying on social fund money to a huge extent. We are being bombarded because of it.'

And James Bolton of Mencap said in his evidence: 'This is a recent case of somebody who turned sixteen shortly after PIP was introduced and, because of his learning disability and other needs that he has, can't go to an assessment centre. When the family member contacted the assessment provider ... it was Atos in this case. When they contacted them to ask for a home visit, they were told that there were no appointments.'

There were many reasons why the contract failed to deliver in the early days. We lighted on the most important ones because of their systemic nature: Atos had made commitments in the tender that they knew when they submitted that tender they could not deliver; the Department for Work and Pensions failed to pilot the new assessment because they were in too much of a hurry to secure the savings; and finally, the department failed to tie down the contract tightly. As a result of these failures, disabled people were forced to wait too long and the government did not secure the early savings they wanted.

In their tender document, Atos claimed to have 750 assessment sites across London and the south-east of England – a mixture of NHS hospitals, private hospitals and physiotherapy centres. They clearly stated that 'each partner has contractually agreed to providing accommodation to the required specification'. In fact, Atos had no contractual agreements in place and two years after it had been awarded the contract had only ninety-six assessment centres open.

The exchange at our hearing was tense.

> MH: 'You said: "We can deliver the PIP service through an extensive estates network comprising 56 NHS, 25 private hospital and over 653 physiotherapy practices." You then went on to name a whole lot of trusts where you said: "We have agreements in place." You named NHS trusts, but did you have agreements in place with them?'
>
> Lisa Coleman (Senior Policy Officer, Atos): 'At the point of writing that tender document, we could not have agreements in place with them because we had not signed a contract with the department.'
>
> Richard Bacon MP: 'In document 4, part 5, at pages 72 and 73 of your tender document it states: "We have agreements in place whereby the contractual commitments of a failing partner can be picked up by another." Are you saying the tender document was incorrect?'
>
> Lisa Coleman: 'No, absolutely not. I know that there have been accusations that we lied in our tender

document, but we did not lie in the tender document. What we set out was what we were talking to the trusts about at the time.'

Richard Bacon: 'Can I just be clear. The reason why I interrupted the chair just then was because your last sentence was that you could not have had agreements in place at that point. My point is that your tender document said: "We have agreements in place." You just said a moment ago that you could not have had agreements in place. I am trying to figure out which of the two is true: the sentence you uttered just now or the sentence in your tender document. They cannot both be true, can they?'

Lisa Coleman: 'So what we had—'

Richard Bacon: 'They can't both be true, can they?'

Lisa Coleman: 'No, absolutely. The way you have described it, they cannot both be true.'

The problem was that the false promise had repercussions. It emerged from freedom of information (FOI) requests that some health partners named in the tender document had never agreed to be named. Some examples:

North Essex Partnership Foundation Trust said in answer to the FOI: 'The trust did not give explicit permission to be named in the tender document. We had tentative discussions about a potential partnership with Hinchingbroke Healthcare NHS Trust which did not go further.' Ipswich NHS Trust responded by saying: 'The trust did not enter into any agreement in principle to deliver PIP assessments . . . the trust had agreed to discuss the proposed partnership with Atos but never agreed in principle to deliver it . . . The trust wasn't aware that it had been named in the bid submission at the time it was submitted to DWP.' Mid Essex Health Trust provided emails showing that their negotiations with Atos had broken down in March 2012, before the tender documents naming them as a partnership organisation were submitted.

It was also clear that the government, at that time, believed that Atos had the necessary infrastructure in place to deliver the assessments. Lord David Alton, the ex-Liberal Democrat MP, asked a question about the capacity of Atos to deliver the PIP assessments at the end of July 2013, a year after the contract had first been awarded. Lord Freud, a minister in the Department for Work and Pensions, told him in a written answer: 'Atos have demonstrated through their supply chain *contractual arrangements* that they have full geographic coverage with an additional capacity of at least 15 per cent in each of their supply chain partners, as well as back up options across their network, should volumes prove higher than expected.'

That reply was not true. Atos did not have enough centres and health professionals to do the assessments in good time. That led them to break another commitment they had made in their tender:

Nick Smith MP: 'Ms Coleman, it seems that you are
      playing fast and loose with the truth, but may I come
      back to the point you were making about distance to
      attend? You said that it takes up to forty-five minutes
      for 40 per cent of people [to get to an assessment
      centre]. What percentage take more than an hour to
      get to one of your places?'
Lisa Coleman: 'At the moment it is around – I am using
      stats we have got now, but we are doing some more
      analysis—'
Nick Smith: 'Answer my question please.'
Lisa Coleman: 'I will. Currently we are seeing 40 per cent
      at less than forty-five minutes, about another 20 per

cent up to sixty minutes and then over an hour is the remainder, so that is about 40 per cent.'

MH: 'Say that again.'

Nick Smith: 'Slowly please.'

Lisa Coleman: 'It is 40 per cent less than forty-five minutes . . .'

Nick Smith: 'Yes, we got that. How many people take more than an hour?'

Lisa Coleman: 'About 40 per cent take more than an hour.'

MH: 'Again, in your contract, what did you commit to? Just tell the public.'

Lisa Coleman: 'We talked about what we thought we could achieve—'

MH: 'No. What did you commit to? When you submit a tender, it is not just chatting about something. It is saying, "This is the specification that I will deliver." That is what you are responsible for.'

Richard Bacon MP: 'What did you commit to in the tender document?'

Lisa Coleman: 'I have got to be honest. I would have to look at the document—'

Richard Bacon: 'I am looking at it. It is surprising that you are not familiar with it. It says that "because PIP claimants have heightened mobility challenges we have designed a solution which means that between 75 per cent and 90 per cent of claimants will be within thirty minutes' travel of a local centre".'

Atos failed to meet the exaggerated claims that they had set out in the tender. A television company, Hardcash Productions, which made a film about this contract fiasco, got advice on the legal position and were told by Rhodri Williams QC that 'based on the information which is now known about its supply chain, the tender submitted by Atos was misleading and in some cases may have involved actionable misrepresentations, should the Department for Work and Pensions have viewed the situation in that light and decided to take legal action'.

The department's permanent secretary Robert Devereux admitted that people were being let down, but he would not be drawn on the failure of Atos to meet what they outlined in the tender. He brushed aside our questions with the rather silly assertion that 'I have not contracted on the tender, have I? I have contracted on a contract.'

The department was culpable on other grounds. Introducing such a sensitive new benefit should have been managed with proper planning and great care so that it didn't result in a shambles for a very vulnerable group of people. That failed to happen. The Department for Work and Pensions abandoned a pilot for the new assessment after less than three months. They launched the new benefit nationally without testing it, presumably because they were anxious to get the financial savings earlier. So they did not understand how the new assessment would work in practice. They expected that only 75 per cent of the assessments would need to be done through a face-to-face interview. In practice, 97 per cent required a face-to-face assessment. The department thought each assessment would take an average of seventy-five minutes. In practice, the average length of time taken for each assessment turned out to be one hundred and twenty minutes.

Rushing the process, allowing a company that was experiencing difficulties in managing another similar contract to win another large piece of work, failing to hold the company to its tender terms, all these pretty obvious mistakes were made by the department. Nobody was held to account for this, but disabled people were failed. The best we could get out of Robert Devereux was: 'When the chair started by saying that this is about real people, I absolutely agree with that. This level of service is not the level that I want to continue with.'

Department of Energy and Climate Change (as of July 2016, Department for Business, Energy and Industrial Strategy)

Everybody worries that the lights might go out because our energy supply is so fragile. The department tasked with ensuring that this does not happen was until July 2016 the Department of Energy and Climate Change (DECC), working with the energy regulators. They have been overseeing a massive £176 billion investment programme, delivered over ten years, to secure enough energy for present and future generations. The facilities are being built and run by private companies, often foreign companies – the Chinese are poised to develop nuclear power stations; the global investment bank Macquarie, based in Australia, now owns Thames Water; we have the French-owned company EDF, the German-owned companies npower and E.ON UK, and the Spanish-owned Scottish Power; these are all major players in the energy market.

How the government designs and manages the investment programme matters, not just because we want the lights to stay on, but because we, as consumers, will pay for this investment through our bills.

Modelling by the Department of Energy and Climate Change showed that our fuel bills will go up by an astounding 18 per cent in real terms, just to pay for this huge investment programme. Getting consumers to pay is simply another form of taxation, but it is not progressive in the way that income tax is: whether rich or poor, we all pay more or less the same for our energy supply. Furthermore, fuel poverty is a big challenge for many families in the UK. Estonia is the only

European nation with a greater number of people struggling to pay their fuel bills.

So the capability of both the department and the regulators in securing a good deal for consumers is hugely important. If government is ripped off, families struggling with their bills are too.

The Public Accounts Committee examined a range of contracts throughout the five years, from those established to introduce smart meters to the early contracts for renewable electricity. The one that sticks in my mind was one we considered in October 2012. We looked at how the department had privatised the transmission of energy from offshore wind farms into the grid. The energy received from offshore wind farms is set to supply between 8 per cent and 15 per cent of all our energy needs by 2020. The decision to privatise the transmission was taken by the Labour government before the 2010 General Election – in fact, by the then Secretary of State, Ed Miliband. The privatisation was expected to create some £8 billion worth of transmission assets and the companies will receive – and we will pay – some £17 billion over twenty years in our bills.

Moira Wallace was the permanent secretary at the Department of Energy in October 2012. (She left the Civil Service shortly afterwards, at the end of that year, reportedly with an exit deal worth over £470,000, before going on to become the first female Provost of Oriel College, Oxford.) She started her evidence session with the committee by telling us: 'The system is privatised but it is regulated by Ofgem. What I think this report [the Audit Office report] shows is that as we build out the grids to bring in the electricity from offshore wind, we and Ofgem together have tried to innovate to keep costs down and combine the benefits of competition and regulation.'

By the end of the evidence session, we had come to a different conclusion. The Department of Energy and Ofgem had designed contracts to last for twenty years, although offshore wind turbines are unlikely to last for more than ten years. The successful contractors were guaranteed income for the life of the contract, whether or not the energy transmitted was needed and used; their payments were tied to the more expensive and generous retail price inflation index (whereas, for example, benefit payments are tied to the lower consumer price inflation index). If something went wrong with the cables and energy could not be transmitted, contractors would lose only 10 per cent of their expected income, whatever the cause of the breakdown. If they made excessive profits, no provision was included to share these with the consumer by lowering our bills.

'There has been a very lively competition for these licences,' Moira Wallace told us. Of course there was enthusiasm for this contract; the terms were so generous and all the risks lay with the consumer. The profit margins were around 10–11 per cent and when we asked Dr Chris Veal, a director from Transmission Capital, why he had competed for this business, he replied: 'Because the investment opportunity meets the investment criteria of the equity investors that we use for projects. It is an attractively structured regime.' The regime was so attractive to Transmission Capital that they successfully secured four of the first six licences granted. The company secured a fifth licence in Lincolnshire in 2014. This was hardly evidence of 'lively competition' bringing the 'benefits of competition' that Moira Wallace tried to persuade us she had achieved. Indeed, Macquarie, the Australian-based investment bank, which has been very active in the UK PFI market, sold their licence some two months after first winning it. Our scepticism led Moira

Wallace to observe: 'Shall we give this to one company as a monopoly or shall we compete it? We decided to compete it. That was a sensible decision to make. You may think that it was the hottest competition in the world . . . but surely it was an awful lot better than just handing it to someone as a monopoly.'

The committee was unanimous in its criticism of the way this competition had been devised and the terms of the licences. We could not understand why the Treasury, which had all the experience of the mistakes made in awarding PFI contracts down the years, had not intervened. When we asked the Treasury why they had not insisted on a clause that would have enabled customers to benefit from the excessive profits the companies might make from refinancing the deals (a common practice with PFI contracts), their spokesman Marius Gallagher rather pathetically told us: 'Well, I think it was a new type of contract and a new type of business and I think the aim was to get this up and running and not to introduce restrictions or limitations on getting the project off the ground – or off the water, so to speak.'

The lack of commercial nous was frustrating; the failure to prevent consolidation to a small number of companies was unhealthy; and the lack of transparency on the profits earned was an unacceptable repetition of past mistakes. Consumers were being ripped off by poor contracting.

Jackie Doyle-Price MP summed up our despair when she told our witnesses: 'What you have actually done is to create a marketplace that is now profoundly uncompetitive, because with one company getting four out of the first six licences, you effectively created a new monopoly with guaranteed income, with the risk being borne by the public sector, the taxpayer and the consumer, and those businesses are laughing all the way to the bank.'

The NHS and out-of-hours GP services in Cornwall

Serco won a five-year, £32 million contract to run the out-of-hours GP service in Cornwall in 2011. It did not take long for people working in the service to discover that they were manipulating the data – fiddling the figures – on how quickly they answered the telephone, how quickly they got a doctor out to see a sick patient and how often they called out the ambulance service.

However, it did take a long time for the whistleblowers to get their story heard. Their complaints to the company and to the commissioning health authorities went unheard. Stories in the local paper were brushed aside. When Felicity Lawrence of the *Guardian* wrote up the allegations in the national press, Serco responded with a letter from Valerie Michie, then the company's managing director, in which she said: 'We are well aware of a substantial number of allegations considered by the *Guardian*; these have been raised before, fully investigated by us and by a number of independent bodies, and found to be false and without foundation.'

But the determined whistleblowers and committed journalists did not go away. Serco eventually caved in and undertook a forensic audit of transactions over a six-month period and identified 252 instances where the data had been 'manipulated' – falsified – so that the company was seen to meet its performance targets. Serco blamed two maverick employees, whom they sacked, with confidentiality agreements linked to their severance payments stopping them from telling their side of the story. The NHS contract with Serco had been so badly drafted that the company continued to receive payments and was, indeed, still entitled to the bonus payments permitted under the terms of the contract.

Felicity Lawrence contacted me, and the National Audit

Office completed a quick piece of work that enabled us to give the issue a public hearing in April 2013. It seemed that Serco expanded its market share of public sector contracts by undercutting their competitors on price. Whereas Capita focused on takeovers of companies that had won public contracts, Serco bid low to secure contracts. The local Cornish GP co-operative, which had been running the service for £7.5 million a year until that point, lost out when Serco bid just over £6 million.

Serco proved good at winning the contracts but not so good at running the services. With less money in the contract, they employed fewer people so there were not enough GPs and those GPs who were supposed to carry out home visits were redeployed to run the out-of-hours emergency clinics; most shifts were not fully staffed. Similarly there were not enough staff to handle phone calls. In the summer of 2012, when many holidaymakers were visiting Cornwall, Serco's performance was particularly poor. Calls should have been answered within ninety seconds; but one in four took longer and, at its worst, a further 14 per cent of those who tried to reach a doctor on the phone abandoned their calls. The data were manipulated because they failed to meet the firm's performance targets.

Lack of staffing led to more patients being referred to the ambulance service. This meant that Serco was failing to meet another key performance indicator. To avoid that, this extraordinary email went out to Serco's staff: 'Please be aware that once the disposition screen for a 999 response is reached, we have three minutes in which to close the call and phone South Western Ambulance Service Trust. If the call remains open for longer than this three-minute window we fail on our KPIs [key performance indicators]. If you do not want/cannot close the calls immediately . . . please click back to the previous screen and "change answer" as this in essence stops the clock.' In effect, meeting the KPI by delaying the call for an ambulance seemed to take precedence over the patient's health. Again, Serco distanced themselves from the email, blaming their own middle manager for a 'poorly written' and 'regrettable' email.

All of the cheating was blamed on individuals, and Serco refused to accept that the company had any cultural issues, or that senior managers had given staff any instructions, or any financial incentives, that led employees to cheat.

We found that difficult to understand, especially because one of the most shocking aspects of this particular story was the attempt to clamp down on whistleblowers. We were given copies of an email that one of the assistant directors sent to staff which read: 'I am writing to inform you that as stated in the recent Team Brief, an investigation will begin over the coming week due to the recent inaccurate information that has been sent to the local and national press. Serco will be conducting a thorough investigation and will be working with third parties such as Cornwall IT Services for information related to Serco E mail accounts and any content of E mails deemed appropriate to establish the facts related to any false information being passed to others within the organisation or external to the business.'

Serco was trawling employees' emails to identify the whistleblower.

As shocking was the discovery that Serco rifled the staff's personal lockers to try to identify the whistleblower. When I asked: 'Did Serco undertake unannounced staff locker searches,' Serco replied: 'We did, yes . . . Again the individual who instigated that is no longer [with us].'

Once again the focus had been on procurement; the NHS had not focused on monitoring the delivery of the contract.

The performance measures they used actually encouraged poor behaviour, whether it was falsifying data or manipulating computer programs to delay calling an ambulance. The NHS should have developed effective performance criteria, like, for example, measuring how often a GP had to be called out during working hours after a patient had contacted the out-of-hours service. The contract was so poorly written that Serco could still claim bonus payments, despite their bad behaviour; the basic competence in drafting a contract that protected the public interest was missing. In some ways, saddest of all was the bullying of whistleblowers; supporting their rights and requiring providers to have appropriate protocols and practices in place should routinely be incorporated into contract documentation.

Ironically, securing a contract by cutting the price did not serve Serco well. Their undoubted capability in obtaining the business was not matched by an equivalent capability in running the service. The adverse publicity damaged their reputation and, coupled with the revelations on the electronic-tagging contract, undermined their credibility. Serco had to recruit more staff for the Cornish out-of-hours GP contract and therefore lost money on it.

Indeed, they ran into trouble on all three NHS contracts that they had secured. The company lost money on a Suffolk contract to provide community services, like district nurses, physiotherapists and paediatric teams. Again, Serco had undercut the incumbent NHS trust provider but could not supply the quality and number of staff at the price they agreed. Similarly, they took over running Braintree Community Hospital from the Mid Essex Hospital Trust, but could not deliver the appropriate service at the price they had agreed. By the end of 2013, Serco had lost over £17 million on all three contracts. The company pulled out of Cornwall, pulled out of

Private Profit and Public Good   339

Braintree and told the health authorities they wanted to pull out early from Suffolk. In August 2014, they announced that they were withdrawing from the UK clinical services market after making substantial losses. Finally, Serco's share price dropped from 674p in July 2013 to 170p in November 2014.

It was left to the publicly run NHS trusts to pick up the work and deliver the services, showing that the private sector is not always more efficient and effective at public service delivery.

These were not the only fiascos. High-profile failures, such as the army stepping in for G4S to provide proper security for the London Olympics and BT failing to keep its promises on rural broadband, made the headlines in 2012 and 2014 respectively. These stories stand as further evidence of the pitiful waste that can result from poor contracting.

Where next?

Chronicling these stories may well leave one sceptical as to the value of private sector involvement in the public sector. Inevitably our committee focused on catastrophes and so had a rather one-sided view. There are plenty of extremely well delivered public services that are provided by private companies, where taxpayers enjoy good value for money and citizens enjoy good services.

But equally there are too many disasters that demonstrate the systemic challenges that need to be tackled. The private sector's role in the public domain is well established and growing; that is the reality. There is now an urgent need to transform the way in which the state contracts, monitors and challenges its partners so that the taxpayer and service users secure good value. The reforms that I envisage fall into four categories: transparency; Civil Service capability; strong competition; and clear ethical standards firmly embedded in the culture of companies.

Transparency

At present we have an expanding shadow state filled with private providers that is neither transparent nor accountable to Parliament or to the public. Appropriate transparency would allow Parliament to follow the taxpayer's pound. Through greater transparency, we are more likely to ensure both better value and better services.

As Louis Brandeis, an American Supreme Court justice, wrote in 1914 in his book *Other People's Money: And How the Bankers Use It*: 'Sunlight is said to be the best of disinfectants.' David Cameron adopted that mantra before he became Prime Minister. It now needs to be translated into practice.

Too often during Public Accounts Committee hearings both private contractors and government departments hid behind commercial confidentiality to avoid accountability. We saw that in the way the Department for Work and Pensions refused to divulge information on the Work Programme. Similarly, BT and the Department for Culture, Media and Sport refused to reveal details of BT's contracts to provide superfast broadband in rural areas, leaving the committee, the people in rural communities and small businesses (who wanted to provide a similar service) suspicious that the monopoly supplier (BT) was ripping off the taxpayer and the consumer.

Confidence in the private sector's value, integrity and performance will only be secured through greater openness. All government contracts should be 'open-book' contracts so that there is a proper understanding of the underlying costs, profits and savings secured by involving the private sector. Companies do not have to engage in the public sector market, but if they do, they should accept appropriate standards of openness, not for their entire business, but for that part that is funded by the public purse. Clearly those standards would need to protect competition for public service contracts. But it is taxpayers' money that is being used to fund the contracts and accountability is an essential ingredient in a democracy.

The National Audit Office also needs the right to access and examine the contracts and all the relevant information in detail to assess whether value for money is being secured for the taxpayer. At the moment, the Audit Office can only look at departmental accounts, and cannot examine a government department's contracts in detail.

Finally, extending freedom of information provisions to public sector contracts would help to protect the public's right to know how our money is being spent and whether officials have secured a good deal on our behalf.

There is a growing recognition of the need for transparency. The CBI has promoted it, with John Cridland, its director-general in 2014, arguing: 'To improve transparency in outsourcing, the public services industry wants a presumption in favour of open-book accounting. The government needs to do its part too as it often pushes for closed contracts, which should now become the exception not the norm.'

Ruby McGregor-Smith, the chief executive of Mitie, an outsourcing company, said at the same time: 'Quite often we get bashed over the head and want to put our side of the story, but there's a term in our contract that stops us from speaking. The more openly transparent we can be, the better in the long run.'

When Serco, Atos, G4S and Capita gave evidence to us on this issue at the end of 2013, they all accepted the need for greater transparency. Paul Pindar of Capita actually said in his evidence: 'I think you should require open-book accounting. The simple principle for that is that if you are a contractor – as

I believe all of us are – that wants to do a good job and make a reasonable return but not to profiteer, there is no conceivable reason why you would not agree to open-book accounting. The second thing that I think you should think about is having the power to put third-party auditors in on any contract at any time. Again, if you have nothing to hide, why wouldn't you be prepared to do that?'

Given the broad consensus, it should be relatively straightforward for this to happen. However, I asked the Prime Minister about transparency directly on a number of occasions at the regular meetings held between the Prime Minister and chairs of all the select committees. He always avoided committing the government to further transparency and so this remains on the to-do list.

Civil Service capability

Transparency on its own is not enough. Civil servants need to have the capability to understand and act on what they are told. They also need to write tighter and more clearly focused contracts. Their ability to act as intelligent customers on the public's behalf remains all too often inadequate. A recurring theme from our inquiries was the lack of appropriate capabilities to commission and manage contracts. Bill Crothers, the government's chief procurement officer, told us: 'In a recent sample of large contracts, about a third were open-book, although most of the open-book clauses were not used. What we have are appropriate clauses, but for some reason, the departments were not enacting the open-book with them.' Only with the right contract-management expertise will transparency be properly used and therefore effective.

We came across one contract with one hundred and fifty key performance indicators, far too many to manage the contract properly, demonstrating another failure of contract management. At the same time, G4S's chief executive admitted that: 'it must be obvious that historically we have not had all the controls we needed in place'; again, a failure on the part of government, as well as on the part of the contractor, to agree the right terms.

Commissioning and managing contracts is not seen as a rewarding and important job by senior civil servants. When we looked at the fiasco surrounding the letting of the £5.5 billion franchise to run the West Coast Main Line train service, we found that not a single member of the project team came from the senior Civil Service. In the same vein, the chief executive of Capita told us: 'If I look at the biggest contracts that we have signed in the private sector, almost invariably the chief executive or the finance director is pretty intrinsically involved, certainly in the latter stages. Equally, looking at our local government relationships, we will be pretty close to the chief executive and the director of finance. If you carry that across into central government, we tend to be dealing with a lower level of seniority.'

Raising the priority and profile of contracting is important. This might also help to avoid government writing contracts where the penalties for failure are inappropriate, so that they do not repeat the mistakes of the Serco out-of-hours GP service contract in Cornwall or the Capita contract to provide interpreter services to the courts. Those charged with monitoring contracts should also rigorously implement the penalty clauses that are so often ignored. Clauses that enabled the taxpayer to benefit from excessive profits might be more widely incorporated, as lessons are learned from the over-generous PFI contracts and the privatisation of the transmission of electricity from offshore wind farms. Again, the private sector is ready to accept a profit-sharing agreement. Paul Pindar of Capita: 'There is a third thing that we can do as an industry, which again from Capita's perspective we would be very happy to do and is a far more imaginative and creative solution to the issue of companies making too much money. I get concerned when I hear people having a debate about the amount of margin that businesses like us make, because actually our margin is a by-product of efficiency. The best way of rewarding it is to say: "Let's agree what is a reasonable margin and then, above and beyond that, let's share that margin with the client.'" Government needs to grasp the opportunity to get better value offered by outsourcing companies like Capita.

Strong competition

If real value is to be secured from the private sector's involvement, we need to ensure that strong, competitive markets exist. Too often a small number of large contractors develop and dominate a particular service; that happened with the Work Programme, the offshore wind farm contracts and the rural broadband contracts. The big operators secure their market share through acquiring companies that have obtained public contracts (Capita and the interpreters' contract) or by undercutting other providers (Serco and the GP out-of-hours contract) or by making it impossible for competitors to bid (BT and the rural broadband contracts). Once they have secured their quasi-monopoly position in the market, it is much more difficult to guarantee strong competition and so eke out best value for the taxpayer. The powerful companies may be good at winning contracts but all too often they prove less than satisfactory at running services and yet they have become too big for the government to allow them to fail. We saw that with Serco and G4S after the electronic-tagging scandal.

The growing domination by a few large players in the public sector market squeezes out the thousands of small and medium-sized enterprises and the voluntary organisations that often have a far better record on public service delivery. The Coalition and the present government have been committed in principle to ensuring that small businesses and charities secure 25 per cent of the public sector market, but in practice government has failed to deliver on that commitment. Even where the big companies are encouraged to subcontract to small businesses, not enough happens. We saw how A4e creamed off 10 per cent of the fee without adding much value in the Work Programme contracts. Our study of the four big outsourcing companies found that Serco only subcontracted out 3 per cent and Atos only 7 per cent of the value of their contracts.

Small businesses often describe how difficult it is to break into the public sector market. One company, Buddi, had wanted to deliver the electronic-tagging contract, as we saw earlier; the chief executive expressed total frustration at the procurement process. She had spent eighteen months working on the tender and was asked to provide the equivalent of twelve A4 boxes of information. She told us that it took four days, working twenty hours each day, simply to print the documents. Buddi compared the UK procurement process with that of Michigan's Department of Corrections, where the preferred bidder was announced within five months of the competition being launched. Very few small businesses can take the risks involved in this complex and lengthy tendering process, and so get squeezed out of the market.

So government needs to ensure effective competition if it is to secure the benefits of private sector involvement in public service delivery. It should resist concentrating contracts in a small number of large companies, and it should enable small companies to enjoy a fair share of the business.

Ethical standards

Finally, those who choose to make their money in the public sector market should demonstrate appropriate ethical standards. Manipulating data, cheating, failing to meet acceptable quality standards by cutting corners, or exploiting the taxpayer by taking excessive profits, is simply unacceptable and should not be tolerated. There should be damaging financial penalty clauses in the contracts if any of these unethical behaviours are discovered. Appointments to boards should be vetted so that any allegation that the non-executive directors influence those who award contracts is avoided. Those who aggressively avoid tax should not secure contracts paid for by other taxpayers. Whistleblowers should not be feared and hounded; they need to be listened to and their rights should be protected. Supporting government in its policies on issues like the minimum wage, apprenticeships or working with small businesses and charitable organisations should become par for the course. All of this is basic common sense; it should not be politically contentious and it will simply help to bring about less waste, better services and a wider acceptance of the role of private sector companies working in the public sector.

18

Government Fit for Purpose

There are hundreds of thousands of brilliant and dedicated public servants working tirelessly to further the public good. Every day fantastic teachers transform children's opportunities; doctors and nurses save lives; police officers and the security services prevent terrorist outrages; families and individuals find their lives enhanced by a great play, a stunning piece of art, a countryside walk on a nature trail or a visit to a part of our national heritage – all of this is made possible by public services funded by the taxpayer.

There are also many talented and effective civil servants working at the heart of government. Yet week after week the Public Accounts Committee scrutinises projects and programmes where precious money is quite simply being wasted. The failure to achieve better value for money is not a party political issue. Both the main parties have an equally dismal record on waste and my comments are not designed to absolve politicians from their share of the blame. This is not about the public sector performing worse than the private sector; both waste too much public money. Importantly, it is not about questioning the commitment of public servants.

It is simply about believing that we can and must do better. Doing better is obviously a tough challenge. Were it easy, previous generations would have succeeded in securing sustainable improvements. But there is a worrying complacency and resistance to change at the heart of the Civil Service – sadly combined with a lack of interest by our political leaders, who never prioritise Civil Service reform. So change is slow and limited, and high levels of waste recur time and time and time again.

This is not because the people who work in the public sector are incompetent, lazy or bad; they are a reasonably talented and able bunch of people trying to work in a system that has fundamental flaws. It is those systemic faults that need to be tackled. Civil Service capability, accountability and organisation need to change.

Sadly there is no one magical silver bullet that can resolve the ingrained and systemic flaws and I know that some of the proposals I set out below are deeply controversial. But at the very least, we should confront the challenges and debate these proposals alongside alternative ideas that others have developed. Without an obvious answer, it may be that we need a perpetual revolution, in which we are always changing, adapting and improving in the quest for better value and better services.

None of this is new. Anthony Trollope in *The Three Clerks*, written in 1858, said: 'It was too notorious that the Civil Service was filled by the family fools of the aristocracy and middle classes, and that any family, who had no fool to send, sent in lieu thereof, some invalid past hope. Thus the service had become a hospital for incurables and idiots.' A cruel and unfair judgement, expressed in language that is unacceptable today, but he was expressing a frustration then that many still feel now.

So the first set of reforms concerns how we develop people's skills and expertise, what is valued in the Civil Service and who we promote. When people of my generation entered the Civil Service in the 1960s and 1970s, the job was all about developing advice for ministers on new policies. Today the emphasis has shifted from policy to practice, from dreaming up new ideas to actually running public services or letting and managing contracts.

If the job has changed, the skills required and the way civil servants work must also change and that has yet to happen in any profound way. It must start from the top.

Senior civil servants

Much good work at less senior levels is undermined by weaknesses at the top of the Civil Service. It has always seemed to resemble a masonic lodge, full of people from a similar background, who have mostly been lifelong civil servants and whose main purpose is to protect themselves and each other. When I checked on the background of the current cohort of permanent secretaries, all bar two went to Oxford or Cambridge, and one of the two went to an American university. They come from the same tight professional and social group. They hold traditional views about the Civil Service and fight like tigers to resist change.

Gus O'Donnell, the suave ex-Cabinet Secretary, had been an Oxford Blue. He claimed good interpersonal skills and was awarded with a seat in the House of Lords when he retired. He gave the game away in his evidence to the Public Accounts Committee. He was telling us about a newly recruited independent tax commissioner. He wanted to assure us that after the Goldman Sachs shambles, the government had established proper separation between those who negotiated tax deals with companies and those who authorised them, and was keen that we should know about the new man they had just appointed. He said [my italics]:

'Simon Bowles, the chief finance officer in the department who is an accountant by profession, for which I forgive him *because he was at Trinity College where he read economics – that is close to my heart.*'

Simon Bowles was 'one of them'.

The top civil servants look out for each other and dispense pretty quickly with any outsiders brought in to stimulate change. Talented individuals from the private sector or local government never last long at the top of the Civil Service tree. This is in part because the Civil Service has its own strongly entrenched culture with particular ways of working, talking and behaving. Unless you adopt the conventions, you are quickly isolated, ignored and removed. Michael Bichard, who was a radical and effective departmental leader, with a background in running local authorities and government agencies, was overlooked to become Cabinet Secretary, although he was the obvious person who might have brought about much-needed reform under Tony Blair. Bob Kerslake, an extremely successful local authority chief executive, managed just over two years as head of the Home Civil Service under the Coalition government before he was propelled into the House of Lords. Bill Crothers, who had worked in Accenture before joining the Civil Service, survived for only a few years as the government's chief commercial officer. Ian Watmore, with a strong background in IT in the commercial world, lasted less than two years as head of the government's Efficiency and Reform Group, leaving, he said, to support his wife in the north-west of England when she became a vicar there. Mike Bracken, who had been brought in to lead the government's Digital Service, said of the Civil Service in an exit interview with the Global Government Forum: 'Well, its greatest strengths are its resilience, its people – I will say that the people are lovely. Yeah, they're the major strengths. Its major weaknesses are its resilience and its people!'

The current cadre of permanent secretaries may have good academic qualifications, but most of them have neither the life experience nor the skills needed in the twenty-first century. When we questioned the permanent secretaries from both the Home Office and the Ministry of Justice, they admitted that they had never managed or run a contract. Indeed, too many permanent secretaries spend more of their time managing their secretaries of state than they do running their departments.

If they fail it doesn't seem to matter – failure is regularly rewarded at the top. For instance, despite the shambles over Universal Credit, the Work Programme, the introduction of Personal Independence Payments, the fitness-to-work assessment for people claiming disability benefits, and on and on – despite all those shambles, Robert Devereux, the permanent secretary in the Department for Work and Pensions, was in 2016 awarded a knighthood. Despite presiding over questionable performance at HMRC – with an increase in the tax gap, a dreadful service to the public (when the phones were often simply not answered), and poor morale among her staff – the permanent secretary, Lin Homer, has been anointed a Dame.

This is simply nonsense and demonstrates a worrying complacency and arrogance among those at the top of the Civil Service. It needs strong political determination from our political leaders to challenge and change the status quo and allow true reform to take place. Indeed, transforming the machinery of government should be a cross-party endeavour. We should all get behind the Prime Minister of the day on this. There is much consensus across the parties and if we worked together, the impact of the electoral cycle would no longer be in the way of progress.

With clear political determination, transforming the leadership of the Civil Service could happen so that the club is broken up, new people with different skills and experience are brought in, and a new culture with different ways of working is developed. We need a new and different leadership.

Civil Service organisation and skills

Lower down the Civil Service, new recruits are mostly the brightest and best young things, who arrive with a strong commitment to public service. The culture of the Civil Service, perpetuated by the permanent secretaries, thwarts their progress. No serious and sustained effort is made to develop the financial, commercial, IT and project management skills that modern government demands. All too often, the ability to advise on policy is celebrated while the ability to steer a project or programme through to successful completion is ignored.

This reflects the cultural tension that exists at the heart of the organisation between policy formulation and programme implementation. The same is, of course, true of politicians, who are much more obsessed with creating new ideas than with prioritising good governance. If both the politicians and the senior Civil Service remain gifted but dilettante amateurs who prefer to dabble in new policies, then efficiency and effectiveness inevitably suffer. Both need to change.

The way that jobs are organised and the way that people are promoted reflect the bias towards policy-making. If you want to climb the career ladder, you are expected to change jobs every couple of years to broaden your knowledge, rather than deepen your experience. Just as you become useful in one job you are encouraged to move to a different one and the person who takes over from you has to spend time coming up to speed. I spent just over two years as Minister for Children, and at the end of that time I had longer institutional knowledge of the subject than most of the officials with whom I worked, because they had all moved on to different jobs.

A common feature of the regular disasters we examined was the frequent change of personnel. The FIReControl project was led by ten different people over a five-year period; no wonder it ended in disaster. On the other hand, the prison rebuilding programme had the same official running it for years and the new prisons were completed on time and within cost.

It cannot be beyond the wit of the Civil Service to devise a career progression ladder with appropriate financial rewards and opportunities for promotion that encourages all civil servants to develop expertise and to stay to see jobs through to their conclusion.

Other divisions of responsibility impede efficiency and effectiveness. One group of people devise and negotiate contracts and then pass the task of monitoring to another group of officials. The first task has higher status than the second. From the electronic-tagging contract to the out-of-hours GP service contract in Cornwall, this unfortunate division of labour has led to shocking waste. Those responsible for writing the contracts so badly were nowhere near the monitoring of their implementation because monitoring performance was seen as mundane and unimportant, with nobody listening when concerns were raised.

In a similar vein, those responsible for framing and taking legislation through Parliament then hand the implementation over to another group who are left to pick up the pieces on stuff that just cannot be implemented. Universal Credit is a strong example of that disconnect. A radical rethink around how civil servants work should be part of a fundamental reform programme.

Doctrine of ministerial accountability

However, it is the relationship between Parliament, government and the Civil Service that is in most serious need of reform and modernisation.

The prevailing convention is that civil servants are accountable only to ministers who are then accountable to Parliament. This principle is strongly defended by all the senior Civil Service – and by some ministers – for the secrecy it provides. Indeed, just before his departure from government at the end of 2011, the Cabinet Secretary Gus O'Donnell wrote to me to complain about our inquiry into HMRC when we had required General Counsel Anthony Inglese to give his evidence on oath. You will remember that we wanted to test the veracity of a document containing the minutes of a meeting held to discuss the deal reached with Goldman Sachs that the whistleblower Osita Mba had sent to us. I quote from this letter in the chapter on Goldman Sachs.

It was as if Gus O'Donnell had taken on the role of shop steward for aggrieved senior civil servants. You will recall that he argued that the doctrine of ministerial accountability was vital to preserving political impartiality in the Civil Service. He also strongly maintained that the advice given by general counsel to the head of tax was protected by legal privilege. It is odd, is it not, that a lawyer, whose salary is paid by the taxpayer, gives advice to an official, whose salary is also paid by the taxpayer, yet Parliament has no right of access to that advice, even when it pertains to an issue (the Goldman Sachs sweetheart deal) where the taxpayer lost millions of pounds? It is also odd in a modern democracy that Parliament has no right to ask questions of civil servants who are directly responsible for a particular matter.

It is the doctrine of ministerial accountability that is broken and needs fixing. If less money is to be wasted, government must be more open to parliamentary and public scrutiny, and officials who are responsible for implementing policies should be held to account for their efficiency and effectiveness in doing so. The conventions around ministerial accountability need to be revisited and revised.

The convention of accountability is steeped in our history. It was the Northcote-Trevelyan reforms, promoted by William Gladstone in the 1850s, that first articulated the idea of a non-partisan Civil Service, selected on merit and ability and not on patronage and influence. This idea formed the basis of the Civil Service we have today.

Then, in 1918, Viscount Haldane was appointed by David Lloyd George to review the machinery of government. It was he who introduced the principle of ministerial accountability. He argued that civil servants and ministers were interdependent, with impartial civil servants providing advice to ministers who were then responsible for exercising their authority to decide. In many European countries and in America, the power of the political class and that of the administrative class is separate. In the UK, we consider them inseparable.

This principle has regularly been confirmed down the years, most recently articulated by Robert Armstrong, Cabinet Secretary in 1985, in what is known as the 'Armstrong Memorandum'. In it he said: 'Civil servants are servants of the Crown. For all practical purposes, the Crown, in this context, means and is represented by the government of the day ... the executive powers of the Crown are exercised by and on the advice of Her Majesty's ministers, who are in turn answerable to Parliament. The Civil Service as such has no constitutional personality or responsibility separate from the duly constituted Government of the day ... The duty of the individual civil servant is first and foremost to the Minister of the Crown who is in charge of the Department in which he or she is serving.'

But these arrangements were agreed in a very different world. When Haldane reported in 1918, there were twenty-eight civil servants in the Home Office. By December 2014, despite all the staff cuts brought about by the deficit reduction programme, there were around 28,000 full-time equivalent civil servants in the Home Office. The idea that any Home Secretary can be held to account for the actions of so many civil servants is absurd; it makes a nonsense of the important accountability that we really need in order to secure better value.

The impracticality of the doctrine is already changing things. Charles Clarke was a victim of it when he was sacked as Home Secretary in 2006 after it emerged that his officials had not carried out a government pledge to deport foreign prisoners freed at the end of their sentences. Simon Hughes, a Liberal Democrat MP, said at the time: 'In politics, if things go wrong then somebody has to carry the can and that is the person at the top.' The failure had not been a failure of policy but a failure of administration.

Five years later, Theresa May ignored the doctrine of ministerial responsibility and blamed the head of the UK Border Force, Brodie Clark, for improperly relaxing passport checks at Britain's borders to better manage the growing passport queues. He was forced to quit and she got away with it. He felt unjustly treated and said so publicly: 'I am saddened that my career should end in such a way after forty years' dedicated service. My employer has disregarded my right to reply in favour of political convenience.' He claimed that Theresa May's statements on the matter 'were wrong and were made without the benefit of hearing my response to formal allegations. With the Home Secretary announcing and repeating her view that I am at fault, I cannot see how any process conducted by the Home Office, or under its auspices, can be fair and balanced.'

These two incidents demonstrate the difficulties that can arise with the historic convention. They show the frustration felt by both civil servants and politicians. Politicians have to take responsibility for the actions of others over whom they have no control and civil servants cannot answer in public for what they have or have not done.

It is almost a hundred years since the principle of ministerial accountability was introduced. The world has changed and the Civil Service bears very little resemblance to the one that existed then, making a mockery of existing conventions. Also, the way in which public services are delivered has changed and this makes it hard, for instance, to hold ministers to account for what happens in independent hospital trusts or academy schools. Equally, are ministers culpable when G4S is found to have physically and mentally abused children held in secure detention centres that it manages under contract? The days of big government and large departments, when it was more straightforward to hold ministers to account for all that happened on their watch, are gone.

Contemporary expectations lead one to further question the traditional conventions. The Freedom of Information Act and the role of the Parliamentary and Health Service Ombudsman have helped to open up the Civil Service to public account. The public's demand for transparency and twenty-four/seven media create pressure for more openness. Yet while the government has imposed greater transparency on other bodies, such as local authorities, it has failed to impose similar standards on itself. It's not that transparency of itself will improve services, but it is a means by which actions and performance can be challenged, judged and improved.

There is, further, a flaw at the heart of the doctrine of ministerial accountability. Ministers are deemed responsible for the actions of civil servants, yet they have no say in the recruitment, the promotion or the dismissal of civil servants, for that is seen to offend the principle of impartiality. How can anybody be held responsible for the actions of people they can't hire or fire?

In fact, civil servants escape external accountability because they are protected by the convention of ministerial responsibility, and they escape internal accountability because ministers are powerless to hold them to account in any meaningful way.

Incremental reforms reflect the essential fracture in the convention on ministerial accountability. Francis Maude, when he was at the Cabinet Office, introduced extended ministerial offices, giving ministers the power to personally appoint their own civil servants, special advisers and external policy experts to work directly to them in a much larger private office. Permanent secretaries are being moved on to fixed-term contracts. The Civil Service has accepted that the responsible official for a project can give evidence to select committees as opposed to the permanent secretary being the only civil servant answerable to Parliament. They have also accepted that permanent secretaries who have moved to a different job can be brought back to account for their actions in their previous role.

These reforms are welcome, but they are tinkering at the edges. The lack of transparency and accountability has frustrated many for a long time. The Scott Inquiry into the arms for Iraq affair reported: 'The enforcement of accountability depends largely on the ability of Parliament to prise information from governments which are inclined to be defensively secretive where they are most vulnerable to challenge.'

I agree. We need to rethink the relationship between the Civil Service and ministers, and the Civil Service and Parliament. Settling on a new convention is not easy and there are many tricky issues that need to be resolved, but simply clinging to the past because it is difficult to devise the future is no answer either.

If civil servants were more directly accountable to Parliament, and through Parliament to the public, that would open up some of the debates around policy decisions which are presently private and secret. We would know whether civil servants warned ministers that implementing Universal Credit in two years was impossible. We would know whether Brodie Clarke or Theresa May was responsible for relaxing the checks at our borders. We might understand who took the crass decisions on the aircraft carriers.

Creating a new protocol, through which civil servants were more openly and directly accountable for their actions, would link responsibility much more clearly with accountability. The idea that there is a clear division between decisions around policy and actions around implementation is flawed. In holding to it, we miss the huge arena of discretion open to civil servants. I learned that from my years as a minister.

Opening all of this to public account by making civil servants more directly answerable to Parliament is controversial and difficult. It means that the debate about policy would be more transparent and that the policy debates between ministers and civil servants would be more visible. But that need not undermine the authority of ministers, and opening the process up might make for better policymaking.

I cannot pretend to have all the answers to the questions this radical change would throw up – that would take another book. But those challenges should not become an excuse for sticking with the status quo, which no longer holds good. We need to consider and debate change.

A positive and pragmatic approach by all concerned would help surmount the hurdles and lead to a modern framework of accountability that would better serve the taxpayers who fund public services and the citizens who use them.

A strategic centre

Another major reform concerns the role of the centre. Government has a centre that is both divided and weak; this impinges on the efficiency and effectiveness of the whole. There are three departments at the centre: the Treasury, the Cabinet Office and the Number 10 Policy Unit. Between them they employ over 3600 people directly, with a further 1000 working in agencies linked to the departments. They spend far too much time arguing with one another and engaging in power struggles at the expense of coherence and good administration. No other big organisation would be fragmented at its heart in this way. No other organisation would boast an institutional structure that encouraged turf wars rather than constructive debate about tricky issues. No other big organisation would have a central finance department that did not fulfil a finance function but simply carved up the budget and distributed it.

So, merging the three parts of the centre under the Prime Minister, working with the Chancellor of the Exchequer, would strengthen the authority of the centre and that could help improve efficiency and effectiveness. This need not undermine the welcome move to decentralise services. Indeed, a strong, strategic centre can actually better enable clear powers to be decentralised.

The centre needs to be strengthened not to manage departments, but to join up thinking so that good practice is copied across government and lessons are learned from past mistakes and failures. A more effective centre could ensure that government takes advantage of its size and reach in purchasing goods and services. A more effective centre could ensure better co-ordination across departments on cross-cutting issues so that services are not based on departmental priorities but are built around the needs of citizens and that decisions taken by one part of government do not adversely impact on another part. A more effective centre could take responsibility for some back-office government-wide functions, such as human resources or information technology, securing best value for those services. A proper finance capability at the centre would be able to use financial incentives to drive change and secure a more corporate rather than departmental approach.

There have been moves to strengthen the capability at the centre. Tony Blair's government introduced the Prime Minister's Delivery Unit and the Coalition government created the Major Projects Authority, now merged to create the Infrastructure Projects Authority. But the senior Civil Service is entrenched in its opposition to any challenge to the autonomy of departments, even though it understands the problems that creates.

Bob Kerslake, when he was head of the Home Civil Service, told us in 2014: 'It is nirvana. Of course people protect their own budgets and of course people will try to play games.'

More concerning was a letter I received that same year, after one of our hearings, from Bob Kerslake as head of the Civil Service, Nick Macpherson as permanent secretary to the Treasury, and Richard Heaton, who was permanent secretary for the Cabinet Office. It read:

Your committee urges the Cabinet Office and the Treasury
to take a strong strategic lead, as the government's
corporate centre. This is what already happens on a range

of cross-cutting and common issues . . . However the
high degree of central direction and integration that you
appear to recommend does not reflect the model that this
government and previous governments have operated. This
is a matter of policy, on which the government differs from
both the NAO and the PAC.

This arrangement reflects the reality of Cabinet
government, with Secretaries of State each responsible
for areas of policy where he or she enjoys considerable
autonomy subject to collective responsibility. This
is complementary to the century old model of the
Accounting Officer, who is personally responsible for the
activity the organisation he or she leads. On this is founded
our system of accountability to Parliament, notably to your
committee and to other select committees too . . .

The centre does not and cannot take decisions or set
a strong direction on every item of the £720 billion of
public expenditure. So long as the essentials – such as
the controlled spending totals and collective agreement –
are delivered and upheld, there is considerable freedom
about implementation. Experience has shown that this
approach is the most effective method of securing good
governance . . . While it would be possible to redesign
our model of government to operate as you suggest, the
government must be free to choose its own policy path.

We were, of course, suggesting strong strategic oversight by
the centre, not interfering controls. I had had several conversations with Francis Maude who as Minister for the Cabinet
Office was in charge of Civil Service reform. We agreed about
the need for a stronger strategic capability at the heart of government to improve efficiency, so I was surprised to receive
this uncompromising rejection of the idea from his senior

officials. When I raised the matter with Maude, it emerged that neither he nor his private office had been given sight of the letter. He strongly disagreed with what the letter said, yet the civil servants used ministers in arguing their case. After my conversation with Francis Maude, I received a different sort of letter signed by him and Danny Alexander, in his role as Chief Secretary, endorsing our view . . . but Francis Maude stepped down a year later after the General Election and the senior Civil Service triumphed – again.

Public service standards

There are a range of other reforms that would enhance the integrity and quality of public administration.

The relationship between the Civil Service and vested interests in the private sector can be too close. It was Stephen Kelly – the man brought in from the private sector to create greater efficiencies – who told us in evidence: 'A thing that still worries me, because I still think it is the tip of the iceberg, is that almost £500,000 is spent on hospitality, entertaining civil servants, and I think that is wrong. But it is changing. Certainly the old days of the Wimbledon men's final and all those sort of things are diminishing.'

I wonder.

There are also too many individuals who take advantage of the revolving door too quickly, using their knowledge and experience in the Civil Service to get more money for themselves and help to secure more money and better deals for the private sector. The case of Dave Hartnett moving swiftly from HMRC to jobs with HSBC and Deloitte was remarkable but not unique. Alan Cave was a senior official in the Department for Work and Pensions in charge of the Work Programme one week. The next week he was sitting at a desk in Serco, one

of the companies he had been overseeing. His move to Serco
had not been vetted because he was not considered sufficiently
senior within the Civil Service.

We investigated the project to construct an additional lane
on the M25. The National Audit Office suggested that this
had been achieved at a potential unnecessary extra cost of £1
billion to the taxpayer. Ian Scholey had been the official in
charge of the project for five years. When we asked whether
he could give evidence we were told that he had left the
Highways Agency and joined Parsons Brinckerhoff, one of the
consultants commissioned to work on the M25 improvement
programme. Parsons Brinckerhoff earned nearly £5 million
in fees from 2005 to 2008 from working on the M25 project
for the Highways Agency.

We identified too many cases where individuals were
declared redundant by one public organisation and received
a generous redundancy package, only to emerge elsewhere in
the public sector in a new job with a good salary. One egregious example of this practice was revealed when we examined
a disastrous set of decisions in relation to Hinchingbrooke
Hospital in East Anglia. Rather than take the tough decision
to close the hospital, as there were too many hospital beds in
that area, the regional strategic health authority, led by Sir
Neil McKay, decided to bring in a private company to run
it. That venture failed and Sir Neil McKay signed off the
disastrous contract with the private healthcare provider. He
was rewarded soon after with a redundancy package worth
£1 million when strategic health authorities were abolished
and then popped up again as the chair of Manchester's cardiac
management board.

A similar sort of unacceptable carelessness in the relationship
between the public and private sector emerged during our
inquiries into tax. So Accenture, who signed a £10 million

deal with HMRC in 2010 to support the department's IT infrastructure, paid no corporation tax in either 2009 or 2010, although they claimed profits of over £180 million in their accounts. They were making money from contracts funded by the taxpayer, yet getting away with not paying their fair share into the common pot.

This tendency towards double standards was brought into stark relief after an investigation screened by the Channel 4 *Dispatches* programme in July 2012. It alleged that two non-executive directors of the HMRC board were themselves avoiding tax. Phil Hodkinson chaired HMRC's ethics committee; at the same time, he worked for a FTSE 100 firm, Resolution Ltd, which was based in Guernsey to avoid UK income tax and corporation tax. He left HMRC six months after the programme aired. Similarly, John Spence, who chaired HMRC's audit committee, was also chairman of a major estate agent and financial services group, Spicer Haart. An employee of his company told a Channel 4 undercover reporter that he had facilitated stamp-duty avoidance for millionaires from India and China. George Osborne had attacked this as 'a major source of abuse – and one that rouses the anger of many of our citizens'. John Spence left the HMRC board at about the time that Channel 4 broadcast its programme.

All these examples demonstrate that government should have tougher rules for civil servants (and for politicians) on revolving-door appointments. All public appointments and government contracts need to be fearlessly scrutinised to ensure that no double standards are practised; those who fail to adhere to a basic set of standards should not be employed by government.

Government also needs to get tougher on itself in its role as the employer and demonstrate the highest standards of propriety in its employment practices. We uncovered extensive use of off-payroll arrangements with staff in the Civil Service, the NHS and the BBC. They were employing staff through personal services companies rather than on the PAYE system, thereby avoiding both National Insurance and income tax. More than 2400 senior civil servants were working on this basis for central government and an incredible 25,000 off-payroll contracts were being used by the BBC. Government responded swiftly to our findings to stamp out this practice, but too many people working for the public sector, whose salaries are funded by the taxpayer, are still using personal service companies as a way of avoiding tax.

Similarly, an inquiry into how government used severance payments with confidentiality clauses to dispense with the services of employees – and keep it secret – showed unacceptable practice. The National Audit Office found that during a three-year period to March 2013, the Treasury approved over a thousand special severance payments at a cost of £28.4 million and that 88 per cent of those compromise agreements contained a confidentiality clause. This audit did not cover the NHS, local government and other public bodies. There were some shocking examples, where it seems to me that individuals should have faced disciplinary action rather than benefiting from a pay-off. For example, the chief executive of Morecambe Bay Hospitals Trust was paid his salary for a year and was seconded to a charity, weeks after a high-profile police inquiry into deaths at the trust's maternity unit. The Mid Staffordshire NHS Foundation Trust signed compromise agreements to secure the departure of both the chair and the chief executive, despite the serious failings that came to light in the 2013 Francis Report. The Department for Media, Culture and Sport made a payment of £16,000 to someone working for one of the organisations funded by the department after serious allegations of gross misconduct had been made against him. All of this lack of transparency and accountability is allowing taxpayers' money to be used to reward failure and allowing public bodies to avoid implementing disciplinary processes that might attract unwelcome publicity.

Sometimes compromise agreements were, and probably still are, being used to silence whistleblowers. The stories in this book have shown the vital contribution whistleblowers make to exposing appalling waste and poor-quality services. From A4e to Osita Mba in HMRC and from Google to Mid Staffordshire Trust, legitimate concerns would not have been exposed without whistleblowers. But the evidence from whistleblowers can be very challenging for bosses, who may prefer to sweep the issues under the carpet. Surveys across Whitehall demonstrate that the culture of too many public organisations discourages whistleblowing. A Ministry of Defence survey found that only 40 per cent of those who responded felt they would not suffer reprisals if they raised concerns. A survey among Department of Health staff found that just 54 per cent felt confident that they could speak up about concerns they had about the service in which they were working. So obviously we found it very difficult to encourage people to give evidence in public about their experience as whistleblowers.

These issues can be put right if people want to put them right. It requires the confidence to admit that problems exist and the commitment to prioritise reform. As John Browne, the highly intelligent ex-chairman of BP who helped both the Labour government and the Coalition government in a variety of roles, observed: 'People say not that something went badly, but that it went "less well" than they had hoped.' Only when we really face up to the systemic failures that bedevil the public sector will we be able to deliver what every voter, every taxpayer, every customer and most public servants want – better-quality public services giving us best value for every pound spent.

19

Final Reflections

Over the five years I spent calling to account those people who spend your money, I learned a great deal. But I hope this book is not just a rant against the waste, profligacy and bungling we uncovered. I have written it because I know that things can be different and better. There are thousands of dedicated and talented men and women who spend their lives on the front line of our public services doing brilliant work. We have all experienced that excellence in the classroom, in the A&E department, at the council helpdesk and from our local police officer. The Public Accounts Committee also saw some first-rate projects and well-run services during the course of our work.

But we owe it to the thousands of brilliant public servants, to the millions who struggle each month to make ends meet while paying their taxes without question, and to those who depend on public services in their daily lives, to do better.

As I reflect on what we uncovered, a number of consistent themes emerge:

There is mind-boggling waste of taxpayers' money right across government. This book has covered only the tip of the iceberg;

we held hearings on far too many other Ministry of Defence disasters where the determination to buy the newest and the best, rather than tried-and-tested equipment, led to waste; we uncovered unnecessary waste in the Department of Transport, from the cancellation of the West Coast Main Line contract to the public private partnership contract with Metronet for the maintenance of the London Underground. We identified scandalous waste in the NHS, in the Home Office, in the Department for Energy and Climate Change, in the Department for Work and Pensions, in the Department for Business, Innovation and Skills, and in many other departments. We found that the private sector performed no better than the public sector in delivering public services.

We identified an alarming and deep-rooted culture where all too often the responsible officials displayed a nonchalant attitude to spending the hard-earned money we entrust to them when we pay our taxes. They felt no sense of personal responsibility because it was not their own money. Sometimes they could not distinguish between their public responsibility and their private and personal interest. Or they dealt with the waste by simply shifting the blame to another person or another institution. The NHS blamed the hospital trusts or the Care Quality Commission, the Home Office blamed the Border Force and the Department for Education blamed the schools and local government. The chapter on the BBC in this book gives just one example among many such cultural issues. I think in particular of the case of a primary school in Lambeth, the Durand Academy, where the headteacher had established private leisure centre facilities on school land gifted to the academy by the state. He said that the facilities had been created to raise money for education. While some of the profits were invested in education, he set up a separate company to run the leisure facilities and paid himself over £160,000 a year from the company. This was on top of enjoying one of the highest headteacher salaries in the country, so that he earned in total around £400,000 a year. Astonishingly, he also set up a dating agency that was originally registered at the school. When questioned about whether this was appropriate, he retorted: 'This is my private life and has nothing to do with this. A few friends and I decided to start a small business in which I have a minor stake . . . because I live on the site doing my job five days a week the mail comes there.' Here was a man who had been a successful head but who it seems to me could no longer distinguish between his responsibilities as a public servant entrusted with public resources and his interests as a private individual.

All too often government seemed institutionally incapable of learning from its past mistakes. Whether we looked at PFI contracts, major IT investment programmes or the management of the government's massive debt, just to name a few examples, the same things seemed to go wrong time and time again. This was, in part, because the cycle of politics, coupled with the career structure within the Civil Service, created no institutional memory and a very short-term approach. Nobody seemed to care about the cost to future generations of nuclear waste or student loans or medical negligence, because they would no longer be there; it would become somebody else's problem. Also, silo working in Whitehall departments with a very weak centre at the heart of government made it much more difficult for the whole organisation to learn the lessons from past failures – and past successes.

The Civil Service continues to lack the appropriate skills and expertise required for modern government. In a world where most public services are run and managed by private providers, the skills needed to specify, commission, manage and monitor contracts were too often not there. The talented young people recruited

into the Civil Service did not receive enough appropriate
training to succeed. Their success was measured and rewarded
by how swiftly they moved to another job, rather than by
how effectively they completed the task to which they had
originally been assigned. Their ability to develop new policy
ideas commanded greater respect and value than the financial,
project management, commercial or IT skills needed to reform
and manage public services efficiently. The top of the Civil
Service was filled by people from a small elite who themselves
had neither the experience nor the skills required in today's
public sector world and who excluded or rejected outsiders
who might have filled the gaps. Politicians must shoulder
responsibility for what happened on their watch, but so too
should the bureaucrats who are responsible for both advice
and implementation. The Civil Service rightly celebrates its
strengths of professionalism and impartiality, but is reluctant
to accept the fundamental changes in career structures or
accountability that are necessary to develop an organisation
fit for purpose in the twenty-first century.

*The link between being responsible for a project or service and
then being held to account for its performance was simply too weak.*
The long-established convention that civil servants are only
accountable to their ministers who in turn are accountable
through Parliament to the public does not make sense in the
modern world. Government has become both big and fragmented, and there is a much broader range of diverse private
and public bodies responsible for delivering public services.
The notion that any individual minister can be called to
account for all that happened in this complex and disjointed
environment is wrong.

*Public confidence that the government, the tax authorities and the
tax system treat all taxpayers equally was questioned by our hearings.*
Our investigations based on evidence from whistleblowers and

the investigative work of journalists started to lift the lid on how the tax system actually worked, on the role and power of tax professionals and multinational companies, and on the efficiency and effectiveness of Revenue and Customs both in securing the tax revenues necessary to fund public services and in demonstrating fairness in the administration of tax. When the vast majority of people unquestioningly pay their regular contributions while multinational businesses and very rich individuals seek successfully to avoid tax, trust in the system is undermined. Since the 2015 General Election, we have had Google's UK tax settlement which was greeted with scepticism. It did not achieve what both the company and the government intended, namely to convince the public that Google is paying a fair amount of tax on the profits they earn from their economic activities in the UK. The extraordinary leaks from the Panamanian law firm Mossack Fonseca showed how far-reaching tax avoidance and potential tax evasion remains, with extensive collusion by banks, lawyers and advisers in helping rich individuals hide wealth and avoid or evade tax. Both these revelations show that there still needs to be enormous change to convince the public that our system is fair.

Securing change

Securing better value for money can be achieved but it does require change. That means that our political leaders must prioritise the necessary reforms and the Civil Service must be willing to embrace change. Securing that commitment is a tough ask, as politicians do not like to focus on delivery and the Civil Service is hugely resistant to change. Personally, I would concentrate on three areas of reform: transparency, accountability, and training and management in the Civil Service.

We should enjoy much greater openness in the public sector, so that we can properly follow the taxpayer's pound. By simply revealing what is happening, we would incentivise improvements in both efficiency and effectiveness. For example, a step change in the transparency required of private companies financed by the taxpayer to deliver public services could transform things. If their contracts were opened to inspection by both the public and the National Audit Office, we could more easily see whether money had been properly spent and whether excessive profits had been made. If the companies were subject to freedom of information requests for their publicly funded business, they could be held to proper public account. If government stopped hiding behind claims of commercial confidentiality to suppress information, value for money would improve. It was absurd that the Public Accounts Committee was prevented from seeing data on the performance of the companies providing support to unemployed people on the Work Programme or information on the aircraft carriers when the government changed course.

Similarly, if there was greater openness around the negotiations between multinationals and the tax authorities, so we knew how they arrived at their tax deals, we could judge whether Google, Vodafone or Facebook had paid their fair share of tax. Everyone has hidden behind taxpayer confidentiality for too long. There is a great difference between respecting confidentiality in relation to an individual and maintaining confidentiality in relation to companies. Companies have a legal status that is separate from the individuals who own them and a company's finances are separate from the personal finances of the owners, so opening companies' negotiations with Her Majesty's Revenue and Customs to public account would in no way offend the privacy of any individual. However, only by being transparent and by being seen to be fair will confidence in our tax system be assured.

The issue of accountability was another constant and recurring theme of our inquiries. Trying to call to account those who were directly involved in a particular project was often impossible. In part that came about because of the doctrine of ministerial responsibility, which I have argued is in serious need of reform. Civil servants and ministers should both answer to Parliament and to the public for their actions. And when things go well, or badly, individuals should be accountable – but the public sector culture rarely apportions either praise or blame. During our five years, some civil servants did leave their jobs following criticism of their performance. The head of tax Dave Hartnett suddenly retired early, as did the chief executive of the Charity Commission and the chief executive of the Care Quality Commission. But at the same time, Sir Neil McKay is just one example of an NHS administrator who escaped responsibility for poor decisions. The chief executive of NHS Midlands and East received a pay-off reputed to be worth £1 million and then reappeared chairing Manchester's cardiac management board. G4S and Serco were not 'punished' for putting in false claims to the Ministry of Justice on the tagging of prisoners' contract. They just secured more government contracts.

The proposition is quite simple: the people who are responsible for executing a particular policy or programme should be properly accountable for their actions, rewarded when they perform well and admonished and supported to improve when things go wrong. If you know you are answerable for your actions that influences your approach. There are those who argue that this would stop innovation and create a risk-averse culture. I think that is just a convenient excuse for maintaining a status quo that obscures accountabilities. Experimenting with new ways to deliver services is hugely important when we are trying to secure more and better services with less money. Some experiments are bound to fail, but the public will accept that, if they can see that a project was properly planned and efficiently run and that the decision to stop was taken in a timely manner; what frustrates them is the constant repetition of mistakes and the poor planning and execution of new ideas. So defining and reforming accountabilities should constitute an element of the reform agenda.

Finally, there is a wide consensus on the need to develop new skills within the Civil Service, but the pace of change is painfully slow. There are simply not enough civil servants with good commercial, financial, IT and project management skills, and the cadre of top civil servants remains stuck in the past. Training people to give them the right skills is not rocket science, but it does require determination and commitment. A bold and brave Prime Minister might do well to recruit a strong group of new top Civil Service executives from outside the Civil Service to take it in a new direction, employing effective leaders from elsewhere in the public sector, like local government and the NHS, and bringing in others with a private sector background. New leadership would help to challenge and change the deeply embedded Civil Service culture. Government does not have to be as it is and good government can make a real difference to people's lives.

Parliamentary scrutiny

The Public Accounts Committee succeeded in reaching many people through our work. We showed how important and effective parliamentary scrutiny can be. The issues we investigated and the style of our committee hearings may have infuriated those who appeared before us, but they resonated with voters and taxpayers, who felt we were asking the questions they wanted us to ask.

We operated as a strong team determined to secure consensus. We could not have succeeded without the high-quality reports and briefings prepared by the National Audit Office. At the same time, as we have seen, we were also helped by the efforts of brave and determined whistleblowers and by the persistence of committed investigative journalists. One can argue that our regulatory and accountability protocols should be stronger so that Parliament and the public automatically receive more comprehensive, open and reliable information. But it is a tribute to our democracy that good journalists and courageous and determined individuals exist and can work with MPs to expose wrongdoing.

I hope our work did help to restore a little trust in the role of parliamentarians. We pushed the boundaries on how select committees work, for instance by insisting that permanent secretaries who had moved on to new jobs came back to account for their previous work. We widened the net on the people we asked to give evidence. In the past the committee had only taken evidence from accounting officers, mainly the permanent secretaries. We required private companies to give evidence in public on their tax-funded work. We also heard from voluntary organisations and charities that worked with and represented the consumers of public services. We ventured in greater detail into areas that had not previously been called to proper account, investigating the stewardship of the Duchy of Cornwall and the Sovereign Grant, examining the BBC, and, of course, focusing on the issue of tax avoidance and tax collection. We undertook landscape reviews of departments to give us a broader framework through which to assess whether they were operating efficiently and we regularly tracked the large reform programmes like Universal Credit and the Probation Service. Much of this approach was new and it helped to strengthen the accountability of the executive to Parliament and the public.

While some castigated us for grandstanding, others cheered us on. We were forthright and hard-hitting but fair in our questioning, and our style ensured that important issues we covered hit the media agenda and created public debate. We did not use publicity as an end in itself, but for a purpose – to expose waste and to encourage better government. We had to ask the uncomfortable questions and, indeed, if people had liked me, I think I would have failed in my job.

Parliament has a hugely important job of holding the executive to account, yet our political system still allows the executive and the political parties to exert excessive control over how MPs work and vote. The presumption that the only route to success in politics is through ministerial preferment still holds true in too many quarters and prevents MPs from acting independently. There are, however, welcome signs that the new generation of politicians from across the political spectrum are increasingly independently minded and want to focus their energies in different ways by representing their voters through the work they do in Parliament. Let's hope this trend is here to stay and will be reinforced over time.

The scorecard

In the five years between 2010 and 2015, the Public Accounts Committee helped to secure change. Our work with tax campaigners, whistleblowers and journalists helped to put the debate about tax avoidance on the map. Our hearings on the role of the private sector in public services helped to create greater transparency and accountability. We secured a raft of welcome changes from our focus on specific issues. For instance, the present chief executive of NHS England, Simon Stevens, announced at the start of one of our hearings that he would embark on a closure programme of the residential homes for adults with learning disabilities. Clearly, preparing for the Public Accounts Committee hearing convinced him that he should do this, much to the satisfaction of campaigners who had come and asked for the investigation and who had been arguing for these closures for a long time. In another example, the powerful evidence given to the committee by the late Lisa Jardine, when she was chair of the Human Fertilisation and Embryology Authority, stopped the government from abolishing this important body, which they had intended to do. We convinced government to instruct all public bodies to stop using premium phone lines; we helped to stop public bodies employing people through off-payroll arrangements to avoid tax and National Insurance; we helped to convince the government that it should terminate the contract with the private consortium running the Sellafield site. These are just some examples; all in all, the committee staff reckoned that 88 per cent of our recommendations were implemented.

But we had some defeats. We failed to convince the Department for Culture, Media and Sport that they should not give BT all of the £2 billion of public subsidy for the rollout of broadband to rural areas, which we thought represented extremely poor value for money for the taxpayer. We did not persuade the government to think again about the Work Programme or Universal Credit. We have not stopped PFI. Taxpayers' money continues to be wasted on ill-conceived and badly planned capital projects, IT investments and major reform programmes. We have not secured the reforms to the Civil Service that we thought were necessary to achieve better value.

So the work of the Public Accounts Committee must go on.

I am sure that my successors will pursue the agenda on behalf of taxpayers with great vigour and determination. I hope they will push the boundaries beyond what we achieved to further strengthen and deepen the work of calling to account those who are responsible for spending our money, and to place the interest of all taxpayers at the heart of our public sector ethos. That matters to different people in different ways. For myself, my passionate belief in the power of government to transform people's life chances lies at the heart of my preoccupation with value for money. My frustration comes from seeing value for money relegated to the backburner by too many people for too much of the time. That has to change. As I said at our final hearing with tax officials in February 2015, when we were looking at the progress they had made in tackling aggressive tax avoidance: 'Honestly, I want to put a bomb under you guys.' Sadly, my final words before thanking them were: 'Kicked into the long grass.'

Index